At War With Wellington

At War With Wellington

The Peninsular War Letters of William, George and Charles Napier

Gareth Glover & Robert Burnham

FRONTLINE BOOKS

First published in Great Britain in 2024 by
Frontline Books
An imprint of Pen & Sword Books Limited
Yorkshire – Philadelphia

Copyright © Gareth Glover & Robert Burnham 2024

ISBN 978 1 39905 991 6

The right of Gareth Glover & Robert Burnham to be identified as Authors of this Work has been asserted by them in accordance with the Copyright, Designs and Patents Act 1988.

A CIP catalogue record for this book is available from the British Library

All rights reserved. No part of this book may be reproduced or transmitted in any form or by any means, electronic or mechanical including photocopying, recording or by any information storage and retrieval system, without permission from the Publisher in writing.

Typeset by Mac Style
Printed in the UK by CPI Group (UK) Ltd, Croydon, CR0 4YY.

Pen & Sword Books Limited incorporates the imprints of After the Battle, Atlas, Archaeology, Aviation, Discovery, Family History, Fiction, History, Maritime, Military, Military Classics, Politics, Select, Transport, True Crime, Air World, Frontline Publishing, Leo Cooper, Remember When, Seaforth Publishing, The Praetorian Press, Wharncliffe Local History, Wharncliffe Transport, Wharncliffe True Crime and White Owl.

For a complete list of Pen & Sword titles please contact

PEN & SWORD BOOKS LIMITED
47 Church Street, Barnsley, South Yorkshire, S70 2AS, England
E-mail: enquiries@pen-and-sword.co.uk
Website: www.pen-and-sword.co.uk
or
PEN AND SWORD BOOKS
1950 Lawrence Rd, Havertown, PA 19083, USA
E-mail: uspen-and-sword@casematepublishers.com
Website: www.penandswordbooks.com

Contents

Foreword		vi
Chapter 1	Early Military Years	1
Chapter 2	Copenhagen 1807	13
Chapter 3	The Corunna Campaign 1808–09	20
Chapter 4	Talavera Campaign 1809	54
Chapter 5	From the Border to the Lines of Torres Vedras 1810	57
Chapter 6	The French Retreat into Spain 1811	86
Chapter 7	Ciudad Rodrigo, Badajoz and Salamanca 1812	112
Chapter 8	The Advance to the Pyrenees 1813	139
Chapter 9	The Chesapeake Campaign 1813	155
Chapter 10	Southern France 1814	171
Chapter 11	1815	188
Chapter 12	Later Life	192
Notes		194
Bibliography		207
Index		208

All artwork by Charles Napier.

Foreword

Beyond such household names as Arthur Wellesley, Duke of Wellington, and Sir John Moore, few other names are more well known than the three Napier brothers, who fought under these two renowned generals in Denmark, Portugal, Spain and France between 1807 and 1815. The individual biographies of Charles, George and William Napier have been published over the last century; but these works often concentrate a great deal on their later lives, when they independently attained greater things and when their achievements were not overshadowed by the glory of their illustrious commanders. When dealing with their military careers during the Napoleonic wars, some of these biographies have published a selection of their letters and journals, but these were published in Victorian times and are always edited to avoid offence or scandal, obscuring the names of individuals who are heavily criticised or removing much that would be of great interest to military historians. The brothers were also very politically aware, particularly William, and his later political affiliations certainly tainted his famous six-volume *History of the Peninsular War* and colours his attitudes towards various actors in the *great game*.

The editors have therefore gone back to the original letters and journals (where they still exist[1]) and have transcribed them in full to ensure that all material of interest to the military historian is included for the first time and the views and experiences of all three brothers are brought together. However, the entire scope of the Napier letters and journals is well beyond the remit of this publication and judicious pruning of lengthy discussions on purely family matters; incessant complaints regarding financial issues and heated commentary on the political situation in both Britain and across Europe has had to be curtailed (perhaps to the great relief of the reader). But what remains is everything they wrote about the military life they led and the experiences they underwent in relation to it. Their views on the current military situation are often enlightening; their comments on the actions of their various commanders are incisive and often barbed; they are also not beyond openly criticising their commanders, their fellow officers, their men and their allies. Their political stances often led them to admire Napoleon and his military skills; esteem the abilities of their French foes, while unabashedly censuring the French Emperor and soldiers for the inhuman atrocities they were guilty of enacting.

It is hoped that the reader will gain a great deal by reading the contemporary thoughts of these three brothers, often at variance with their later writing, but first we need to provide some background to the three brothers and where they came from.

Background

They were three of the sons of Colonel the Honourable George Napier (1751–1804); who had been commissioned in the 25th Regiment of Foot in 1767, rising to captain in the 80th Foot by the time of the American War of Independence; where he served on the Staff of General Sir Henry Clinton. He sold his commission in 1781 but re-joined the Army the following year and rose steadily to the rank of colonel in 1800. He served as Comptroller of Army Accounts in Ireland from 1799 until his death in 1804. In 1775 he had married Elizabeth Pollock and they had three children, Louisa born 1776, Sarah 1777 and Henry 1778, but unfortunately Elizabeth died in 1778. He remarried in August 1781 to Lady Sarah Lennox, daughter of the 2nd Duke of Richmond (who had previously married Sir Charles Bunbury – the marriage was annulled in 1776 after Sarah's adultery with Lord William Gordon, by whom she had a daughter, Louisa), having another eight children: Charles, born in 1782; Emily, born in 1783;[2] George, born in 1784; William, born in 1785; Richard, born in 1787;[3] Henry Edward, born in 1789;[4] Caroline, born in 1790;[5] and finally Cecilia, born in 1791.[6]

Charles, the elder son, was born in London on 10 August 1782, but at the age of 3 the family moved to Celbridge, 10 miles from Dublin. On 31 January 1794 (at the age of 11) he received a commission as ensign in the 33rd Foot and he became a lieutenant in the 89th Foot on 8 May 1794. Charles joined his regiment at Netley camp,[7] but as he was too young to accompany the force forming under Lord Moira[8] for foreign service, he was exchanged into the 4th Foot and went home to be schooled. In 1799 Charles became aide-de-camp to Major General Sir James Duff commanding the Limerick district, but in 1800 he resigned his Staff appointment to join the 95th Regiment, or Rifle Corps, which was being formed at Blatchington in Sussex. He was quartered for the next two years at Weymouth, Hythe and Shorncliffe and in June 1803 he was appointed aide-de-camp to his cousin, General Henry Edward Fox, Commander in Chief of the forces in Ireland. He then accompanied Fox to London when he was transferred to the command of the Home District.

On 22 December 1803 he was promoted to captain in the Staff Corps, a newly organised body of artificers to assist the Royal Engineers and the Quartermaster General, and he was quartered at Chelmsford and Chatham. In the middle of 1805, he went with his corps to Hythe, where he was employed in the construction of the Royal Military Canal and came under the personal supervision of Sir John Moore. On 29 May 1806, Charles Napier was promoted to a majority in the Cape Corps, from which he exchanged into the 50th Regiment, then quartered at Bognor Regis in Sussex. During the next two years he moved with the regiment to Guernsey, Deal, Hythe and Ashford, being frequently in command of the battalion.

After the battle of Vimiera in August 1808, Charles was ordered to join the first battalion of the 50th at Lisbon as the colonel had obtained leave of absence, and he found himself on arrival at Lisbon in command of the battalion. Sir John Moore incorporated the regiment in his force marching into Spain; the 50th were in Lord William Bentinck's Brigade and on 16 January 1809, at Corunna, Charles was wounded five times. Eventually he was taken prisoner; his name was returned among the killed, but his life was fortuitously saved by a French drummer. He was taken to Marshal Soult's quarters, where he received every attention; Marshal Ney, who succeeded in command at Corunna, set him at liberty on 20 March 1809; being on parole not to serve again until exchanged. It was not until January 1810 that an exchange was actually effected, and Charles was able to re-join his regiment. Finding the 50th in quarters in Portugal, he obtained leave of absence to join (as a volunteer) the Light Brigade in which his brothers George and William were then serving. He acted as an aide-de-camp to Brigadier General Robert Craufurd at the Action on the Coa, where he had two horses killed under him. Charles was then attached to Lord Wellington's Staff. At the Battle of Busaco he was shot through the face, his jaw broken and his eye injured. He was sent to Lisbon, where he was laid up for some months, but in March 1811 he left to re-join the army, his wound still bandaged up. He was engaged at the Battle of Fuentes de Oñoro and at the second siege of Badajoz.

On 27 June 1811 he was promoted to lieutenant colonel of the 102nd Regiment, which had just arrived at Guernsey from Australia. He embarked for England on 25 August and spent some months with his mother before joining his regiment in Guernsey in January 1812. In July he embarked with the 102nd for Bermuda, where they arrived in the September. In May 1813 he was appointed to command a brigade, composed of the 102nd, a body of Royal Marines and a corps of Frenchmen enlisted from prisoners of war, to take part in the expedition under General Sir Thomas Beckwith engaged in coastal operations against the Americans. In August his force was attached to Admiral Sir George Cockburn on the coast of Carolina, where further minor operations took place. He then proceeded with the regiment to Halifax in Nova Scotia, but being anxious to serve in the Peninsula again, he exchanged back into the 50th Foot. However, he did not arrive in Europe before the war ended. In

December 1814, he was placed on half pay, Charles immediately entering the military college at Farnham, where he was soon joined by his brother, William.

In March 1815, when Napoleon escaped from Elba, Charles went to Ghent as a volunteer. He later took part in the storming of Cambrai and entered Paris with the allied armies. While on his way home from Ostend in 1815 the ship sank and Charles was nearly drowned. He re-joined the military college at Farnham and remained there until the end of 1817. For his services in the Peninsular War, he received the Gold medal for Corunna and in 1848 he gained the Military General Service Medal with two clasps for Busaco and Fuentes de Oñoro.

George Napier was also born in London, on 30 June 1784, and moved to Ireland with the family. George was not particularly scholarly and when aged 15 he was appointed as a cornet in the 24th Light Dragoons in January 1800. He became a lieutenant in the 46th Foot on 18 June 1800 and went on half pay during the Peace of Amiens in 1802. George transferred into the 52nd Foot in 1803 and became a captain in the regiment on 5 January 1804. He was a favourite of Sir John Moore, serving with him at Shorncliffe, Sicily and Sweden before becoming one of his aides-de-camp at Corunna. George then served with the 52nd in the Peninsular campaigns of 1809–11, being slightly wounded at Busaco. George became a major and volunteered for the command of the stormers of the Light Division at the assault on Ciudad Rodrigo on 19 January 1812, losing his right arm, which had been broken by a fragment of shell at Casal Nova ten months prior. He received a brevet lieutenant colonelcy. George went home to recuperate, married Margaret Craig of Glasgow and was appointed Deputy Adjutant General in the York District. He re-joined the 52nd still as a major at St Jean de Luz in the beginning of 1814 and was present at the Battles of Orthez, Tarbes and Toulouse. Immediately after the latter battle, he was appointed lieutenant colonel of the 71st Highland Light Infantry, with which he returned to Scotland. On 25 July 1814 he was appointed captain and lieutenant colonel of the 3rd Foot Guards. He had received the Peninsular Gold medal for Ciudad Rodrigo, and in 1848 he received the Military General Service Medal with four clasps (for Corunna, Busaco, Orthez and Toulouse).

William, was born at Celbridge and although he received some education at a school there, he was far more keen on field sports. William initially received his commission as an ensign in the Royal Irish Artillery in June 1800, but was soon transferred to the 62nd Foot. He was promoted to lieutenant on 18 April 1801, but was reduced to half pay like his brother with the Peace of Amiens. On the resumption of the war, his uncle the Duke of Richmond got him into the Royal Horse Guards, but Sir John Moore suggested that William should transfer into one of his light regiments, to which William eagerly agreed. A series of quick hops saw William appointed captain in a West India Regiment in June 1804, then into a battalion of the Army of Reserve, before finally becoming a captain in the 43rd Foot on 11 August 1804.

In 1807 William participated in the expedition to Copenhagen and took part in the Battle of Køge. In September 1808 he embarked with his regiment at Harwich for Spain and arrived at Corunna on 13 October, taking part in the campaign of Sir John Moore. On his return home William was appointed aide-de-camp to his uncle, the Duke of Richmond, Lord Lieutenant of Ireland, but gave up the appointment to go with the 43rd back to Portugal in May 1809.

At the fighting on the Coa in July 1810, William highly distinguished himself; towards the end of the action he was shot in the left hip; but the bone was not broken, and he continued with his regiment until the Battle of Busaco, where both of his brothers were wounded. On the retreat of the French army, he took part in the actions of Pombal and Redinha, but at the combat of Casal Nova on 14 March 1811, William was dangerously wounded. It was after this action that his brother Charles met the litters carrying his two wounded brothers and was incorrectly informed that William was mortally wounded. William re-joined the army with a bullet sitting near his spine and his wound still open. He was appointed brigade major to the First Brigade of the Light Division. He took part in the Battle of Fuentes de Oñoro and on 30 May was promoted brevet major for his services. He continued to serve until after the raising of the second siege of Badajoz, when he was attacked by fever; ill as he was, he would not quit the army until Lord Wellington directed his brother to take him to Lisbon. William was sent to England in the autumn of 1811 and in February 1812 he married Caroline Amelia, daughter of General the Honourable Henry Fox.

Only three weeks after his marriage, William sailed for Portugal on hearing that Badajoz was besieged again. Before he reached Lisbon he learned that Badajoz had fallen and his dearest friend, Lieutenant Colonel Charles Macleod, had been killed. William took command of the regiment, having become a regimental major on 14 May 1812 commanding the regiment at Salamanca. William obtained leave to go to England in January 1813 and remained at home until the August, when he re-joined his regiment. He landed at Passages (Pasaia) and found the 43rd Regiment encamped above Bera in the Pyrenees. On 10 November 1813 at the Battle of the Nivelle, Colonel Hearn fell sick and the command of the regiment once again devolved on William, who was directed to storm La Rhune mountain, which the 43rd carried with great gallantry. During the Battle of the Nive he was twice wounded; he was promoted brevet lieutenant colonel on 22 November 1813.

William was present at the Battle of Orthez, but his wounds and general ill-health compelled him to go to England again. On his recovery from a protracted illness, he joined the military college at Farnham, where his brother Charles was also studying; but on the return of Napoleon from Elba, William made arrangements to re-join his regiment and embarked at Dover on 16 June 1815, too late for Waterloo. He followed the army to Paris and remained with the 43rd, which was quartered at Bapaume and Valenciennes, and then remained in France with the Army of Occupation until 1818. William was granted the Gold medal with two clasps for Salamanca, Nivelle and the Nive; and in 1848 he received the Military General Service Medal with three clasps for Busaco, Fuentes de Oñoro and Orthez.

Chapter 1

Early Military Years

Previous to the commencement of the Peninsular War, we have a number of statements and letters from the Napier brothers briefly outlining their early military careers.

We begin with George, who wrote about his early career until he joined the 52nd Foot in 1803:

> I was at first determined to be a sailor and was entered on the books of the '*Invincible*',[1] Captain Thomas Packenham,[2] but as the sea disagreed with me, I did not join the ship. I then thought I would be a clergyman … However, after working at Latin, I was so idle and disliked it so much, that I would not go into the Church, but said I would be a soldier, as I liked fighting, a red coat, and a sword! …
>
> Being, as I said, determined to enter the army, I studied, or rather flattered myself I studied Mathematics and French, but … what I did learn was very superficial, and I soon forgot it all, to my inexpressible sorrow… Charles, on the contrary, being very clever, persevering, and of a studious turn of mind, learned so well and so thoroughly, that he soon got over all difficulties, and made himself master of the theoretical part of his profession by the time he was a captain and was appointed to a regiment called the '*Staff Corps*', which only such officers as are good mathematicians, understand fortification, military drawing and are fit for the Staff of the army, are allowed to enter, and it is a great feather in a young officer's cap to get a commission in that distinguished regiment. There he studied still harder, and has, in consequence of his attention to the study of his profession, distinguished himself as an officer in a double ratio to me … William, being fond of reading and studying his profession in various ways and also a very clever man, gifted by nature with great abilities and much talent …
>
> Lord Cornwallis,[3] who was one of the best soldiers and most excellent, humane, high-minded, honourable, and virtuous men that ever graced the annals of English history, being an old and long tried friend of my father and mother, gave me a cornetcy of Dragoons on 1 January 1800, I being then fifteen years and a half old; … in the Gazette, '*George Thomas Napier, gent, to be cornet in the 24th Light Dragoons.*' …As soon as I had

got all my things and bought some horses I joined my regiment in Dublin Barracks, and you will easily imagine what a happy fellow I was to be my own master at fifteen, with a fine uniform, a couple of horses, a servant, and about fifty pounds in my pocket. ... In the dragoons I remained only six months, where, I must acknowledge, however painful the confession, that except to ride and get a tolerable knowledge of horses, paying well in my purse for the same, I learned nothing but to drink and enter into every kind of debauchery, which is disreputable to a gentleman. ...

My father, being an old soldier, was convinced I should go to ruin if I remained any longer in the dragoons and therefore, procured me a lieutenancy in the 46th Regiment of Foot, then quartered in Limerick, in the south of Ireland ... The general commanding the district was an old and most intimate friend of my father's (Sir James Duff),[4] to whom ... Charles was at the time aide-de-camp, so that on joining the 46th Regiment in June 1800, I was under Sir James's eye, and also my brother's, who ... was a very steady fellow and never drank any wine or committed follies of any kind ... From Sir James I learned that although a man was wild, and drank as our officers did, yet if he was an honourable man and had the feelings of a gentleman, he never would, even in his drunken moments, do a cowardly or unmanly act.

About six months after I joined the 46th, Sir James Duff was made a Lieutenant General, and my brother Charles having gone to join the Rifle Corps, I was appointed, with Lady Duff's nephew, James Douglas[5] to be one of his aides-de-camp. I remained very happy in that situation till the year 1802, when Sir James Duff was removed from the Staff, and my battalion being also reduced in consequence of the Peace of Amiens, I was placed on half-pay, and went to England for a few weeks.

George continued his statement up until 1805:

On my return to Ireland [in 1803] I was appointed to the 52nd Regiment of Light Infantry, which was Sir John Moore's and commanded by Colonel MacKenzie.[6] And now I come to that period of my life from whence I may date the commencement of my military career, as till I entered the 52nd Regiment I had learned nothing of my profession. ... While at Limerick with ... Charles, going out one day to shoot snipes, he ... shot one, and springing over a deep ditch in order to get it, he fell and broke his leg, which gave a crack like a whip. Upon my running up to him he laughed and called out to me, *'Though I have broken my leg, I've got the snipe!'*

The 52nd Regiment was quartered at Chatham, under the immediate command of Sir John Moore, and when I called upon him to pay my respects upon joining, he received me very kindly, turned me round, looked at me, and then laughingly said, *'Oh, you will do; I see you are a good cut of a light infantryman, come and dine with me.'* ... From that time he treated me like a son. Very soon Colonel Kenneth MacKenzie took the command of the regiment, to which Sir John Moore had him appointed as the officer at that period best adapted to form a light infantry regiment, ours being the first of that description of force ... Colonel MacKenzie was an old, experienced and skilful officer, ... and particularly distinguished himself in Egypt in command of the 90th Regiment, and indeed, was generally considered the best commanding officer in the army ... and by the system then commenced and afterwards perfected, the 52nd Regiment was considered as a model for the rest of the army, and was the nucleus from which that beautiful brigade, consisting of the 43rd, 52nd and Rifle Corps, was formed at Shorncliffe camp under Sir John Moore's own eye ...

We marched from Chatham to Canterbury ... During the time we were quartered at Canterbury, having been extravagant and got into debt with the Paymaster of the regiment, two other young officers, who, like myself were in debt, agreed that as it was very uncomfortable and disreputable to owe money, we would no longer live at the mess, but be content to live in our own lodgings upon plain bread and milk till we should be able to pay off our debts; and it was three months before we again joined the mess. The two officers, my companions in this, were brothers, Robert and Charles Rowan ... We marched from Canterbury to Hythe on the coast of Kent, and remained in that neighbourhood ... for about three years, as the French ... had assembled a large force in the camp of Boulogne, on the opposite coast, and Napoleon Buonaparte threatened to invade England with this immense army ...

The whole male population of England was armed; at least, all those who were capable of using arms; and organised in corps of cavalry and infantry, and the regular and militia force was ready to move at a moment's warning to any particular spot where Napoleon might land, or attempt to land. There would have been collected at Shorncliffe and along that coast from Deal to Hastings in a few hours, no less than 40,000 excellent troops to oppose the enemy, principally under Sir John Moore, ... and in case of this first line being obliged to fall back, there was another line ready to support the first of 50,000 troops, besides large bodies of armed peasantry, all breathing defiance and rage against the French ...

About this time, January 1804, I purchased a company in the regiment over the heads of many lieutenants, by which I got a great advance in my profession. I had been four years a subaltern and was nineteen years and a half old, which was very young to be a captain. At the time the company became vacant, I could not get the money to buy it and was very sorry to be obliged to give up all idea of it, when an intimate friend of mine, a captain in the regiment, and whose subaltern I was, without saying a word to me, went off to London and lodged the 950 l[7], (the regulation price) in the agent's hands upon my account and I was immediately gazetted as captain ... this friend was Lord Frederick Bentinck[8] ... I was enabled to pay him back the money he lent me to purchase my company some years afterwards, but, had I not done so, it would have been all the same to Frederick Bentinck, for he never would have asked me; on the contrary, often did he wish me to accept the money as a proof of friendship.

In the autumn of 1804, William, who was in the Blues, exchanged into the 52nd, and was my lieutenant. Sir John Moore, who was fond of William, very soon got him a company for nothing and had him appointed to the 43rd Light Infantry, in which regiment he remained ... Soon after I was a captain I was sent to get volunteers from a militia regiment in Ireland, and ... William was also sent from his regiment for the same purpose, so we went off together to Limerick. One day there came [to William] and me ten very handsome militia soldiers, six feet high, who said they would volunteer with whichever officer of the line (for there were a number of us all on the same duty) could beat them in running and jumping. Of course, in order to get these fine fellows, we all tried and exerted ourselves to the utmost. [William] and I were the two most active of all the officers, and we had a hard struggle with Pat; but I was beat by them. Not so [William]; with his cursed long legs he beat the men both in running and jumping, and they being honourable fellows, as most Irishmen are, kept their word and he took them all ten to the 43rd, and probably most of them found their graves in Spain, poor fellows! We returned to our regiments, and I was immediately sent off to Guernsey on the same duty, and afterwards to the Isle of Wight, where there was a Reserve battalion from which Sir John Moore expected to get a great number of men for the 52nd, as it was commanded by one of the finest fellows and best officers in the service, who he knew, would do all in his power to make the men volunteer. So he did, for I got an immense number. The officer I allude to was then Lieutenant Colonel Samuel Gibbs[9] ... who had highly distinguished himself in India ...

The number of volunteers we got was so great that a second battalion was given to the regiment; and in consequence of its being in such high order, and at the recommendation of the general, all the promotion was allowed to go in the regiment. At the same time the King (George III) made General Moore a knight of the Bath, at that time only given to such general officers as had particularly distinguished themselves on service. Upon this occasion the officers of the 52nd subscribed a large sum of money and bought a beautiful diamond star, which they presented to Sir John Moore as a mark of their esteem and affection. The star was worth five or six hundred guineas, I forget which. Sir John Moore was highly pleased and gratified with this proof of the respect, esteem, love and gratitude of his officers, and well did he deserve every proof in our power to give, for never did any colonel of a regiment pay such attention to the happiness and interests of his regiment as he did to the hour of his death. But that which gratified him most was the good conduct and zeal of both officers and men in the performance of their duty, and often would he tell us he felt prouder of having such a regiment than he did of his red ribbon.

In this year, 1804, my father died. He had been long ill of a consumptive complaint and the indefatigable zeal with which he attended to the business of his office in Dublin made the confinement too much for the weak state of his health. He was ordered by the physicians to go to Clifton near Bristol, where in a few weeks he breathed his last. My father had a beautiful figure and was six feet two inches in height, with one of the handsomest faces I ever saw, and was the most perfect made man possible. He was in his younger days looked upon as the most active and the handsomest officer of the British army in America, where he was serving with his regiment as a captain against the Americans, who had separated themselves from the mother country. As well as being so fine a looking man, he was as clever and able in mind as strong in body. There were few things that he did not succeed in; he had read a great deal in many languages, was a good classic scholar, well acquainted with all history, ancient and modern, was a good mathematician, engineer, and chemist, and had written several papers and reports upon these latter subjects when he was controller of the Laboratory at Woolwich; he was an excellent regimental officer, and had served through all the American War, and was Deputy Quarter Master General to the army commanded by the Marquis of Hastings,[10] which went to Holland in the year 1794, after which he commanded the Londonderry Regiment.[11] When placed upon half pay in consequence of his regiment being drafted into regiments in the West Indies,[12] he was made Controller of Army Accounts in Ireland by his friend Lord Cornwallis, then Lord-Lieutenant,[13] by whose humanity, skill and judgment in governing Ireland the rebellion in that unhappy country was put an end to; at the same time the horrid cruelties practised with so much barbarity were effectually put a stop to, and while Lord Cornwallis was at the head of that oppressed country, justice was administered impartially to the poor peasant and degraded Catholics.

By 1805 Charles Napier was a member of the Staff Corps in Kent. His first letter recounts his brave determination to stand by his opinion regarding the result of a court martial, despite significant pressure from Sir John Moore to alter his decision:

Hythe, 31 August 1805
I have been on a cursed court martial. Colonel Brown[14] would not approve the opinion, which acquitted the prisoner. There was, as I thought, not proof enough of his guilt, although I was persuaded of his being guilty. He showed it to General Moore who thought as Brown did, I was sent for (they had *no pawn*, but wished it *revised*) and Moore and I were together for an hour by ourselves, he was rather *warm*, I was rather silent but did not *agree*, he grew more eager but friendly though *severe*, and mistaken I thought and I left him *most distressed*, determined not to sacrifice a bit to Moore's opinion unless fully *consistent* with my conscience. This I foresaw, from his violence, would create a *quarrel*, but there was no help for it. Well, I came home cool, decided but unhappy and particularly so as I saw I had been *wrong* in part. I said to myself '*My father I feel your absence*', then I said '*As he would have acted for himself, show yourself his son and do so also for it is your duty, while you were weak God gave you support, now you are strong and he has taken that from you*'.

Charles soon became a major in the 2nd Battalion, 50th Foot, and proceeded to Guernsey. He was not a good sailor:

Portsmouth May [1806] – *Quo fata vocant*,[15] is the 50th's motto, and at present *fata* sends us to Guernsey, while the first battalion will form part of the expedition now fitting out. My single chance now is, the first battalion being cut off and the two eldest majors skewered: a great comfort that would be, and is my brightest prospect.

Guernsey [1806] – We sailed, and never was a wretch more sick than I was, when at night the cry of '*Privateer!*' arose on deck, '*Officers! Officers!*' I was up in a minute and a ludicrous scene opened. I, the major, shouting for the men to come up, the other officers rolling about in the dark, for there was a storm and none could keep steady; the soldiers tumbling up, some sick, some loading their muskets, others doing both, and all rolling about and falling in such heaps as to make me think they would shoot each other before *Monsieur* arrived. However, in a few minutes we got some forty into the forecastle and side next the privateer, which was bearing down and not a hundred yards off, looking very black. She would not answer or fight, but came almost athwart our bows, when our captain called to me, '*sir she is a privateer and trying to get to windward to board, we had better fire a shot*'. No sooner said than done: a man fired by my order, but only into her rigging, as she might not be a privateer. Still she bore down so close as to menace boarding before half my men were on deck and loaded, the latter not easy to effect, from sickness and the holding on to prevent being washed overboard. However, thirty fired, just to say we did not mean to be taken and the argument was found good: she sailed round and went off, answering our hail with '*Guernsey smuggler*'. Our seamen said smugglers avoid other ships: yet she did not return our fire, and probably seeing so many troops, expected *more kicks than halfpence*.[16]

George sailed with the 52nd Foot to Sicily, to form part of the garrison:

In the year 1806, Sir John Moore was appointed second in command in Sicily, under General Fox.[17] In a few weeks the 52nd followed him under the command of Major General Paget,[18] accompanied by the Guards and several other regiments. We embarked at Deal and had a boisterous passage down Channel and in the Bay of Biscay; many of the men-of-war being disabled in the gales, several transports with horses were lost and others driven on the French coast and taken prisoners. One unfortunate transport with horses on board was run down by a large ship, which passed clean over her and not a vestige of her was ever seen again. The ship I was on board of was run foul of by a frigate, but being a very fine new large vessel she suffered comparatively little damage. I was so sick that notwithstanding everyone thought we were sinking, and all hands were trying to escape into the shrouds of the frigate, I could not move, but resigned myself to my fate without the least effort; such is the powerful effect of seasickness on the mind as well as body. In a few days the weather cleared up, and on a fine bright morning, the anniversary of the glorious Battle of Trafalgar, in the very spot where that greatest of all naval battles was fought the year before, in which the immortal Nelson fell, as he had lived, the pride of England's Navy and the successful conqueror and destroyer of the fleets of France, did we meet that same British fleet under the command of that excellent, skilful, gallant and good man Lord Collingwood.[19] Immediately the signal was made by our commander, Sir Thomas Duckworth,[20] for the ships of the convoy to pass under the admiral's stern; the soldiers dressed and paraded on the decks, with bands playing '*Rule Britannia*' and colours flying; and as we passed our colours dropped, and presenting arms, we gave three hearty cheers, the fine sailor-like old admiral taking off his hat and bowing to us, his own brave crew and the rest of his fleet returning our cheers with loud huzzahs. My ship, in which was our band, was, curiously enough, called the '*Collingwood*'[21] after him, and had a fine large figure of the admiral at her head, painted in full uniform, and we led the van in this well-merited compliment as Collingwood himself had led the van in the battle. I never felt more elated or saw a finer sight! From thence we proceeded to the Straits of Gibraltar and on our arrival in the Bay of Tangier, on a beautiful fine evening, we were ordered by signal from Sir T[homas] Duckworth to '*lay to*' till next morning, as he feared the Spanish gunboats would come out as we entered the Straits and snap some of us up. Unfortunately for us, during the night a Levanter (so called from the wind blowing from the Levant down the Mediterranean) came with such force that the fleet was dispersed and driven away to the Atlantic. My ship was twenty-two days cruising off Cape Spartel, on the north-west coast of Africa, before the wind changed and enabled us to bear up and sail through the Straits and anchor in the Bay of Tetuan [Tetouan] (on the African coast, just opposite Gibraltar), where we were to take in fresh meat and water. The poor cattle were bought by the commissaries at the town of Tetuan [Tetouan] from the Moors, and then brought alongside the ships in boats, where a rope being fastened round their horns, they were hoisted on board by a pulley, which is very cruel, for I have often seen the horns completely dragged out of the head and the wretched bullock drop into the boat again writhing with agony.

While at Tetuan [Tetouan], being one day on shore with a watering party, the Moorish captain or chief of the guard placed there to prevent the English soldiers from going into the town asked me in English (for he could speak it a little) to give him some brandy, which I very foolishly did and he got intoxicated; and having given some also to several of his men, the consequence was that our soldiers and the Moors began to quarrel and it ended in a general fight, the English of course, soon beating off the Moors. Then came down a strong reinforcement from the town, with several officers sent by the Governor with orders to make us all prisoners. Of course this we would not submit to for the Emperor of Morocco himself if he had been there in person, but I told the chief in command I would return on board ship again with my party, and he might report the circumstance to the English general; but as to making myself or any of my people prisoners, that he should not do as long as I had command of them, and I immediately drew them up ready to fire upon him if he presumed to attempt any violence. He was very angry and blustered about, but seeing there was no use in trying force, he wisely contented himself with brandishing his sabre, making his men prance their horses and gallop about very actively, for they were all beautifully mounted on barbs, and taking hold of the poor drunken officer said he should have his head cut off immediately for being drunk and neglecting his duty; accordingly they tied the poor devil neck and heels and throwing him across a horse away they galloped to the town, where the poor fellow was degraded as an officer but not put to death, only well bastinadoed.[22] ...

After having completed our water in Tetuan Bay (which, by-the-by, is a beautiful situation, with a magnificent view of the mountains which frown over the town and the strong fort of Ceuta, which belongs to the Spaniards, and of which they are very jealous, as it commands the Straits on the African sides and is in time of war a great annoyance to our merchant vessels when becalmed, which often happens, and then the Spanish gunboats move out under cover of the guns of the fort and whip up our merchantmen at a great rate) we proceeded '*aloft*' (the term used for going up the Mediterranean Sea and in about six weeks we arrived at Messina, in Sicily. It was a brilliant day and I was much struck with the beauty of the coast on both sides of the Straits. The current is so rapid, and there are so many eddies and whirlpools, that although I thought we were near enough to chuck a biscuit on shore, it was many hours before we were able to cast anchor, for just as we thought ourselves safe in harbour, in one minute an eddy carried us off to the opposite side of the Straits, where, on the Calabrian shore, there is a rock called '*scylla*,' so that if you escape the whirlpool of '*Charybdis*,' on the Sicilian shore, you are driven against the rock of Scylla [Scilla]. Messina is a very beautiful old town, full of ancient ruins caused by earthquakes, which have so frequently taken place there that there are many streets in ruins. Our regiment was ordered to go round the island by sea to a town called Melazzo [Milazzo], situated on a promontory, where we remained the whole time we were in Sicily. Nearly all the officers were permitted to go and see Mount Etna except myself. I did not get leave, having consented to take other officers' duty to let them go, and by that means I was delayed so long, that the very day General Paget and I were preparing to go off to Etna, an order came for us to embark on a secret expedition and so there was an end to my hopes of seeing Mount Etna, as well as various other curious places and things, which was very vexatious ...

During the time we remained in Sicily wine was so cheap and plentiful that our soldiers drank so hard that great numbers were in hospital, and many died; but what is worse, many of the men in their drunken fits killed their comrades and were accordingly hung for murder, as it would never do to let drunkenness be an excuse for murder. I was on several courts-martial which sentenced the prisoners to be hung, and although I very much disliked sentencing a fellow creature to death, still it was my duty to do so; but it leaves a very painful sensation on the mind for a long time after.

While in Sicily, I was once detached from headquarters to a place in the hills called Gisso [Gesso], where one day an orderly dragoon arrived and delivered to me the following letter from Sir John Moore:

Messina, 15 July 1807
My dear Napier,
Some people of rather a suspicious description have been reported to have been seen about the mountains over this. They are dressed and armed like the masses of Calabria. Among them are Frenchmen who have spy glasses and are said to have been seen sketching. It is possible they may pass through, or take up their lodgings at night at Gisso [Gesso] or in the village below. It would be well to give orders, if any people of this description are seen in your neighbourhood, that quietly you may be informed of it and then by calling on the magistrate you would find if he knew them. If he did not, and they could not give an account of themselves, they should be arrested and reported, or sent to headquarters.

You are aware how much discretion must be used in obtaining this sort of information so as not to give alarm to those we wish to take, nor to molest others who have no concern with it; but I feel I risk nothing in giving you this information, which will tend to excite your vigilance without tempting you to act unless you see good cause. Believe me, sincerely yours, John Moore.

Immediately upon the receipt of this letter I disguised myself as a peasant, and taking my compass and map with me, as well as my spy glass, I started into the mountains, with a gun on my shoulder and a pair of pistols under my waistcoat and made a tour round my own immediate neighbourhood; and although I did not meet any of these people, I gained sufficient information to have an idea where they were, and that there was a considerable number of them. This information I forthwith transmitted to Sir John Moore, and received the following letter in answer:

My dear Napier,
Many thanks to you for your letter and for the activity you have shown on the subject about which I wrote to you. I only beg that you will not allow your zeal to carry you so far as to risk yourself by putting yourself in the power of any vagabonds should you fall in with them. They should be traced, and then a strong body of soldiers sent to seize them in the night. General Oakes is also employing people to make the same discovery. I shall perhaps see you in a day or two on my passage to Palermo. Sincerely yours, John Moore.

Immediately after this letter came an order from the Quartermaster-General, directing me to proceed, according to a route sent with the order, to a certain place in the mountains with one hundred men and the necessary number of officers, where I should meet and join detachments from the Guards and other regiments sent from different parts of the island on the same service. I put myself and party accordingly en route at nine at night, and marched for many hours over the worst road I ever saw before or since, till we came to a very curious old walled town on the summit of a high mountain, which we passed through without waking the inhabitants, after well examining the town and satisfying myself that none of the people we were in search of were in it. At last, after a harassing night march, we saw, at 11 o'clock a.m., the other detachments in the valley below us, not one of them having seen or heard anything of the objects of our pursuit, so we marched home again.

The whole thing turned out to be that a body of poor Calabrese peasants had passed over from the opposite shore, bringing their arms with them, and were proceeding to Palermo to see the king, and to beg to be allowed to enter the Sicilian army, as they had not the means of subsistence in Calabria.

Soon after this we embarked for England, and touching at Gibraltar, where we remained for a fortnight, we landed at Portsmouth; but in less than three months we again embarked and sailed for Gottenburg in Sweden.

Charles was relieved to be back in England in 1807:

Deal [June?] – Once more in barracks and with little duty, luckily, for Guernsey duty was too much. My poor friend Macleod 78th[23] has been killed in Egypt, and William Stewart wounded. Our first battalion is coming here, and we are to form a brigade under General Spencer, who is a very gentlemanlike and peaceable kind of man: I thought he had been famous as a dasher both in dress and talent.

July – William marched into this place on Monday, and on Tuesday to Ramsgate, and is now on board a transport in the Downs. He is on board a small transport and quite well. You told me our destination depends on which militia regiment we recruit from: therefore I did not work, disliking to have any concern with fixing my own fate in the dark. Meanwhile my orders are to be superintend the volunteering from the militia at one of the stations. It will be a troublesome appointment, but the most troublesome of all troubles to me is having nothing to do – a too easy chair is the rack for me.

Chapter 2

Copenhagen 1807

William and George were the first brothers to see action, being part of the expedition to Copenhagen under General Cathcart. William's letters begin at Hythe a few months before the 1st Battalion, 43rd Foot, were ordered to march:

Hythe, January 1807
My dearest mother,
I had intended to answer your letter in person, but I have unfortunately had my room robbed of my jacket and three guineas, the sum I had intended for my passage. I think there is no chance of an expedition, from the accounts we have received of the Russians being totally defeated by the French.[1] There is a subaltern of mine whom I wish to serve if I could, and his brother who is now an officer in the York Militia, wishes to get an ensigncy in this:[2] if you could by any means get one in this regiment, or point out the way, I would be very glad of it, for to tell the truth I do not see how I can do without you show me the way. Some of your friends might perhaps be able, particularly as Lord Dundas[3] will recommend him as an excellent young man. His brother would have applied to him to get one for him, but he has no other dependence in the world for himself, and he is afraid of asking too much; this is fair because he is an elderly man (!) and therefore has less chance of getting on without interest than his brother of the militia, who is a boy of 18. In case you could not get one in the 43rd, you might in the 35th, as the Duke would probably be glad of a young man of good character &c. &c.

Hythe. One o'clock in the morning. [August 1807]
I have these three days back expected the route to embark, but have been so often disappointed I did not like to flurry you with the news, but the wolf is come at last, this moment arrived, to march in four hours; where I have not heard yet, but it must be Deal. ... God bless you, my dearest mother.

Ramsgate, Tuesday [August 1807]
We this moment embark. You will, I know, excuse my brevity when I tell you that our colonels seem to vie with the transport masters and ministers who can make most confusion, even on our own shores: some of the men faint for want of food, my last sixpence is gone to them; and the second colonel[4] took both my bugles to make a band on board the headquarters ship... Your affectionate son, W. Napier.

Uterslaught [Utterslev] 19 August 1807
We are now before Copenhagen, at the distance of one mile and a half, where we arrived without opposition: we have been here three days. We have had some trifling skirmishing on the outposts, taken some prisoners and killed about 50 I believe, with the loss of an officer of artillery and no men. Tonight, we begin to dig the approaches, as it is intended to be a regular siege. Henry[5] I saw at Elsineur [Helsingør] roads. Some of our generals have dreadful thick skulls, for I never saw any fair in Ireland so confused as the landing: had they opposed us, the remains of the army would have been on their way to England. The country people are like the Irish; give the soldiers everything they want and in return are plundered and abused, for which we hang and flog the soldiers every day. British soldiers fight well but are the greatest scoundrels possible. I shall write again soon, but I have not been in bed or off my legs for four days and nights and my eyes are so heavy I can hardly see to write. We are now in cantonments (at first we lay in the fields), but there is an alarm every hour, which murders sleep, besides the out pickets, which last twenty-four hours at a time. I do not know how you can direct to me. Neither the [Danish] King or Crown Prince are at Copenhagen and the Danes have few troops, and those bad. &c. &c. Your affectionate son, W. Napier.

William wrote to Charles, who still languished in England:

Roeskilde [Roskilde], 2 September 1807
My dear Charles,
The account of our operations is short, being a compound of stupidity, vanity and villainy. We stayed eight days off Elsineur [Helsingør] without landing; at last landed at Webek [Vedbaek] in the greatest confusion; marched in two days to Copenhagen, at which time we might have gone straight into the town, they having only 3,000 regulars in the town or in the island; remained in villages ten days, in which time we erected one battery that on trial was found not to answer, being too great a range. On the eleventh

day a sortie was made by the garrison, when the Germans, Rifles and ours drove them in, in about five minutes; they are the greatest cowards I ever beheld. On the twelfth day 6,000 troops were sent under the command of Sir Arthur Wellesley in two divisions, five companies of ours with each. The German General Linsingen[6] went with the second to disperse the *levy en masse* collected near Roeskilde [Roskilde] and commanded by regular officers. We hunted them for four days; on the 5th Sir A Wellesley fell in with them to the amount of 9,000 near Kioge [Køge]; fired one volley; the 92nd charged and they ran in every direction. Our five companies were upon the right flank and were not within shot [of] the other division, with which I was, [we] ought to have been in their rear and made the whole prisoners, but by General Linsingen halting where he had no business, we were too late and merely had what they called a *gallant action*, but which I call a murder of some poor runaways who did not intend to resist. The number of prisoners and the killed are correct, but all the nonsense that you will see in the Gazette is no more than what I tell you. You may probably see my company put down as missing; everything was in such confusion that the other four companies lost their way and joined Sir Arthur's division and returned me missing. I stayed with my own general and did the same by them. They have now I understand, collected 5,000 or 6,000 more and we are to have another hunt after them in a day or two. It is damned easy to be a general; no disparagement to the *big wigs*. I understand they have now erected 63 mortars with which they are bombarding the town, in which case they will have it in three or four days and then all is over. I fancy plunder is the order of the day and the Germans add murder to it.

Roeskilde [Roskilde], 1 October [1807]
My dear Mother,
I received your two letters, but you must not be surprised that I do not write often, as we are in the interior and not always able to procure paper. You will have seen by the letter I wrote to Charles that I did fight a battle, such as it was. People say here we are to winter in the island.[7] Reports fly as thick as the generals' skulls. Copenhagen is extremely like Cork, which you know as much about as you do of Pekin [Peking]; however, there is a very fine collection of pictures in it and seven millions worth of French property, which our clever generals contrived to have put down as private property in the capitulation and great quantities of prize money, which I don't believe we shall get. Henry was gone to England before your letter came. Tell the Duke of Cumberland[8] that we are the Reserve; that is, men reserved for the most dangerous service. I saw General Spencer,[9] and gave

him the Duke's letter, and I never met with so much real civility in so short a time from anybody. &c. &c.

In November 1807, Charles wrote regarding rumours of the disgraceful conduct of the 43rd Foot at Copenhagen:

There is a report that Captain William Napier has taken sixty prisoners! But it is said also that the poor 43rd had twelve men hanged; and Lord Cathcart said twenty successful campaigns cannot wipe off their disgrace! He praises the Germans highly. Now if the 43rd had behaved so ill, it is the fault of General Richard Stewart, their late lieutenant colonel. Nevertheless, if they have behaved so ill, Lord Cathcart is right to stigmatize them; but he talks nonsense if he thinks those Hanoverians are equal to Englishmen. I wish the fate of England lay on the issue between five thousand of them and the 43rd alone!

William arrived back at Gravesend in early November:

Gravesend, 9 November 1807
As I did not know exactly when I landed whether you were at Goodwood or London, nor do I know now, I wrote to Charles desiring him to write to you of my arrival; but neither seeing him or hearing from him in answer, made me imagine that the letters must have failed. I write to you at hazard of it reaching you. We are now on our march to Ipswich Barrack, being in number two companies parted from the regiment in a gale of wind off Yarmouth. I expect three hundred pounds prize money; people tell me I shall get six hundred; I am not sanguine myself.

When I arrive at Ipswich I intend to write a journal of my warfare, interspersed with witty anecdotes, sound remarks, and severe military criticisms interspersed with moral and political reflections to be dedicated to the Right Honourable Lady Sarah Napier.[10] &c. &c.

He responded to Charles' reported outrages:

Ipswich, 15 November 1807
I am extremely surprised at your account of our marauding, but what puzzles me most is that you seem to have heard something particular about my company and talk as if some of them had been hanged. All I can say is, that our regiment did plunder now and then, particularly at the beginning, but certainly less than most; but unfortunately the 43rd officers considered it

their duty to punish the men that did it and the other regiments passed it over in silence, by which means all the mischief they did was placed to our account also. The Germans, being foreigners and therefore incapable of plundering, were taken under Lord Cathcart's particular protection and extolled at the expense of the British; but I can assure you, from sad experience, that the General Linsingen of the Germans down to the smallest drum[mer] boy in the [King's German] Legion, the earth never groaned with such a set of infamous murdering villains and that being highly laudable, Lord Cathcart returned them thanks for their conduct ...

William later wrote a fuller response to the rumoured outrages of the 43rd, strongly criticising General Linsingen:

Two soldiers of the regiment, one a black musician, a deserter from the French; the other a deserter, as he acknowledged from a ship of war, outraged a woman and were instantly discovered and tried by a general court martial. They were condemned, but the proceedings went home, for confirmation and were declared by the judges [as] illegal: the men thus escaped, but the matter was mentioned in the House of Commons with the usual errors ... to the detriment of the regiment ...

As to the sixty prisoners noticed in the correspondence, there is also a new but true tale to be told about them. A company of the 43rd under my orders being separated from the rest of the regiment, acted on the right, at what was called the Battle of Kioge [Køge]. General Linsingen commanded, and the following atrocities were perpetrated under the name of fighting. Advancing through a thick wood, the Hanoverian red skirmishers, not their green, were in front and a heavy fire was heard although no enemy was perceived; dead men were however soon come upon, one or two having sword [wounds]; more had musket [wounds] and it was evident that a butchery of poor peasants was taking place. At the foot of one tree lay six unhappy creatures; they had climbed it to hide and were shot down. Five were dead, the sixth still alive but mortally wounded and the upper part of his arm being broken, the bone was driven half a foot out through the flesh from the fall! Every British soldier shuddered at the cruelty.

Next day a large village was occupied and there General Linsingen set some soldiers to dabble in a common sewer for money said to be hidden; and he excited others with ladders, to enter a church by the roof, the doors being too strong to break open: I saw him in the streets without his hat, stimulating the men. All this time the 43rd remained immovably abstinent, with the exception of one man, who obeyed the general's call to search the sewer; he was instantly recalled by his captain [William Napier], who expressed to General Linsingen in terms scarcely reconcilable with discipline, his disgust and determination to rejoin his regiment. He was not opposed and all the prisoners were then put under his charge, with orders to take them to headquarters: not sixty, but four hundred were given over. But what prisoners? More than three hundred were women and decrepit men! Few were able to bear arms! With this column a march of three days was made, across the country directed by the churches, which in Zealand are all on rising knolls and seen from afar. Hourly the poor prisoners cried out *'There is my village/my house'* and when they did so, the women and old men were released; the column was thus reduced to sixty young men who perhaps bore arms, but [who] did not appear to have done so.

Charles now found himself back in England:

September 1807 – The 50th Second Battalion will not go to Ireland: some regiments are not permitted to take Irish volunteers, which appears as if they were especially appropriated for half hanging and floggings and cutting of throats; for burnings and robberies, and other little government details. What an intolerable system of ruling.

September 1807 – Thank you dear mother for my two brothers' letters from Copenhagen: they are worth reading. One is from a man who reflects on the scenes before him in a moral point of view; the other with not less humanity, notes only what relates to the progress of the action. It might be thought the younger mind [William] would feel most the horror of war; but the one has seen dead bodies and perhaps some burning and pillage; the other has only seen the noise and spirited part of a battle, which he expected and would have been disappointed not to [have] seen. A dying man in pain, a bad wound, the cries of the hurt, are things he does not expect to affect him, as they will when he sees them, and as they have his brother; he [George] is therefore all eagerness to fight and only thinks how things favour or retard success. All this is quite natural and the other probably felt the same, but when writing, his thoughts were chiefly occupied by a higher consideration. He saw the injustice of the action: he saw men dead in defence of their homes; he saw a people ill-used by another nation in the first instance, and in the second ill-used by individuals; his ideas are therefore raised above the considerations of success. Why are they so raised when he is not accountable for the event beyond his own duty? Why should his mind dwell on what he thinks unjust when he cannot help it? Because his wish to succeed is not so great as his wish to save!

This Copenhagen expedition, is it an unjust action for the general good? Who can say that such a precedent is pardonable? When once the line of justice is passed, there is no shame left. England has been unjust! What power will now blush to be so also? Was not our high honour worth the danger we might perhaps have risked in maintaining that honour inviolate?

Volunteers pour in and business accumulates: the rascals rob all the country. I chased two fellows a few nights ago and cut one of them down. Thank God he is not hurt to signify, but the affair was uncomfortable for an hour or two, until a surgeon and a light showed that his hat had saved his head and his ribs had preserved his innards. It could not be helped. It was very dark and following them into a lane I could not trust to taking two men prisoners, both grenadiers and neither drunk. He is now well, and it has had a good effect. I am bothered with Sir Neddy Knatchbull[11] and other squires here, who object hugely to their game being shot. I, hypocrite that I am, inwardly rejoice at it, while with the face of a Quaker when a trooper swears in his presence, I condole with them on the impropriety of shooting their birds and the impossibility of preventing it; the last always tacked to my pity for their grievances, as consolation. I do not shoot, but the officers who do send my friends game: so honour and profit combine. In good faith however, though some of the squires behave very ill and are very sulky, which is of no use for it only amuses the mess, good Sir Neddy really behaves very well.

William wrote further at the end of the year, on his thoughts of Staff college and Copenhagen Prize Money, which his brother Henry thought would be minimal:

Maldon, 18 December 1807
Henry I believe is wrong, as we expect six or seven hundred pounds, but nobody can tell what it will be; indeed, some people say that they intend not to give anything.[12] This I think they would be afraid to try, because it would not be very safe to discontent 30,000 soldiers and twenty-six sail of the line.

I would like to go to High Wycome [Wycombe][13] very much, for the sake of the French, drawing and German masters, and also because all the Quartermaster-Generals, &c., are taken from High Wycombe, and there are so many of them that very few are of use on an expedition, and by these means get leave to gallop about where they choose; and I have seen enough service to know that is the best way of acquiring knowledge. Also you learn how to write a despatch, which is the *grand arcana*[14] of a general, fighting have little to do with it.

Chapter 3

The Corunna Campaign 1808–09

In early 1808, Charles was very hopeful of getting on active service and preferably on the Staff:

Ashford, February 1808
As to Moore's putting me on the Quartermaster-General's Staff, dearest mother, he cannot; his interest would of course be great, but I have no right to ask for it, nor would that be a proper way. As to being placed as my father was, it is [as] impossible as to be made commander in chief. The system of the department is now different and so many are fit; and so many more think themselves fit; and so many are employed, that the situation is in fact become a very extensive command and is generally given to lieutenant colonels who are favourites of the Horse Guards. All I want is the name, and leave of absence, with permission to go anywhere; that favour would not be great, and General Fox is the right person to get it granted: but I don't want to go to India.

Sickness in the regiment was serious and the locals were not being very agreeable:

March 1808
Our men have got the ophthalmia very badly and are dying fast, also from the inflammation of the lungs, caused by the coldness of the weather and bad barracks; in some cases typhus supervenes, but is not contagious.[1] There is no raging fever, cold alone is the cause, yet the men go off three or four a day: no officer suffers, they are warmer. You have of course dear mother, by this time got my lungs into a high state of inflammation and put out both my eyes: you shall be duly informed when the typhus begins or if I am to go off with a good pulse.

The people are very disagreeable to us soldiers; but we are taking John Bull in his own way. Some people attacked the 14th Dragoons for keeping hounds and prevented their hunting. In return they indicted the roads, put their enemies to an expense of fifteen hundred pounds,[2] pulled down two mills built too near the highway, and thus taught the gents that if they push [the] law to extremity for trifles we can do so likewise.

The sickness continued for some months:

May 1808
The soldiers have got pneumonia at Hythe and are dying as fast as we folks at Ashford. Only think of the surgeon taking from one man in twenty-four hours, one hundred and sixty ounces of blood and he is recovering![3] They say bleeding to death is the best way of saving them!

He was not a supporter of flogging, but felt obliged to explain his need to impose the punishment:

June 1808
You know my antipathy to flogging; you know that it is unconquerable. It began from hatred of the sight and disgust not yet gone, though habit reconciles one to horrible sights. This antipathy gains strength from principle and reason, as I am convinced it could be dispensed with. Still, as other severe punishments do not exist in our army, we must use torture in some cases, until a substitute is given [us] by our government. Mark this narrative: A robbery was committed in the regiment and the thief was discovered in a few hours, for men seldom suffer an outrage on their own society; no soldier can rob another without discovery. I resolved to make a severe example.

1st Because we are chiefly composed of boys, and if the punishment of robbery were not made terrible, the temptation of gold and impunity might have a great effect on their minds. 2nd Because it was only justice. The man is a pardoned deserter and a hardened villain, very little deserving of pity; and the soldier he robbed was a comrade who put entire confidence in him. It was altogether a villainous affair and I made a great stir when the matter was reported, giving the men to believe I would drink the very blood of the offender and flog the whole regiment unless the robber and his accomplices were discovered. Officers and men were thus worked up and the grenadiers (he was one of them) so cleared their honour by producing him. He was sentenced to nine hundred lashes, yet there was not one positive proof of the robbery, all was presumptive evidence: but I charged him with breaches of discipline, which could be proved and my resolve was to punish or not, according to my own judgment, a commanding officer being in truth despotic. Two days I took to consider every circumstance, thinking if he should be afterwards proved innocent, it would be disagreeable to have bestowed nine hundred lashes wrongfully. However, the thing appeared so clear, my mind was finally made up, but entirely for the good of others and against my feelings. If mistaken in my judgment there was nothing to tax conscience with, for decision is absolutely necessary amongst troops. The man thought me his deadly foe, whereas he had not such a powerful advocate in the garrison, for everyone was outrageous against him, while in my mind, there was not an atom of anger.

Yesterday he was flogged in the square, where no longer appearing angry, I said part of the punishment should be remitted if he would tell of his accomplices; that torture would make him speak and the money would prove his truth; it would therefore be better for his accomplices to confess and be produced. No one spoke. When he had received two hundred lashes he was promised pardon if he told where the money was. No! '*God in heaven was his witness he was innocent*'; many a man prayed for my honour who was guilty of many bad things, '*spare him in God's name who is innocent!*' In this manner he went on. I was inexorable and it is hardly credible that he received six hundred lashes, given in the most severe manner; and which he showed he felt with that acute sense of pain that some men have not; the whole time calling '*God and the saints to witness his innocence*', praying for death to relieve him. It required great resolution to remain inflexible, but it was necessary. Was I right in thinking him guilty, then it was right to do what was done. Was I wrong, then my misfortune could not be greater merely from giving more pain; and unless I went to the full extent it must be wrong, because it would evince doubt, and with doubt not a lash should have been given. Feeling right I was firm, but [after] six hundred lashes he was taken down, with the seeming brutal intention of flogging him again on a half-healed back, which is in a commanding officer's power to do and the greatest torture possible. He was told it should be so unless he confessed in the interim and directions were given that he should be kept [in] solitary to lower his spirits. My troubles were soon over; pain, lowness and the people employed to frighten him succeeded, he confessed all and told where the money was hid.

By the summer, there was great talk of an expedition to Spain to support the patriots. Charles, like many, was an enthusiast and hopeful of success, but realistic as to their chances against Napoleon:

July 1808.
They say Lord Moira is to command the expedition to Spain, Anstruther[4] is going, everybody is going but me: with my untoward luck I ought not

to serve. Will you let me know if you hear of any majority of Militia vacant, for it is better to be one thing or t'other at once. I see no prospect of adversity to try Napoleon's genius, but a great prospect of fresh laurels [for him] and as much patriots' blood as will make rich land and good crops in Spain. Where all is noise and bubble; the slaughter of the patriots is the only substantial thing and that will continue to be so. Still, we are bound to help them, poor people. We have not indeed ruined them by our intrigues, we are guiltless of their blood, but I would rather see England sink with them than refuse her aid in so noble a cause. Let her trust home to my brother Militia men and send her soldiers to the last man into Spain, we may succeed: *God only knows, and He is beyond our ken.* That we shall make some blunder is my opinion, we always do; but the fate of Spain and Europe is settled beforehand; and we shall do as fate ordains. Those fine Spaniards are to be liked and it is fitting we should fall with them rather than leave them without help. I have heard no military man's opinion yet, but it appears madness to make diversions as they call them: if they intend to fight, let fifty thousand men be sent and all the officers who speak the language to form their men. We have but one chance, which is to annihilate the French army in Spain before succours [sic] can cross the Pyrenees; but this requires a rapidity of action which we never exert, although we have the power.

Why should we attempt Italy? If we succeed in Spain it will be the best diversion in favour of Italy; for Napoleon will draw troops from there and the north to restore his power: then will be the time for attacking him nearer home. If he leaves Brest[5] defenceless, as he has often done, we could strike a blow, which you have often heard of, before he could help himself. In this mode we might help ourselves, but his arms will crush everything in Spain that they can reach. Nevertheless, a hostile population is a powerful weapon and no man can say what it will effect.

George had gone to the Baltic with Sir John Moore in 1808, but it soon became clear that nothing could be achieved there and the force returned to Britain, only to be moved on rapidly to Portugal:

We remained at anchor at Gottenburg for several weeks, while Sir John Moore, whose army was about 10,000 men, went to see the King at Stockholm, to consult with him as to the operations of the force under his orders. But finding Gustavus[6] to be full of wild impracticable schemes, and that he would not listen to reason …, Sir John Moore refused to co-operate with him …, [saying] that his master had given him the command, and that to him alone would he deliver it up. Upon this Gustavus flew into a violent rage, put Sir John Moore under arrest with a sentinel at his door, and swore he would take command of the British army in spite of him. Sir John Moore, knowing that he had a madman to deal with, made his escape during the night in the dress of a peasant; and one day a number of us were on board the '*Victory*,'[7] Sir James Saumarez's flagship,[8] at a ball given by the officers of that ship ... when a fishing-boat came alongside, and a peasant ran up the side and sprang on the quarter-deck! All the officers looked astonished and wondered who the devil that impudent fellow was, when I looked at him and instantly recognised the general! He laughed, and taking off his peasant's cap, asked the admiral if he did not know him. Of course we were all delighted to see him back, as we had heard a rumour of something having gone wrong. Had he not been able to get away, I believe it was the intention of the admiral and Sir John Hope,[9] the second in command, to have sailed round to Stockholm and demanded his release forthwith. Colonel Colborne,[10] who had accompanied him, was left there for some time and joined us at sea on our way back to England ...

In about ten days after we came to anchor at Spithead, we got orders to sail again, Sir John Moore being superseded in the command by Sir Harry Burrard, whom Lord Castlereagh sent down from London to take charge of the army, Sir John Moore remaining as second in command, which was not at all what the Ministers wanted, for they expected that General Moore would not serve as second, ... he went with the army to Portugal, where we arrived too late to take part in the battle of Vimiera ... The consequence of this battle was that the French entered into a treaty with the British commander-in-chief, Sir Hugh Dalrymple, who had arrived from Gibraltar, by which the French troops were permitted to embark on board British ships with their arms and baggage and were to be landed at a French port as soon as possible. This convention was loudly and ignorantly decried as cowardly and disgraceful to the British army, and this shameful and most unjust outcry was supported and encouraged by the Ministry; whereas, nothing could be more useful to the great object of sending troops to support and aid the Spanish nation, by clearing Portugal so immediately of the French that the British army could instantly commence preparations for moving into Spain.

Very soon after this convention was put into execution Sir Hugh Dalrymple was recalled, and went to England to account for his conduct before a court of inquiry; and, as Sir Arthur Wellesley was as much implicated in the business, he was sent for too; so that the army was deprived of his valuable services for a long time. Sir John Moore was appointed by the King's positive command to be commander-in-chief of the army ordered to enter Spain … he made me his aide-de-camp, which was the highest honour I could receive at that time, and proved that I had, by constant zeal and attention to my duty, gained his approbation.

Before giving up the command of my company and joining the general, I went with a detachment of my regiment under the command of Major Arbuthnott[11] to escort the French garrison of Elvas to Lisbon, where they were to embark and be conveyed to France. We had a very agreeable march, but part of the French troops, a Swiss regiment[12] (whose colonel[13] the Portuguese had attempted to assassinate), behaved very mutinously and riotously, and attempted to plunder the inhabitants; so we were obliged to threaten them with punishment. I saw a French soldier behave ill, and on speaking to the commander of the troops he went up to the man, who was rather mutinous and insolent, upon which the colonel instantly pulled out his pistol, presented it at the soldier's head and snapped it at him; luckily it did not go off, or he would have shot him dead. This could not be done in our army, as no officer can either shoot or flog a British soldier upon his own authority …

Upon our arrival at Lisbon with the French garrison, I joined Sir John Moore and commenced my duty as aide de camp. One day I was going to purchase a sabre, when Sir John Moore told me not to do so, but to buy a straight sword, sharp on both edges. The reason he gave was this: when a colonel, he commanded a storming party at the fort of Calvi, in Corsica, and just as he mounted the top of the breach and was forcing his way in, a French grenadier… was on the point of plunging his bayonet into him, when Moore, seeing his only chance of life was to run his sword through the man, he did so and killed him on the spot … So I did as he desired me, and purchased a straight one; but, thank God, I was lucky enough never to use my sword in the same way as Sir John Moore was forced to use his (…he told me he never should forget the horrid sensation it gave him when drawing the sword out of the man's body, and that it was always a painful recollection to him…)

At the same time, William was also hoping for foreign service, but was frustrated in his bid for further promotion:

Colchester, July 1808
My dear mother,
I cannot tell yet whether we are to embark or not, as we have been countermanded for some time, I suppose to belong to Lord Chatham's

division[14] or some other man who delights in having handsome showy guards for himself, and to take the credit of making the regiment to himself, and consequently ask for all the promotion that ought to go in it for his friends. We have now been for five years considered as the best regiment in England, and the reward is to put everybody they could think of over the heads of our officers and to finish it all they are now going to give a Lieutenant Colonelcy in the regiment to some friend of Colonel Stewart,[15] whose neck may the Lord break! And in order to make room for him they send the Major, whose claims they could not get over, into another regiment, notwithstanding he is an excellent officer and has been 20 years in this regiment,[16] by which you will perceive, my dear mother, that the worst regiment I could possibly have got into is the 43rd, and that I never can have any chance or promotion or real service in it.[17]

William wrote a few months later, still frustrated awaiting the order to march:

Colchester, 11 September 1808
My dear mother,
We are still vexed by the ministry: instead of marching on Monday, here we are on Friday, and no chance of our going at all that I can perceive. The first order was that we should embark the moment the transports had arrived; they have been there a week and we have not even got orders to march, and yet the first order was so peremptory that we broke up our mess and have been living ever since on pounds of raw meat per day, for those who have not got money or gridirons of their own. It certainly is the most plaguy [sic] disagreeable government in the world: they give orders to a number of troops they never intend to employ, break up their messes and half ruin the officers, and then congratulate themselves on their vigour and foresight. Precious rascals! In short, my dear mother, you may damn the Ministry, but believe me your affection son, W. Napier.

However, William was able to add a postscript to his letter, as he could report that they were finally to sail:

Sunday, 13 [September 1808]
The post did not go on Saturday, so that I have opened the letter to tell you that we have at last received the final order for sailing. We do really march this night at 12 o'clock for Harwich: the north of Spain is I believe our destination, as we are victualled for six weeks only. &c. &c. W.N.

Deal (in the Downs),[18] 22 September [1808]
After being windbound for a week at Harwich we have arrived here, where we shall stay about two days and then sail for Falmouth. I think Sir Arthur's laurels and talents for war are eclipsed by his talents for negotiation:[19] They will now be called Portugal laurels by way of eminence and the convention of Dalrymple and Wellesley. I am perfectly well. The boat is waiting. &c. &c.

Falmouth, 1 October [1808]
I received both your letters, but I could not answer them before, although I have been here four days, and we are likely to wait a fortnight longer. Sir David Baird[20] arrived here on Tuesday last, but we are to wait for cavalry. The 95th Rifle Corps and the 1st Battalion 43rd, are to be in one brigade under [Robert] Craufurd, who has the rank of Brigadier. I am very glad Charles has got two steps.[21] I must conceive that General Moore's approbation of Sir Arthur Wellesley was given before the convention was made, as he never could have praised a man who signed his name to the first agreement, which is worse than the final one;[22] in short, my dear mother, somebody must be hanged. I have not the least idea where we are going to; the Spaniards I think will not allow us to go to them, as they must be afraid we should endeavour to force them to give up their prisoners not taken in war, according to the promise of *Sir Scoundrel* Dalrymple in the convention. &c. &c

William also wrote to Charles, discussing who would now command the army in the Peninsula:

Falmouth, 3 October 1808
Since writing to my dear mother we have received an order to sail to-morrow or next day, for Corunna it is thought. I have not heard anything worth writing since the last, except that Sir Harry Burrard remains in Portugal[23] and General Moore goes to Spain, where it is probably we shall be under him, as Sir David is a younger officer; I hope so with all my heart.[24] This is a detestable place, the sooner I get out of it the better. I am quite well, and well stocked with provisions and a stomach. &c. &c.

William's next letter was from Corunna, where his battalion had arrived with Baird's force. Whether they would be allowed to land by the Spaniards was doubtful and how they would coordinate with Sir John Moore's force was unknown, but he hoped to see his brothers, who were already in the Peninsula:

Corunna, 14 October 1808
We arrived at this place yesterday after an uncommonly fine passage of four days; we are to stay here for some time, as there are couriers sent to Madrid about us, the answer to which can't arrive under ten days. The French have got possession of Bilbao again but are surrounded and can't escape. ... People say we are to be encamped here until Sir John Moore arrives, but nothing is known certainly as yet. ... I do not think I am likely to see Charles, but George I think I shall.

A week later William announced that they were landing:

Corunna, 23 October 1808
We have just received orders to land to-morrow and march to Lugo, a town about 40 miles from here, where we are to be cantoned until the arrival of General Moore, who takes the chief command, bringing with him an army from Lisbon; we shall then commence active operations. I think that both Charles and George will be with him, George certainly. The people are very good natured to us; I have been several times at the play, was introduced to several ladies, and been every night at balls, where I danced the waltz, which is their chief dance. It is a mistake to say Spaniards are jealous; so far from it that the women are extremely attentive to us, endeavouring to teach us the language, which is very easy, and also delighted if we dance with them, and the men equally so. In short, we are on very near the footing with them that we should be with old friends in England, that is some of us, for some of the Guards and others are very impertinent and not liked. The men are poor frippery little apprentice-looking people, but the women have all beautiful black eyes and generally very good figures. Do not be afraid of stilettoes, for they only use them when people behave ill, which I have no inclination to do; some however have, as two officers have been already stabbed, but both have recovered. The peasants who are training here are extremely well drilled to the use of the firelock and if they have the courage to fight, they are as good troops as our militia, that is in discipline, for they are of a very inferior race of men to the English in point of personal appearance, except the carmen, who are the strongest-looking men I ever saw. As I have a good deal to do, I must conclude, and I think it very probable I shall not be able to write again for a long time, as the orders about baggage are very strict and I shall not be able to carry my writing desk, besides which, the posts will not be regular when we go nearer to the enemy, who are however not nearer than 300 miles. If you could get me some letters [from] Lord Holland[25] they would be used

to introduce me to good company, by which I shall learn the language better than any other way. I forgot to say that the religious processions are magnificent and beautiful, and the nuns old, ugly, and loquacious to a great degree. We go the convents often and talk to nuns and monks, who are handsome, dirty, good-natured men.

William continued to write during the long march to join Sir John Moore, but he already had little faith in the Spanish:

Villafranca [del Bierzo], 10 November 1808
My dear mother,
I take the opportunity of an express going to Corunna to write to you. We marched in here yesterday after a very fatiguing one of 120 miles, raining the whole way and our quarters are worse than anything you can conceive from the worst description of the worst inns in the very worst part of Spain. The march however was pleasant because the romantic scenery of the mountains of Galicia and Leon is beautiful. I am perfectly well, and having made acquaintance at Corunna with some families, they gave letters to Lloyd[26] and me of recommendation to the next town, which was four days' march, called Lugo; there we met with more attention and pleasant parties than I ever saw before in anybody to strangers. The girls teach me the language fast, and we were such favourites that they gave us more letters to this place, where we meet with the same kindness; *à propos*, the only way I can repay them is to give them some toothbrushes and powder, as they complain they have no method of cleansing their teeth, to their sorrow. Whenever you have an opportunity, pray send me a large assortment of the above articles. The women and the upper class of men are as far as I can see good, the men proud and dirty; the lower class cruel, dirty, cheating, proud and crafty; they ought to be exterminated for their treatment of animals and flogged for their laziness. We have just heard of a proposition from Bonaparte and Russia for a general peace:[27] this has put us in a fright, because we have 300 miles more to march, and we are afraid of coming back without fighting; the only consolation we have for our long marches, because then we punish those who caused them. I think however that Napoleon will conquer Spain, because I observe that all the prisoners that I have seen are Germans, the troops that he has from the Rhenish confederation, and not one good soldier among them; thus the Spaniards will imagine that they can beat French soldiers, and when Bonaparte comes himself with his good troops they will [be] wofully [sic] mistaken. I hope I am no prophet; but if the British troops don't

save Spain, I think the Spaniards can't, for so vain are they that already they talk of invading France, forgetting that the best general and 300,000 of the second-best troops in the world are to be conquered first. They all seem to be well inclined to throw off the yoke of the priesthood; and as they are up to any kind of villany [sic], I should not be surprised if they murdered the monks and destroy the convents. By the bye, the aforesaid monks are the fattest people in Spain, and there are 200,000 of them, and their bishops very impudent, refusing to allow British officers into their houses although they were regularly billeted, for which the Spanish officers who accompanied us called them damned crooks and wig-makers to their faces; ... I like our General Craufurd much; he is very attentive to the men.

George recorded his experiences of the campaign:

After a great deal of bother and much labour on the part of Sir John Moore ... we all joined at Salamanca ... Sir John Moore made a forward movement towards the enemy, in order to form a junction with Sir David Baird's corps ... towards Sahagun, where he expected Sir David would join him, and then he would make a forced march and attack Soult[28] at Saldanha ... The very morning of our arrival at Sahagun Lord Paget had given them a dressing, making several prisoners, besides a number being killed and wounded. I found a number of the prisoners confined in a large cellar, where they were badly off, many wounded and nothing to eat or drink. Of course, I immediately mentioned this to the general and he desired me to order the commissary to provide them with wine and bread. This being done, the poor fellows were as merry as possible and began dancing and singing; and one of them, to my great amusement, took a little fiddle from his pocket and commenced playing quadrilles with as much energy and life as though he was playing to a parcel of ladies in a ballroom.

The next night we were joined by Sir David Baird's corps, and the head of the column was in motion to move on Marshal Soult's corps of the French army, which we were to attack at daylight on the following morning, when just as Sir John Moore was mounting his horse, and I was actually giving him his pistols, a Spanish peasant came up and asking for the general in chief, put a note into his hand from the Marquis de Romana[29] ... which gave information that Napoleon had changed his plan of operations ... and was marching with great speed on the British army with an immense force ... He immediately ordered the troops to counter-march, and we commenced our memorable retreat to Corunna ...

At Benevento [Benavente], a large town where we halted for one night, one of Napoleon's generals, and a relation of his own, called Lefevre Desnouettes,[30] commanding a division of cavalry of the Imperial Guard, crossed the river and formed up his troops on a plain, upon which our hussars under Sir Charles Stewart[31] attacked them with great spirit and in a very short time completely upset them, killing, wounding and taking many prisoners, among whom was the general himself, who being attacked by a couple of our hussars as he made an attempt to gain a ford and being slightly wounded in the head, surrendered himself just as Sir Charles Stewart came up, who sent him to headquarters, where he arrived magnificently dressed in scarlet and gold as general of the Imperial Hussars.[32] Sir John Moore received him in the kindest manner and seeing he was bleeding, immediately sent for some water and washed the wound himself, gave him fresh linen &c, and sent in a flag of truce to request that his baggage might be allowed to come to him, which was permitted by Napoleon and that night it arrived, with several horse's and servants &c, for the French generals have always a great proportion of baggage. When General Lefevre was dressed, and just before we sat down to dinner, Sir John Moore asked him if there was anything he wished, upon which Lefevre cast a glance at his side (his sword having been taken from him when made prisoner) and then looked at Sir John Moore, who, comprehending what he meant, with all the high feeling of a soldier and the grace of a perfect gentleman, unbuckled his own sword from his side and presented it to his prisoner ...

We proceeded on our retreat towards Corunna. Our march was made with great rapidity, and the men and officers were obliged to be eternally under arms, as the enemy pursued us as quickly as possible ... There never was any want of provisions, but great want of time to cook them, and this it was impossible to prevent, as the enemy gave us no respite till we got to Astorga, where ... we found the town crammed full of Spanish troops, and of course the arrival of our army made the confusion beyond anything. And here the army was in a highly disorganised state, breaking open stores, plundering the houses, &c, and a horrid scene of drunkenness in all the corps except General Paget's[33] and the Guards at Villafranca [del Bierzo]. The general found it necessary to make an example by shooting a private of the 15th Hussars, whom Captain Pasley[34] and myself caught plundering a house; and upon our laying hold of him he was most insolent and struck Pasley. The facts being stated to the general, he was shot that morning; and this had some effect, but not much, I am sorry to say.

At Lugo, the French having only pursued us from Astorga with Marshal Soult's corps ... we made a halt in order to rest the troops and if possible to give battle and cripple Soult's corps, which would enable us to retreat more leisurely and consequently more regularly. Sir John Moore took up an excellent position and offered battle to the Marshal, who after a slight demonstration and a smart skirmish, in which we lost a few killed and wounded, thought it the most prudent thing to leave us quiet, as he felt sure we must move off the next day, and that he could not fail to have us at Corunna. As I was riding along the position in the morning with some orders in a great hurry, and as I passed that part of the line where … Charles, who commanded the 50th Regiment, and his friend Major Stanhope[35] were eating a famous dish of '*Irish stew*' for breakfast, these two fellows, knowing that I dared not stop, ran up and put this savoury dish to my nose by way of tantalising me, who had been on horseback nearly all night and had not eaten anything for many hours, and then shouted out, 'You dainty dog, you can't eat Irish stew!' This will show you what merry fellows soldiers are, for we were then every moment expecting to be attacked by the enemy and knew not if any one of us three should ever eat any dish again …At night the army was ordered to be put, as silently as possible, in movement, and we recommenced our rapid retreat, leaving the picquets to keep up the fires all through the night in order to deceive the enemy and gain several hours' march upon him, which we accordingly did, and the picquets joined us by a forced march before we halted for the night. The men however, being very much disappointed at not having a battle, and being fatigued with the length and rapidity of the retreat which was absolutely necessary to save the army from destruction, became totally disorganised, and disregarding all discipline and throwing off the authority of their officers, detached themselves in large parties, straggling, drinking and pillaging in the most shameful and infamous manner. I saw several fellows quit their ranks and go off across the fields to plunder, and on riding up to one of them and ordering him to return instantly to his regiment, he swore he would not be ordered by me, and presented his rifle at my head; but luckily for me it missed fire, or I should have finished my career on the spot. I ought to have shot him with my pistol on the instant, or to have brought him a prisoner to the commander in chief, who would have ordered him to be shot, but I felt a dislike to have a fellow creature put to death on my account …

On that very day Sir John Moore halted the whole army and addressed each division upon its infamous, disgraceful conduct; he called upon the soldiers to recollect they were Englishmen, and not to disgrace their country and the bright lustre of the name of Britons by such disorders and such beastly drunkenness! He told them that rather than command men who behaved in such an infamous manner, he prayed to God that the first bullet fired by the enemy might enter his heart, for he would much rather be dead than command such an army! This seemed to produce some effect, and I do think their conduct improved after that day. But the men were not so much to blame as the officers; for I fearlessly assert that, generally speaking, the officers of that army were more engaged in looking after themselves and their own comforts, and openly murmuring against the commander in chief, than in looking after the soldiers and keeping up proper discipline. I know that there were many exceptions to this censure; notably Sir John Hope, Lord William Bentinck,[36] and Sir Rowland Hill,[37] who exerted themselves in every way to keep up the discipline; and the reserve under General Paget, which, as forming the rear-guard, had double the work and fatigue of any other division; for every officer and man, from the general who gave the example to the youngest soldier in the regiments, did their duty with spirit and with zeal. I from being on the Staff, had many opportunities of observing the conduct of the various divisions of that army, and the more I reflect upon what I witnessed, the more convinced I am that the great cause of the disorganised state of the troops was mainly owing to the supineness of the general officers and to the imprudent language they used themselves, and permitted their Staff to make use of, when speaking of the retreat and the conduct of it by the commander in chief.

During the retreat I was one night sent by Sir John Moore with despatches of great importance to Sir David Baird, which were to be forwarded by him to General Fraser[38] who commanded a division[39] which was to march by another route and this despatch was to countermand the former order and desire him to resume his place in the column. This despatch was delivered by me, after riding all night in a heavy storm of rain, sleet and snow, at four or five o'clock in the morning, Sir John Moore having told me that if I did not ride fast I should be too late to catch Sir David [Baird] before he had marched, as his division would be under arms before daylight and moving off the ground. However, as I said, I arrived just after day had broke, about five o'clock and going direct to Sir David's quarters I found him and his aide de camp, Captain Alexander Gordon[40] in bed in the same room and not thinking of moving. Sir David having read the despatch, asked me if I was to carry the one enclosed to General Fraser, or was he, Sir David, to forward it. I replied I received no orders to do more than deliver my despatch as speedily as possible to him, but that if he had no officer to send and would give me a fresh horse (my own and the dragoon's who accompanied me being completely knocked up), I was perfectly ready to go on. He said, '*Oh, no, if you were not ordered to go, I shall send it on by an orderly dragoon.*' I then repeated I was not ordered but was perfectly ready to do so if he had not an officer to send, as I knew it was of consequence. Sir David replied in a very gruff manner, '*sir, that's my business; I shall send it by a dragoon.*' Of course I was silent, and then asking him if he had any commands, I took my departure (after resting my horse) on my way back to meet the general, and in a few hours I was overtaken by an officer who told me that the orderly dragoon sent by Sir David had got drunk and lost the despatch, so that by the time Sir John Moore was informed of this and a fresh despatch written and sent off, many hours were lost and the division of General Fraser quite knocked up with the length of march it was forced to make in order to regain the main body. Sir John Moore was deeply vexed at this, but as the thing was done and could not be undone he said very little about it to Sir David. Not so Colonel Graham[41]... who was very angry indeed and made no scruple of loudly expressing it both before Sir John Moore and to Sir David Baird. At length we arrived at Corunna after a most arduous and harassing retreat, the rear-guard under General Paget being almost constantly in action with the enemy's advance. Upon arriving at Corunna there were no transports, as the wind and stormy weather had delayed them in Vigo Bay, where it had been Sir John Moore's first intention to have retreated and embarked the army; indeed, one division of the troops under General Robert Craufurd did go by that route and embarked there.[42] The transports not having arrived was very unfortunate, as had they been all ready as Sir John Moore fully expected, the whole army would have been embarked without fighting that battle which, although so glorious for the honour of the army, was the cause of England losing Sir John Moore, the best general she had except the Duke of Wellington ...

As soon as the troops were in position, they commenced preparing for embarking the stores and heavy artillery which were unnecessary in the camp. Then the order was given for shooting the dragoon horses, as there were no horse ships to embark them in; besides, had there been ships, there was no time, and the poor animals were all half-dead already from fatigue and want of food, and were all foundered and suffering great pain. Now, if they had fallen into the hands of the enemy or of the Spaniards, the unfortunate brutes would have been worked to death, so it was better that they should be at once shot than left to live a few weeks longer in pain and misery.

The troops received fresh ammunition, as what they had was wet and bad; also the unserviceable muskets were exchanged for new ones found in the Spanish stores and which had been sent from England long before for the use of the Spaniards, who instead of distributing them to the peasantry or to their troops, coolly locked them up in store! There were two powder magazines at some distance from the position of the army. These Sir John Moore very properly ordered to be blown up, as they would otherwise have fallen into the hands of the French. I never saw a more beautiful sight; but I am sorry to say, a fine fellow, an officer of engineers who had the execution of this, was unfortunately blown up by going too near the place to see that the train was properly laid, and he had not time to escape before the whole blew up, and of course, he was destroyed, poor fellow![43]

The same evening the transports arrived under convoy of several men of war, and immediately everything was embarked, such as the sick and wounded, the stores, heavy artillery, baggage, and Staff horses; that is, every Staff officer was allowed to embark one horse if he had one that was sound and worth embarking. That morning, before the ships arrived, as I was attending Sir John Moore riding to the position, he said to me: *'I have often been thought an unlucky man by my friends in consequence of being generally wounded in action, and some other events of my life, but I never thought so myself till now; and if the transports do not arrive this day, I shall certainly be convinced I am an unlucky fellow, and that fate has so decreed!'*

The Battle of Corunna

Charles wrote later a long description of his experiences at the battle:

On the 16 of January 1809, the British Army was opposed to the French at Corunna. The Imperial troops on higher ground, hung over us like threatening clouds and about one o'clock the storm burst. Our line was under arms, silent, motionless, yet all were anxious for the appearance of Sir John Moore. There was a feeling that under him we could not be beaten, and this was so strong at all times as to be a great cause of discontent during the retreat wherever he was not. *Where is the general?* was now heard along that part of the line where I was, for only of what my eyes saw and my ears heard, do I speak.

This agitation augmented as the cries of men stricken by cannon shot arose. I stood in front of my left wing on a knoll, from whence the greatest part of the field could be seen, and my picquets were fifty yards below, disputing the ground with the French skirmishers; but a heavy French column, which had descended the mountain at a run, was coming on behind with great rapidity and shouting *En avant, tue, tue, en avant tue!* Their cannon at the same time, plunging from above, ploughed the ground and tore our ranks. Suddenly I heard the gallop of horses and turning saw Moore. He came at speed and pulled up so sharp and close he seemed to have alighted from the air; man and horse looking at the approaching foe with an intenseness that seemed to concentrate all feeling in their eyes.

The sudden stop of the animal, a cream coloured one with black tail and mane, had cast the latter streaming forward, its ears were pushed out like horns, while its eyes flashed fire and it snorted loudly with expanded nostrils; expressing terror, astonishment and muscular exertion. My first thought was, it will be away like the wind! But then I looked at the rider and the horse was forgotten. Thrown on its haunches the animal came, sliding and dashing the dirt up with its fore feet, thus bending the general forward almost to its neck; but his head was thrown back and his look more keenly piercing than I ever before saw it. He glanced to the right and left, and then fixed his eyes intently on the enemy's advancing column, at the same time grasping the reins with both his hands and pressing his horse firmly with his knees; his body thus seemed to deal with the animal while his mind was intent on the enemy and his aspect was one of searching intenseness beyond the power of words to describe; for a while he looked and then galloped to the left, without uttering a word. I walked to the right of my regiment, where the French fire from the village of [San Vicenzo de] Elvina was now very sharp and our picquets were being driven in by the attacking column; but I soon returned to the left, for the enemy's guns were striking heavily there and his musquetry also swept down many men. Meeting Stanhope, I ordered him to the rear of the right wing, because the ground was lower, it was his place, he was tall, the shot flew high and I thought he would be safer. Moore now returned and I asked him to let me throw our grenadiers, who were losing men fast, into the enclosures in front. *'No'*, he said *'they will fire on our own picquets in the village.'*

'Sir our picquets and those of the 4th Regiment also, were driven from thence when you went to the left.'

'Were they, then you are right, send out your grenadiers' and again, he galloped away. Turning round I saw Captain Clunes[44] of the 50th, just arrived from Corunna and said to him, *'Clunes, take your grenadiers and open the ball.'* He stalked forward alone, like Goliath before the Philistines, for six feet five he was in height and of proportionate hulk and strength, his grenadiers followed and thus the battle began on our side.

Again, Sir John Moore returned and was talking to me when a round shot struck the ground between his horse's feet and mine. The horse leaped round and I also turned mechanically, but Moore forced the animal back and asked me if I was hurt? *'No Sir!'* Meanwhile a second shot had torn off the leg of a 42nd man, who screamed horribly and rolled about so as to excite agitation and alarm with others. The general said *'This is nothing my lads, keep your ranks, take that man away; my good fellow don't make such a noise, we must bear these things better.'* He spoke sharply, but it had a good effect; for this man's cries had made an opening in the ranks and the men shrunk from the spot, although they had not done so when others had been hit who did not cry out. But again, Moore went off and I saw him no more! It was a little in front of this spot that he was killed. The French pointed out the place to me two months afterwards. There it was he refused to let them take off his sword when it hurt his wound! That dreadful wound! Poor fellow!

Lord William Bentinck now came up on his quiet mule and though the fire was heavy, began talking to me as if we were going to breakfast; his manner was his ordinary one, with perhaps an increase of good humour and placidity. He conversed for some time, but no recollection of what he said remains, for the fire was sharp and my eyes were more busy than my ears; I only remember saying to myself *'this chap takes it coolly or the devil's in it'*.

Lord William and his mule, which seemed to care as little for the fire as its rider, sheltered me from shot, which I liked well enough; but having heard officers and soldiers jeer at Colonel Walker[45] for thus sheltering himself behind General Fane's[46] horse at Vimiera, I went to the exposed side; yet it gave me the most uncomfortable feeling I experienced that day. Lord William borrowed my spyglass, it had been Lord Edward Fitzgerald's[47] and was a very fine one, I never saw it more. He went to the 4th Regiment and was not seen by me again during the fight; nor did I receive an order from him or anybody, unless Sir John Moore's permission to move my grenadiers forward can be called one; neither did I see a single Staff officer during the battle, except Sir John and Sir William.

When Lord William went away, I walked up and down before the regiment and made the men shoulder and order arms twice to occupy their attention, for they were falling fast and seemed uneasy at standing under fire.[48] The colours also were lowered, because they were a mark for the enemy's great guns; this was by the advice of old John Montgomery, a brave soldier who had risen from the ranks. Soon the 42nd advanced in line, but no orders came for me. *'Good God! Montgomery'* I said *'Are we not to advance?'*

'I think we ought' he answered,

'But' said I *'No orders have come.'*

'I would not wait' he said.

The 4th did not move, the 42nd seemed likely to want our aid, it was not a moment for hesitation and John Montgomery, a Scotchman said laughingly *'You cannot be wrong to follow the 42nd'*. I gave the word but forbad any firing and to prevent it and occupy the men's attention, made them slope and carry arms by word of command. Many of them cried out *'Major let us fire'*.

'Not yet' was my answer, for having advanced without orders, I thought to have them more under command if we were wrong, whereas firing once begun, we could not change. At that moment, the 42nd checked a short distance from a wall and commenced firing and though a loud cry arose of *'Forward, forward!'* no man, as I afterwards heard, passed the wall. This check seemed to prove that my advance was right and we passed the 42nd. Then I said to my men *'Do you see your enemies, plain enough to hit them?'*

Many voices shouted *'By Jasus we do!'*

'Then blaze away!' and such a rolling fire broke out as I have hardly ever heard since.

After passing the 42nd we came to the wall, which was breast high and my line checked, but several officers, Stanhope one, leaped over, calling on the men to follow. At first about a hundred did at a low part, no more and therefore leaping back, I took a halberd and holding it horizontally pushed many over the low part; and again getting over myself, run along, followed by my orderly sergeant, Keene, with his pike. As we passed, four or five soldiers levelled together from the other side, but Keene threw up their muskets with a force and quickness which saved me from being blown to atoms, as it was my face was much burned; then all got over, yet it required the example of officers and the bravest men to get all over.

Now the line was formed beyond the wall and I, recollecting Voltaire's story of the Guards' officers laying their swords over the men's firelocks to keep their level low, did so with the halberd to show coolness and being cool, though the check at the wall had excited me and made me swear horribly. We then got to marshy ground close to a village, where the fire from the houses was terrible, the howitzers from the hills pelting us also. Still I led the men on, followed closely by Ensigns Moore and Stewart[49] with the colours until both fell, and the colours were caught by Sergeant Magee and another sergeant. My sword-belt was shot off, scabbard and all, but not being hit I pushed rapidly into the street, exactly at the spot where soon after, I was taken prisoner. Many Frenchmen lay there, apparently dead, but the soldiers cried out *'Bayonet them, they are pretending'*. The idea was to me terrible and made me call out *'No! No! Leave those cowards, there are plenty who bear arms to kill, come on!'*

At this place stood the church and towards the enemy a rocky mound, behind which and on it, were the grenadiers; but no officer met my sight, except Captain Harrison,[50] Lieutenant Patterson and Lieutenant Turner[51] and my efforts were vain to form a strong body; the men would not leave the rocks, from which they kept up a heavy fire. No time was to be lost, we could not see what passed on our flanks, we had been broken in carrying the village of [San Vicenzo de] Elvina and as a lane went up straight towards the enemy, I run forward calling out to follow; about thirty privates and the above named officers did so, but the fire was then terrible, many shells burst among us and the crack of these things deafened me, making my ears ring. Halfway up the lane I fell, without knowing why, but was much hurt, though at the moment unconscious of it; a soldier cried out *'The major is killed.'*

'Not yet come on'.

We reached the end of this murderous lane, but a dozen of those who entered it with me fell ere we got through it. However, some shelter was found beyond the lane; for Brooks of the 4th[52] had occupied the spot with his picquet the day before and had made a breastwork of loose stones, which was known to me, having been there and nearly killed the evening before, when visiting the picquet as officer of the day. The heap remained and about a dozen of us lodged ourselves behind this breastwork and then it appeared to me that by a rush forward we could carry the battery above; and it was evident we must go on or go back, we could not last long where we were.

Three or four men were killed at my side, for the breastwork was but a slender protection and two were killed by the fire of our own men from the village behind. The poor fellows kept crying out as they died *'Oh God! Major, our own men are killing us! Oh, Christ God I'm shot in the back of the head!'* the last man was so, for he fell against me and the ball had entered just above the poll. Remembering then that my father had told me he saved a man's life, at the siege of Charleston,[53] by pulling a ball out with his finger before inflammation swelled the parts, I thought to do the same, but could not find it and feared to do harm by putting my finger far in. It made me feel sick and the poor fellow being laid down, continued crying out that our men had killed him and there he soon died.

The misery shook us all a good deal and made me so wild as to cry and stamp with rage, feeling a sort of despair at seeing the soldiers did not come on. I sent Turner, Harrison and Patterson, the three officers with me, to bring them on, and they found Stanhope animating the men, but not knowing what to do and calling out *'Good God, where is Napier?'*

When Turner told him I was in front and raging for them to come on for an attack on the battery, he gave a shout and called on the men to follow him, but ere taking a dozen strides cried out *'Oh my God!'* and fell dead, shot through the heart. Turner and a sergeant who had been also sent back, then returned to me, saying they could not get a man to follow them up the lane. Hearing this, I got on the wall, waving my sword and my hat at the same time and calling out to the men behind among the rocks; but the fire was so loud none heard me, though the lane was scarcely a hundred yards long. No fire was drawn upon me by this, for a French captain afterwards told me and others, he prevented their men firing at me; he did not know, nor was he told by me who it was, but he said, instead of firing at him I longed to run forwards and embrace that brave officer. My own companions called out to jump down or I should be killed: I thought so too, but was so mad as to care little what happened to me.

Looking then along the field, from the height of the wall, our smoke appeared to be everywhere retiring; but the French smoke was not advancing, which gave me comfort. However, it was useless to stay there and jumping down I said to Harrison *'stay here as long as you can, I will go to the left and try to make out how the 42nd get on.'* No one was to be seen near our left from my standing place near the wall; but there was some brushwood and a ridge with a hedge on the top, which debarred further sight, and the thought came to me that instead of being foremost, we might be in line with some of the 42nd and though the 4th had not advanced, if fifty men of the 42nd and 50th could be gathered, we might still charge the battery above us: if we failed there was a house near, into which we could force our way and as it was conspicuous from the English position Moore would send me support.

Telling this to Captain Harrison, I went off along a lane running at right angles from the one we were in and parallel to our position; this exposed me to the English, not to the French fire, but being armed with only a short sabre, useless against a musket and bayonet and being quite alone, short-sighted and without spectacles, I felt very cowardly and anxious. Pursuing my course however for about a hundred yards, I came near a French officer lying on his back wounded and being myself covered with blood and my face smeared, for two of the killed men had fallen in my arms, my look was no doubt fierce; and though I approached him out of pity, he thought it was to kill him: his feet were towards me and as he raised his head he cried out to some comrades above him, pointing with a quick convulsive motion towards me. Those whom he addressed could not be seen, for the ridge was about six feet high, nearly perpendicular, with the thick hedge at top; but my danger was soon announced through the roots of the hedge by a blaze of fire poured so close as to fill the lane with smoke. All went over my head, being evidently fired without seeing me, or my body must have been blown to pieces.

Giving myself up for lost, the temptation to run back was great, but the thought that our own line might see me, made me walk leisurely, in more danger indeed yet less alarmed than when going forward without knowing what would happen. The whole excursion along the lane was the most nervous affair I ever experienced in battle; nor was my alarm lessened on getting back, for Harrison and the others were gone! They could not stand the fire. I felt very miserable then, thinking the 50th had behaved ill; that my not getting the battery had been a cause of the battle being lost and that Moore would attribute all to me. The English smoke had gone back and my only comfort was that the French smoke had not gone forward. The battle seemed nearly over, I thought myself the last man alive belonging to our side who had got so far in front and felt certain of death and that my general would think I had hidden myself and would not believe me to have done my best. I thought also my little party had been taken. Lord William Bentinck afterwards told me that he had ordered my regiment back, in direct contradiction of Moore's design, who had he admitted, told him not to recall me, but send men to my assistance!!!

In this state of distraction and still under a heavy fire, I turned down the lane to rejoin the regiment and soon came on a wounded man who shrieked out, *'Oh praised be God Major! My dear Major! God help you my darling, one of your own 50th.'*

'I cannot carry you' was my reply *'Can you walk with my help?'*

'Oh no Major I am too badly wounded.'

'You must lie there then till help can be found.'

'Oh Christ God, my jewel, my own dear Major, sure you won't leave me.'

The agony with which he screamed was great, it roused all my feelings and strange to say, alarmed me about my own danger, which had been forgot in my misery at finding Harrison was gone from the corner and thinking the battle lost.

Stooping down, I raised the poor fellow, but a musket ball just then broke the small bone of my leg some inches above the ankle; the pain was acute and though the flesh was not torn, the dent made in my flesh remains to this day and is tender to the touch! Telling the man of my own wound, my course was resumed; his piteous cries were then terrible and fell bitterly as reproaches for my want of fortitude and courage. Yet what could be done by a man hardly able to walk and in great pain, with other duties to perform?

I felt it horrible to leave him, but selfishness and pain got the better and with the help of my sword, limping and with much suffering, I arrived at a spot where two other lanes met at the corner of a church: there were three privates of the 50th and one of the 42nd, an Irishman there, who said we were cut off and indeed Frenchmen were then coming up both lanes, one party from the position of the 50th, the other from that of the 4th. The last appeared the least numerous and the nearest, they were not thirty yards from us and forgetting my leg then, though I had not pluck to do so for the poor wounded man left behind, I said to the four soldiers, *'follow me and we'll cut through them'*; then with a shout I rushed forward.

The Frenchmen had halted, but now run on to us and just as my spring and shout was made, the wounded leg failed and I felt a stab in the back: it gave me no pain, but felt cold and threw me on my face. Turning to rise I saw the man who had stabbed me making a second thrust; whereupon letting go my sabre I caught his bayonet by the socket, turned the thrust and raising myself by the exertion grasped his firelock with both hands, thus in mortal struggle regaining my feet. His companions had now come up and I heard the dying cries of the four men with me, who were all bayonetted instantly.

We had been attacked from behind by men not before seen, as we stood with our backs to a doorway, out of which must have rushed several men, for we were all stabbed in an instant, before the two parties coming up the road reached us: they did so however just as my struggle with the man who had wounded me was begun. That was a contest for life and being the strongest, I forced him between myself and his comrades, who appeared to be the men whose lives I had saved when they pretended to be dead on our advance through the village.

They struck me with their muskets clubbed and bruised me much; whereupon, seeing no help near and being overpowered by numbers and in great pain from my wounded leg, I called out *Je se rend[re]*,[54] remembering the expression correctly from an old story of a fat officer, whose name being James, called out *'Jemmy round'*. Finding they had no disposition to spare me, I kept hold of the musket, vigorously defending myself with the body of the little Italian who had first wounded me, but soon grew faint, or rather tired. At that moment, a tall dark man came up, seized the end of the musket with his left hand, whirled his brass hilted sabre round and struck me a powerful blow on the head, which was bare, for my cocked hat had fallen off. Expecting the blow would finish me, I had stooped my head in hopes it might fall on my back, or at least on the thickest part of the head and not on the left temple; so far I succeeded, for it fell exactly on the top, cutting into the bone but not through it. Fire sparkled from my eyes, I fell on my knees, blinded yet without quite losing my senses and holding still on to the musket. Recovering in a moment, I regained my legs and saw a florid handsome young French drummer holding the arm of the dark Italian, who was in the act of repeating his blow. Quarter was then given, but they tore my pantaloons in tearing my watch and purse from my pocket and a little locket of hair which hung round my neck; they snatched at everything; but while this went on, two of them were wounded and the drummer Guibert ordered the dark man who had sabred me to take me to the rear.

When we begun to move, I resting on him, because hardly able to walk, I saw him look back over his shoulder to see if Guibert was gone; and so did I, for his rascally face made me suspect him. Guibert's back was towards us, he was walking off and the Italian again drew his sword, which he had before sheathed. I called out to the drummer, *'this rascal is going to kill me! Brave Frenchmen don't kill prisoners.'* Guibert run back, swore furiously at the Italian, shoved him away, almost down and putting his arms round my waist supported me himself: thus this generous Frenchman saved me twice, for the Italian was bent upon slaying.

We had not proceeded far up the old lane, when we met a soldier of the 50th walking down at a rapid pace; he instantly halted, recovered his arms and cocked his piece, looking fiercely at us to make out what it was. My recollection is that he levelled at Guibert and I threw up his musket, calling out. *'For God's sake don't fire, I am a prisoner, badly wounded and can't help you. Surrender.'*

'For why would I surrender?' he cried aloud, with the deepest of all Irish brogues.

'Because there are at least 20 men upon you.'

There were five or six with us at the time. *'Well if I must surrender, there'* said he, dashing down his firelock across their legs and making them jump. *'There's my firelock for yez.'* Then coming close up he threw his arm round me and giving Guibert a push that sent him and one or two more reeling against the wall, shouted out, *'stand away ye bloody spalpeens, I'll carry him myself, bad luck to the whole of yez.'*

My expectation was to see them fall upon him, but John Hennessy was a strong and fierce man and moreover looked bigger than he was, for he stood upon the higher ground. Apparently, they thought him an awkward fellow to deal with, he seemed willing to go with me and they let him have his own way. In this manner, we proceeded about a hundred yards beyond the corner where Harrison and the rest had left me and found a large force under General Renaud,⁵⁵ afterwards governor of Ciudad Rodrigo and captured by Don Julian.⁵⁶ He asked me my rank and how I was taken? My reply was *'taken because my regiment would not come on!'* I was in great anger and altogether ignorant of Lord William Bentinck having ordered them back; for the Staff officer sent by him had not chosen to come up to me. My thought was that the regiment had given way, which made me very unjust in abuse of the glorious old 50th, for they had gone further than any other corps in the army. Had Moore's orders for the 42nd and 4th to support us, been obeyed by Lord William, we should have carried the hill in a few minutes: that this was the cause of their going back is true, for Lord William Bentinck afterwards told me so himself. General Renaud ordered a surgeon to dress me and he put a plaister [sic] on my head; but my leg was so swollen he could not get off my boot without cutting, which I would not allow, hoping to escape, in which case the loss of a boot would be irreparable. They took me up the hill to where the Spanish magazine on the top had been exploded.

Soon after leaving [San Vicenzo de] Elvina, being supported by one of his officers and Hennessy with a guard, we passed a large gap in a wall, on which the English fire was still very heavy. The French soldiers cried out, *'Don't cross there except on your knees, or you will be shot,'* whereupon the French officer desired Hennessy and me to do so, but we refused and Hennessy said low *'Be Jasus they're afraid.'* My desire was to be seen by our own people and therefore my walk with Hennessy and the officer was erect and slow; but seeing the French Guard crawl on their hands and knees, I said to the captain *'Crawl you too, or you will be hit, I can't run away.'* This anxiety for an enemy greatly amused the Frenchmen and it was afterwards told to the Marshals Soult and Ney; Renaud also mentioned it when a prisoner in London; however, the officer would only stoop and none of us were hit. On the summit of the position my bodily agony was so great, that Hennessy and the French captain, seeing some straw near a fire laid me on it; my leg and side were giving me excruciating pain, it was dark and Hennessy went away for a while with the captain: then a French officer came and stood over me, a tall handsome man; he looked at me for some time and said *'War! War! War! My God, will this horrid work never cease! Poor young man, I fear you are badly wounded.'* He gave me some drink and tears rolled down his cheeks; but then he turned away and several others sat down round the fire without noticing me. Soon however came the man whose straw I had been laid upon; he gave me two kicks and dragged me by the neck off his bundle, hurting me much. I said nothing, except *'God damn you'* and two or three Frenchmen starting up took my part.

Then the tall officer returned and was very angry, but the beast who kicked me would not let me be put back on the straw, which he claimed. The officer told them to take me into the ruin of a blown-up house or magazine, where some officers had had a fire in the remains of a room, the fireplace being indeed nearly all that existed of the building; but he left me and then the men took me into another ruined room and threw me into the filth with which it was filled and began to laugh at me. I was very angry, wished myself dead at once and said something violent, whereupon they seemed to consult about killing me and my hopes of life fled; indeed, my wish was not to live, but at that moment the officer came back with two or three more and with two soldiers who had before left the place, I think to call them and save me.

These officers were very angry, but my understanding was faint and my desire was to be put out of misery, for I thought we had lost the battle and my pain of body was past bearing. They however carried me to the other part of the building near the fireplace and there was Hennessy. They offered me broth and wine, but I could touch nothing from the agony of my wounds and groaned at times, for the pain was no longer supportable even before an enemy. Not being able to lie down, Hennessy held me in his arms in an upright posture. The French officers did all they could for me, as far as kind words went and soon one of their own officers was brought in wounded; it was the captain who had been with me when first taken. General Renaud also now sent an officer with my sword, desiring me to wear it for I had used it well. I wrote my name and rank on a piece of paper, with a stick dipped in his blood and requested the officer to give it and my sword to Marshal Soult, with a request to speak to him. That officer did not return. Hennessy having occasion to go out of the ruin, set me in an angle of the fireplace, but never came back, being seized and marched off, as he afterwards told me. Before he left me, he unbuckled my spurs and *whispered 'The spurs are silver, the spalpeens would murder you for them.'*

When he did not return, my idea was that he had made his escape and took the spurs with that intention; at least my hope was so, that he might tell my brother George where I was, for what fretted me most was, that no flag of truce came in for me. I thought Moore was angry, that myself and the regiment had been disgraced and therefore he would not send in, nor let George come: then the fancy came that George was killed, but my thoughts were all mild and sad that night. Very wretched in body and mind was I now and in about two hours after Hennessy had gone, the French officers went away, one after another. The fire was out and it was dreadfully cold, yet pain kept me from feeling it so much and all that long and horrible night and next day, did I lay wishing for death and expecting it if a stray soldier should see me. There was no roof, only a few feet of wall standing and the following evening, about dusk, being in less pain, I crawled out, reckless of being killed or not. Outside there was a Frenchman cooking, he was a kind man and gave me some broth, but I could not eat it. He went away, but returned with another soldier and they made up a little more fire, rolled themselves in their greatcoats and other warm things and lay down. Pain kept me waking and the fire went out soon, for there was no fuel. I had no waistcoat or drawers, only a uniform coat and torn trousers and the cold was dreadful, for it was January and the hill high. An oilskin was on my hat and I pulled it off to cover my head and face; then putting my hands on my mouth warmed myself with my breath, but could not lie down. My feet and legs lost all feeling and the wounded leg ceased to pain me, except when moved. About midnight the two Frenchmen went their way and promised to tell their commandant of my state, yet the second dreadful night passed and no one came.

Next day about three o'clock a musician came near me and I persuaded him to take me to his regiment, but to walk was agony. I was however very kindly received by all the French officers, who were seated round a fire and especially so by their commander, a man with a very red face and perfectly white *moustachios* and hair; they treated me well and finally forwarded me on to Marshal Soult's quarters. We passed through [San Vicenzo de] Elvina amidst all the bodies of my poor 50th soldiers scattered about; and many wounded were still alive in a house and very clamorous for food. Scarcely able to speak from weakness, I was supported by two men, yet at last reached Soult's quarters and being shown into the kitchen sat down in much suffering. Monsieur de Chamont, *aide de camp*, to Soult, came to me; he was all kindness and attention and offered me money, which was declined, but I told him his men had been expert in robbing me; that everyone who met me as I was borne to the rear had asked '*est il pille?*' [Is he looted?] and the reply always was '*oh pour ca oui, joliment*' [Oh yes, nicely].

It was impossible to be kinder than De Chamont and that kindness was continued by the Marshal[57] and his Staff and again by Ney and his Staff. On my telling Soult of the wounded starving English soldiers lying in the village, he promised to have them helped immediately, and sent me to his quarters, where a bed was provided and food; the latter was in truth much needed, for none had been taken since my breakfast on the 16th and this was the 18th.

The pain in my side gave me little rest and next morning, being ordered to go into Corunna, I was put on a horse attended by a dragoon and entered the town with the troops. At the gate there was a crowd and a Spaniard hustled against my leg, which put me to such torture I cursed him aloud in English and gave him a blow on the head with as great force as the pain left me strength to do. The stupid brute knew of my wound, for I had pushed him twice away before and showed him how my leg was tied up. The delight of the French soldiers at my striking the Don was very great; he deserved it, but I was now very well treated. My billet was on Monsieur Barriere, a banker who lived with his brother in law, Marchesa, an excellent kind fellow with a pretty Spanish wife. There my state was as comfortable as kindness on the part of my host and the French officers, particularly Baron Clouet,[58] Ney's *aide de camp*, could make it, but I was a prisoner!

Before the 50th advanced, while standing under the cannonade, the balls at first went about a foot or two over our heads, the men stooped, or as it is called by soldiers ducked. Standing in front I said laughing. *'Don't duck, the ball has passed before you hear the whiz.'* The ducking however was continued, by all but one little fellow, who stood erect and I said to him aloud *'You are a little fellow but the tallest man in the 50th today for all that, come to me after the battle and you shall be a sergeant.'* Everyone heard me, yet strange to say no one afterwards knew who he was, nor could his name be learned; we supposed he fell and the agitation of the moment had made others forget, or not notice him.

George also wrote of his experiences at the battle:

On the morning of the battle ... I had just returned from delivering some orders in the camp, when the commander in chief desired me to order the horses and accompany him to the position. We had just mounted when we heard a shot from a gun and we instantly galloped off, and arrived as the troops were all under arms and the whole line preparing to sustain the attack of the enemy, who was advancing in strong columns down upon us under cover of a heavy fire from their batteries which commanded our position, and a cloud of sharpshooters in their front. The fire from the artillery was destructive and killed many of our brave fellows; but nothing could shake the steadiness or disturb the order of our troops; and as the enemy closed upon our line, the general gave the order to advance and placed himself in front of the 42nd Highlanders, to whom he was addressing himself and telling them not to forget what he had seen them so often do under his command in Holland and Egypt. He had just ordered me to go and bring up the Guards to the support of Lord William Bentinck's Brigade (consisting of the 4th, 42nd and

50th Regiments), where he was himself, and which was most furiously attacked by the enemy. I had just put spurs to my horse, when, turning my head to look at what was going on, I saw Sir John Moore's horse give a spring into the air and the next moment the general fell to the ground and was instantly caught up and supported by Captain Hardinge ...[59] My first impulse was to return to him, but in an instant, I recollected that he had sent me with most important and urgent orders for the Guards, and bitter and painful as were the feelings which agitated me at that instant, my duty told me to proceed, though my affections strongly urged me to go back ... On my return, I heard how dreadfully and mortally he was wounded, and that he was carried to the rear. Sir David Baird, than whom a more gallant soldier never breathed, had been severely wounded early in the action and was taken onboard ship, where his arm was obliged to be removed at the shoulder joint, and consequently the command devolved on Sir John Hope, one of the most able officers in the British army, as well as the most noble minded of men.

As it would have been very improper to have left the field, and being aware that Colonel Anderson,[60] Sir John's oldest and dearest friend, was with him, I attached myself to General Hope, who was now in fact, commander in chief. During the battle I had seen ... Charles charging the enemy at the head of ... the 50th, with his friend and second in command, Major Stanhope. They had taken the village of [San Vicenzo de] Elvina, and were driven out again three times, for the enemy, being able to reinforce their attacking troops after every repulse, at last overpowered the 50th, which was forced to retreat. At this period Captain Stanhope[61] a brother of the major and myself, were riding towards the 50th in order to make some inquiries respecting our brothers, and I was just at the rear of the regiment when I met some soldiers carrying the body of an officer who was shot through the heart. I jumped from my horse, removed with trembling hands the handkerchief which was over the face and beheld the pale and ghastly countenance of my valued friend Charles Stanhope. I had no time to shed a tear to his memory, his poor brother was approaching; I quickly remounted my horse and meeting him, said, *'Come along, we must instantly return to General Hope;'* at the same time I seized the bridle of his horse and turned him round before he had time to recognise the bleeding corpse of his gallant brother. As we went along, I told him what had happened and he bore it as every soldier ought, but could not resist the desire of going to take a last look at poor Charles. To this I could not object, but did not accompany him. While riding about with General Hope, we came to a narrow place where we could only pass singly and as the enemy had a vast number of sharpshooters, they fired at every officer as he passed. Captain Woodford,[62] who went before me, got severely wounded in the foot; I crossed without being touched; but the poor fellow who followed me, young Burrard,[63] got shot in the chest and died two days afterwards onboard ship.

We rode about the field of battle, first to one brigade, then another, General Hope directing and encouraging the troops in every part. At last, coming to where the 50th was hotly engaged, Captain Clunes,[64] the eldest captain of the regiment, came up to us, and addressing General Hope, said; *'Sir, our commanding officer, Major Napier, is killed; we have no field officer left; our ammunition is expended; what are we to do?'* …

Towards evening, the enemy having been repulsed in all their attacks, and driven by our position, the battle ceased. Then, the evening being far advanced, Sir John Hope returned to the town to give orders and superintend the embarkation of the army during the night … I did not return to the town with the general, as I heard from some of the officers of the regiment that they thought my brother was only wounded and that he must be lying somewhere on the field of battle. It being now dark, I went over the ground with a torch in my hand and looked at the body of every officer I could find, in the melancholy but vain hope of once more seeing the countenance, though in death, of my beloved brother Charles, and that I might satisfy my mind that he was dead. At last, finding it hopeless to search any longer, and in the bitterness of my sorrow, it came across me that perhaps he had been taken to the hospital in town. As quick as the thought seized me, I went off to the house appointed for receiving the wounded, and on arriving, commenced afresh my melancholy search. Not a wounded man in the hospital escaped my glance but in vain! No dear brother was to be found, and no one could give me any other tidings but that they saw him killed.

With a heavy heart I turned my sorrowful steps to the headquarter house. On entering I saw no light; I heard no sound, no movement; all was silent as the grave. A cold dread chill struck upon my heart as I ascended the gloomy stairs and opened the opposite door from whence I imagined I heard the half-stifled sob of grief. Oh, God! what was my horror, my misery, my agony! Sir John Moore lay stretched on a mattress; a dreadful wound bared the cavity of his chest; he had just breathed his last … Never shall I forget the scene that room displayed on that fatal night. Colonel Anderson, who had been from youth the tried friend and companion of his general, was kneeling, with his arm supporting Sir John Moore's head, with blanched cheeks, half-parted colourless lips and his eyes intently fixed on that face whose smile of approbation and affection had been his pride and delight for years; but the look of keen anguish that Anderson's countenance expressed is far beyond my powers of description. Next in this group stood Colborne, whose firm and manly countenance was relaxed and overcast with thoughtful grief, as though he pondered more on his country's than on private sorrow, for he felt and deeply mourned the amount of England's loss. Then high-spirited, guileless Harry Percy,[65] pouring forth in convulsive sobs the overflowing of his warm and generous heart; and poor James Stanhope completely struck down and overwhelmed by the double loss of his brother and his friend. Although last in this imperfect sketch, not least absorbed in the deep anguish of despair, stood his faithful and devoted servant '*François,*' bending over his master's mangled body, his hands clasped in speechless agony, his face as pale as the calm countenance he wildly gazed upon. That eye which was wont to penetrate the inmost soul was glazed in death. That manly, graceful form, the admiration of the army, lay stretched a bloody, lifeless corpse; the great spirit had quitted its earthly habitation; all around was sad and gloomy. Moore was dead!

… Early on the morrow of that sad and dreary night Colonel Colborne and myself went on board the *Audacious*, 74 gun ship, Captain Gosling[66] having with much difficulty reached her, as in consequence of the enemy bringing some guns to the heights which in fact commanded the bay, and opening a fire on the transports, they were cutting away their cables and were in much confusion, and it was a service of danger to get through them. The day we embarked Colonel Graham (Lord Lynedoch) told me it was the intention of General Hope to send me home with the despatch of the battle, as Colonel Graham knew that Sir John Moore had meant to send me if there was a battle. However, be this as it may, Sir David Baird settled all that by ordering General Hope to make his report of the action to him as commander in chief and saying that he, Sir David, should send his own nephew and aide de camp Captain Gordon home with the despatch, which he accordingly did, notwithstanding the remonstrances of General Hope, Colonels Graham and Murray.[67] … I must do justice to my friend Captain Gordon, by saying that he himself remonstrated with his uncle, Sir David, upon the impropriety of sending him instead of Sir John Moore's staff, but the only reply he got was, *'If you don't wish to go, I shall send Captain Baird.'*[68] Of course, after that, Gordon went. He told me this himself just before he started, and repeated it to me when I met him in London afterwards …

The second day after we embarked, my poor friend and brother aide de camp, Captain Burrard, son of Sir Harry Burrard, died on board of the wound he had got in the chest. He was a fine young man, a great favourite with everybody, and had he been permitted to live, I have no doubt would have distinguished himself as an officer. It was melancholy to see his body consigned to the deep. ... young William Craig[69] (who had been quite knocked up, and was ill onboard one of the ships), the moment he heard the first shot fired by the enemy, got out of his bed, dressed himself and landing, went off to his regiment, the 52nd, where he behaved so gallantly as to attract the notice of his commanding officer, Colonel Barclay[70] and also that of the general commanding the division, General Paget, both of whom praised him highly.

The 50th lost five officers and 180 men killed and wounded at Corunna. George also related a few further details gleaned later from Charles:

... he was taken to a part of the enemy's position from whence he could perceive the British army, the town and the fleet. During the night, as he lay on the ground, he heard from some of the French officers that the English commander in chief was killed. ... He says, when morning broke and he saw all the fleet in the bay beneath, his spirits cheered up, feeling confident that ere long the wished for flag of truce would make its appearance; but when he perceived the ships sailing away one after another and at last the only remaining one in full sail, his heart died within him and he kept straining his eyes looking after them till they were completely out of sight. He then felt in perfect solitude and misery; he was sure I must have been killed; and with the many severe wounds he was suffering from himself, he felt as if he was dying without a human being who cared for him to close his eyes. I can easily conceive the mental pain he endured during these twenty-four hours. However, when he was taken into the town and lodged at the American Consul's house, where every care and kindness was shown to him by that gentleman, as well as by the French officers, particularly Marshals Soult and Ney, he soon resumed his wonted cheerfulness and in the course of some weeks he recovered sufficiently to enjoy himself as well as a prisoner can.

William's battalion formed part of Robert Craufurd's Flank Brigade that marched to Vigo, but he wrote as soon as he arrived back in England of the presumed death of Charles:

Plymouth, February 1809

My dearest mother,

You have before now heard I hope from George himself of the misfortune that has again befallen us all by the death of Charles, but it must be some comfort to you to know that he fell like a soldier fighting for his country, that his regiment distinguished themselves, and more than all that he fell with Moore, the best and bravest soldier that England had. These thoughts, my dearest mother, although they may be lost in the first moments of affliction, will in time have their effect, and you cannot therefore bring them too often to your recollection; they must mitigate your grief, and will I hope. For me, my dear mother, my unlucky fate has still followed me; having been sent to Vigo, I have returned without having an opportunity either of dying like my darling Charles, or of contributing to revenge his and Moore's death. We go round to Portsmouth today, from whence I have got leave to go to London to see you. I long much to do so, for sorrow draws the chords of affection close, and our sorrow is great and with reason, for we have lost the best friend and best brother and son that God ever made. God Almighty bless you, my dear mother! I hope to be with you as soon as this letter.

George later wrote on the investigation to establish what had happened to Charles:

My mother was never quite convinced that Charles was killed, because, as I could not find his body, she thought rightly as it proved, that he was only wounded and must be a prisoner; and as about this time reports had reached us confirming her view in a slight degree, Lord Mulgrave, who was First Lord of the Admiralty, very kindly offered to send a sloop of war with a flag of truce to Corunna to make the necessary inquiries and ascertain the truth of the report.

When the ship arrived they found him recovering from the wounds he had received, which were four; a sabre cut across the top of his head; a bayonet plunged into his back as he lay on the ground; a shot in the leg; and grazed by a cannon ball which broke two of his ribs. So you see, he had a narrow escape. He would have been put to death had it not been for a French drummer, who saved his life by defending him from the fury of the soldiers. This drummer received from Napoleon the cross of the Legion of Honour for his conduct in having saved the life of a British officer. Marshal Soult, Duke of Dalmatia, was very kind to him; sent his own surgeon to dress his wounds; ordered him whatever money he wanted,

Pombal Castle, 1810.

Castle of Leiria.

Celorico from the Guarda road, 1810.

Sabugal Castle, 1810.

Nisa in 1811.

Penamacor, c.1811.

Arronches, 1811.

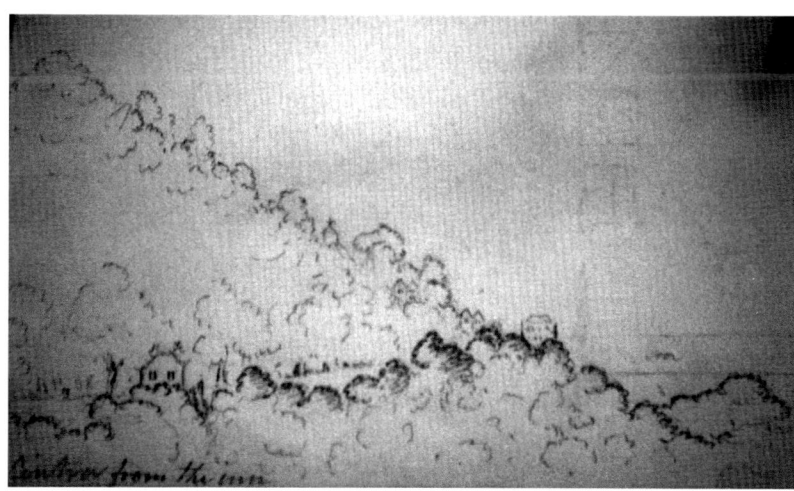

Cintra from the Inn.

Monte Santo.

Vila Velha.

Penamacor in the distance.

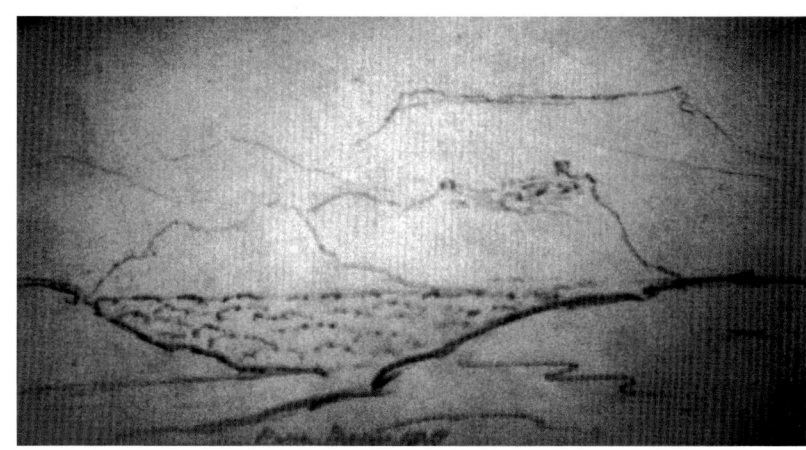

Juan de Castor's house, Cintra.

George Town Bermuda, 1813, from town cut.

Barracks at Bermuda, 1813, from the Narrows.

Chesapeake Bay, 1813.

River Pottomac, 1813.

Boat Attack, 1813.

View in Kent Island, 1813.

Flying fish and other items.

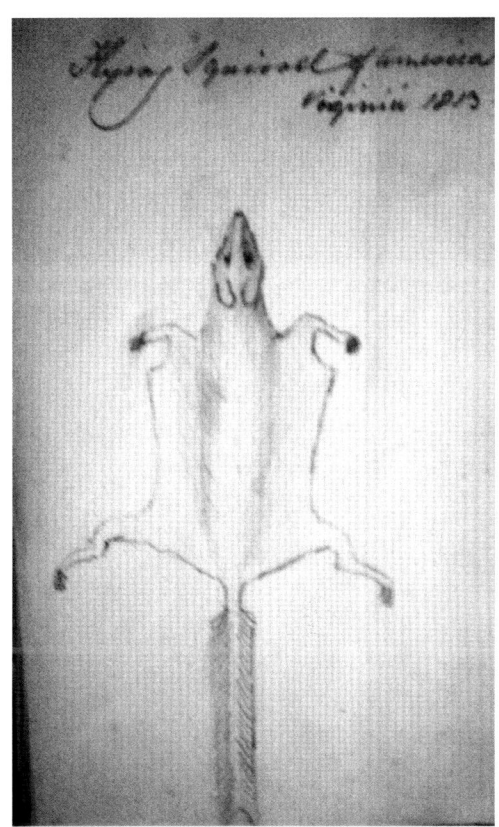

Flying squirrel, Virginnia.

King Crab, Kent Island, 1813.

Halifax Harbour, 1813.

Signal Post, Halifax, 1813.

Lady of Grand Canary Islands.

A Camanista or Lord of the Bedchamber.

Monk.

and to be supplied from his own table with everything necessary to his comfort. When Marshal Soult left Corunna, Marshal Ney commanded, and from him he also received every kindness ... Baron Clouet received the flag and hastened to inform Ney.

'Let him see his friends and tell them he is well and well treated.' Was the marshal's response.

Clouet looked earnestly but moved not, and Ney smiling asked why he waited!

'He has an old mother, a widow and blind.'

'Has he? Let him go then and tell her himself that he is alive!' He also released twenty-five badly wounded English soldiers, jocosely adding *'provided they take all the Englishwomen with them, as they make our French soldiers quarrelsome.'*

Charles was released on parole on 20 March 1809, but was unable to serve against the French until formally exchanged. However, in a letter to his mother, he vainly stated his preference to be exchanged for a major than for two lieutenants; but he would have to be patient before the transaction was officially completed.

Chapter 4

Talavera Campaign 1809

George and William were to return to Portugal in May 1809, Charles still being on his parole. George proceeded on the famous march to Talavera, William having been forced to fall out because of severe sickness, as George related:

We embarked onboard transports at Deal in May for Lisbon, where we arrived in about three weeks, having stopped at Portsmouth for some days on our passage down Channel. As soon as we had completed ourselves in baggage, mules and various other equipments necessary for service, we proceeded to join the army which was marching on Talavera in Spain, on the road to Madrid … One day in the month of August, while marching under a burning sun, an officer of the 43rd told me my brother William was taken very ill and was unable to proceed with the regiment. I immediately went to him and found he was very ill indeed, and in consequence of the quantity of blood the surgeon had found it necessary to take from him, he could not stand; so I got a bullock car, and placing him in it on some straw, I went to Placentia [Plasencia] with him, to the hospital which had been established there. Upon arriving, the commandant gave me a good quarter for him, and the doctors having visited him and ordered medicine &c, I put him into a comfortable warm bed; and in about five or six hours and a good sleep, he being out of all danger, I left him in the care of his servant and the doctor and started to overtake the regiment; which was no easy matter, as an express had arrived with orders for the brigade to make a forced march and join the army as quick as possible, as it was engaged with the enemy.

So, upon my arriving at the village where I expected to find my regiment bivouacked, all was clear, the brigade having moved off as fast as possible according to the orders received. It was then near ten o'clock at night, very dark, and a large forest of many miles long to march through without a guide or companion, and the devils of wolves howling in all directions. About twelve or one o'clock I began to be very tired, when I saw a light glimmering at some distance, and making towards it I was glad on arriving to find an officer of the Rifle Corps in a hut, with some sick men and some baggage. I got some wine from him and a bit of something to eat and lay down for half an hour, when I awoke and jumped up, and seizing my sword and cap I started off, having dreamt that my company was in action with the enemy; and I never halted till about eleven the next morning, when I overtook the brigade and marched on to *'Talavera's bloody field.'*

As we moved on, the road was crowded with cowardly fugitives; Spaniards innumerable, and lots of English, commissary clerks, paymasters, sutlers and servants, to say nothing of a few soldiers and officers who said they were sick; all swearing the British army was cut to pieces. How we did swear at them and hiss every fellow we met! Moreover, these followers of the army were committing every kind of rascality and pillaging with impunity, as they never fail to do when out of reach of punishment ...

At last our brigade arrived on the field of battle, after having marched fifty miles in twenty-two hours,[1] every man having at least forty pounds weight upon his back! But our disappointment was great when we found we were too late, the battle having finished the night before. We took up the line of the advanced posts and were employed burying the dead and saving the unfortunate wounded French from the fury of the Spanish peasants, who murdered them wherever they could find them without mercy. The field of battle was a horrid sight, particularly to us who had not shared either in the danger or the glory, though we did our best to arrive in time. The dry grass had caught fire, and numbers of wounded of all nations were burnt to death, being unable to crawl out of the way of the raging fire; then the dreadful smell from the half-burned carcasses of the horses was appalling. In short, I never saw a field of battle which struck me with such horror as the field of Talavera.

George continues his narrative with the retreat over the River Tagus, forced upon Wellington's army as Marshal Soult's forces threatened to cut off his retreat to Portugal:

We had just time to pass the Tagus by the bridge of Arzibispoa [Arzobispo] before Soult made his appearance, and the Light Brigade under General Craufurd was ordered to gain the bridge of Almaraz by a forced march, in order to prevent the French from crossing there and seizing the pass of Mirabete [Miravete]. This was done exactly as ordered, and the whole of Marshal Soult's plan of operations being frustrated (principally, however, by the jealousy of his brother marshals), Lord Wellington took up his headquarters at Deletoza [Deleitosa]. While the army remained in this position we suffered dreadfully from want of food; nothing but a small portion of unground wheat and (when we could catch them) about a quarter of a pound of old goats' flesh each man; no salt, bread or wine; and as the Spaniards had plundered the baggage of the British army during the Battle of Talavera, there was nothing of any kind to be procured to help us out, such as tea or sugar. Our brigade had to move down from a height every evening to watch the ford and bridge, and as the banks of the river were marshy we soon had enough of sickness. At last Lord Wellington was determined to remain no longer in Spain or to cooperate with the Spanish armies and generals, as they were good for nothing in the field, and only marauded and insulted the British while inactive; so we received orders to march to the frontiers of Portugal. The headquarters were at Badajos [Badajoz] in Spain, and the rest of the army distributed in the various Portuguese towns along the frontier. The Light Brigade went to Campo Mayor [Campo Maior], and never were poor fellows better pleased than we were to be under cover again and get good food &c. I never in all my service felt so completely exhausted and worn out as at Almaraz, and it was there that I got the seeds of the ague which I suffered from for a full year afterwards. The hospital was established at Elvas, and there five or six thousand gallant British soldiers breathed their last. It was really dreadful to see the dead cart go round the town three times a day, loaded with dead bodies all naked, and tumbled into a hole outside the town, from whence the smell was horrid, notwithstanding all means were tried to prevent it.

Chapter 5

From the Border to the Lines of Torres Vedras 1810

George wrote of the early months of 1810:

In the course of a few months we moved towards the north of Portugal and our regiment was quartered at a town called Pinhel. Sometime afterwards, we got orders to march into Spain and were in cantonments along the banks of the River Agueda; the French under Marshal Ney being all round the neighbourhood of Ciudad Rodrigo.

Barba del Puerco, 19 March 1810
George continued:

One night, the post occupied by the Rifle Corps was surprised, the enemy killing the sentry at the bridge and stealing unawares on the picket or advanced post. They were halfway up the bank or hill where the body of the regiment was under Colonel Sidney Beckwith, before the alarm was given, and the regiment had only time to seize their arms and accoutrements, and ran out in their shirts, with their belts and cartouche boxes slung over them; and in this ridiculous dress, with old Beckwith at their head, in his dressing gown, red night cap and slippers, they fell upon the enemy and completely annihilated him, very few getting across the river again.

George continued about life on piquet duty:

One day I was on picket at a ford in front of the village of Gallejos [Gallegos de Arganan], when I observed a general officer and his Staff coming down the road on the opposite bank towards the ford. I called out across the river, which was narrow, to desire them to go back, and at the same time drew up my men and told the French general that I would fire at him if he persisted in coming down to the ford. They seemed to hold my threat in perfect contempt and still moved down; upon which I fired and shot one of their horses. This had the desired effect and they wheeled about and went back at a trot. The general was Marshal Ney, [he] rode a white horse; and as I was not aware at the time that it was he, I made my men do all they could to shoot him. Another day, being on picket at the same place, where opposite to us the enemy had now also a picket, some of the French soldiers asked my leave to come across and get tobacco from our men, as they had none, and could not get any in consequence of the siege. I allowed two of them to come, who immediately stripped off their clothes and swam across (for I would not let them try the ford), got the tobacco, told us all the news from France and returned quite happy. Now this was all wrong, because, when a man is placed in charge of a post, he should never permit his enemy to come within reach of being able to observe what he is about, the strength of his party, or the nature of his defences.

Charles was finally released from his parole in January 1810 and he immediately embarked to re-join the 50th Foot in Portugal. On his arrival, he was disappointed to find the regiment in winter quarters in Portugal inactive and he promptly gained permission for three months' leave of absence, which he used to proceed up to the front, volunteering to serve with the Light Division, which was covering the border and watching French preparations for an invasion of Portugal. He was utilised during this time as an extra aide-de-camp by Brigadier General Robert Craufurd. Charles maintained a journal of this period:

16 April 1810. [Gained] leave of absence for three months.

20 May. After a long passage, this day saw me safely into harbour; may I reach the port now in my mind by next 20 of May! May the omen be good! I augur well of it; what we most wish for we feel most confident of, and I am sanguine.

21 May. Dined with the admiral,[1] a Spanish general and some Portuguese noblesse there; and also the daughter and grandchildren of Pombal.[2] The Spanish general told me that he was the best general they had, he thought, his name was Contreras[3] and he [had] more information than I expected in a don; he had also the honour of having been well thrashed by the French very lately. Men of three nations were at the dinner and it is difficult to say which despised the others most; or which thought most of themselves.

31 May. Once more at Sacavem. On the 28 October 1808, I was here commanding the 50th Regiment. Standing under an olive, my thoughts were of my friend; for under that very tree Charles Stanhope had then

breakfasted with me, and hope of glory and admiration for Moore, were our themes!

Coimbra, June. Portuguese troops here; they are a strong race, and will make good soldiers, but are not so now; it will take Beresford[4] some years to make them good troops, and more English officers are wanted. We shall lose half our army if Lord Wellington risks a battle any great distance from Lisbon; and I fear the French may penetrate by the Tagus and perhaps cut off part of our army. I am inclined to think they want to draw us on to Salamanca for the purpose.

Celorico [de Beira], 14 June. Passed a volcanic country to all appearance; innumerable conical hills, each covered with and surrounded by stones, are scattered in all directions ... Thrashed a *Juiz de Fora* for insolence at Penhanços [Pinhancos].

Charles made some very critical remarks on Wellington's campaign at Talavera and it seems that he was far from alone:

15 June. Waited yesterday for Lord Wellington, who was very civil and signed my certificate of exchange. Dined with him. He told me the French made the most regular retreats he ever saw, at Roriça [Rolica] and Talavera: quere [sic], did he follow their example? People say his march from Talavera to Alemtejo [Alentejo region] was very bad; but those who criticize generals do not always know their motives of action, and often have motives of their own for criticizing. Nevertheless we must think; and I think Lord Wellington committed a great error in that campaign by trusting to the Spaniards after what Moore had experienced; and another in advancing too far, when his retreat might be cut off. He was wrong also I think in fighting when victory did him no good, and defeat must have destroyed him; his information was bad and he trusted it too implicitly. Again, why did he stay in the destructive marshes of the Alemtejo [Alentejo] until nearly the whole of his army fell from sickness? It is not easy to comprehend all this, and I have heard no good answer to it. Every officer I have seen and spoken to about the matter, has told me the same story, viz, that the Battle of Talavera was lost if the French had made one more attack; and that the whole army expected to [be] beaten next day. Now Lord Wellington might have had ten battalions more in the fight, viz. Lightbourne's[5] and the two Craufurds' brigades.[6] Why were they in the rear?[7] The thing is not easily explained to his advantage; he did not expect a battle, and yet had the French delayed a few days he must have laid down his arms, or

been cut to pieces. Altogether his general operations are difficult to be defended. But his conduct in the battle shewed great coolness and the most perfect self-possession; and by what I observe, since I came here, he seems to have gained a lesson from Talavera. Still the whole of the campaign is discreditable to him as a great captain, and he appears to have deserved the epithets of rash and imprudent; not that of fool though, as many say; his errors seem to be more those of inexperience and vanity than want of talent. England has paid dearly in men and money for his education indeed, yet if he has thereby been made a good general the loss is less; we have very few capable of being made worth a straw, though all the blood and gold in Europe and India were lavishly expended on them.

17 June. I see no reason to find fault with Lord Wellington's conduct now in not succouring Ciudad Rodrigo, and his preparations for a retreat are good; they might be however, I think, better, as I have seen many roads almost impassable for anybody, and wholly so for an army, which a few peasants might make good in three days, the materials being on the spot. Perhaps others are good, by which he means to retire, and that I have not seen; I can discover no fault or appearance of rashness, except the having Craufurd so advanced. His remaining so secure at [da Beira] is probably a consequence of good intelligence, but it appears a dangerous post if the enemy should push General Hill. I cannot help thinking the siege of [Ciudad] Rodrigo is to entice him into Spain, and if he does move forward they will push him at Abrantes; should he be so tempted the game is up! But he will not be thus ensnared, the scheme is too evident ...20 June. Examined the works of Almeida. Commanded[8] on the north east, but may make a good defence; guns very small in calibre though large in size, one pounders chiefly, with bad carriages.[9] 21 June. Gallegos [de Arganan]. Saw William and George, the latter not well, heat affects him; he has I believe the best heart alive and beating, and a right good head. I hope to see both safe home after this breeze; if not they are well prepared for a longer voyage, but God forbid they should take it now.

22 June. This morning we fired five shots at a foraging party. At noon Marshal Ney reconnoitered us with some squadrons, driving our posts within the line of the Azava [Azaba] River. Captain Mellish[10] the celebrated sporting Mellish, (a brave fellow, he was on the Staff) and myself were at the outposts; he made a fool of himself and I laughed at him. He made our people give up two posts without a shot, and the lieutenant of the 43rd asked my advice, so did Mellish, and it was to occupy the ground again. This was done easily, as the enemy had made his observations, which

he should not have done if I had commanded the post. Our position is fearfully dangerous here: we expect an attack, and having only three thousand men and the French twenty-five thousand, shall be lucky if we get off; it is uncomfortable.

23 June. Saw the Spanish General Carrera:[11] he showed me his troops, and they are bad enough, like all Spaniards. Don Julian Sanchez, the partisan, has cut his way out of Ciudad Rodrigo; he is an intrepid man they say, and very savage. The French go on slowly with the siege. Lord W[ellington] wisely keeps quiet; he is blamed for this, but is right and it gives me great confidence in the man.

25 June. French opened their batteries, and the fire was returned with spirit. The enemy drove back our picquet from Marialva [Marialba] and Carpio [de Azaba], beyond the bridge and fords of the Azava [Azaba]. Soon afterwards a troop of our German hussars crossed the bridge and skirmished, but using only carbines and pistols, only one man and two horses were killed; the spectacle was as pretty as it was ridiculous. Such trifling work serves no purpose whatever, it risks brave men and teaches them to trifle with service; we should fight or let it alone; the latter is most to my taste. Everything convinces me that light cavalry has no business with carbines. The Germans understand outpost work better than our cavalry, but if the English err they will fight themselves through; and though Germans are brave enough, they certainly have not the fire of our men, wherefore, taking all risks from drinking and ignorance, I would rather have two British regiments [of] infantry or cavalry than three German regiments, and that is saying a great deal.

26 June. The 16th Light Dragoons come up. The town fires bravely; the cannonade was tremendous last night, and this morning the place is on fire. Three explosions in the trenches; but a breach is to be seen, though small. Lord W[ellington] reconnoitered in a slight way, and saw the town from Molina da Flores [Molinos de Los Flores]. Marshal Ney is supposed to have passed the ford where my brother's picquet was, and the men fired at him without George's orders, wounding one person of his suite. Had Ney been hit it would not have been creditable; it is not right to fire at people without necessity, like Indian savages. The marshal or whoever it was, had rode up the river and crossed safely, so no end was answered by pelting him as he was going home. Brigadier General McKinnon,[12] Colonel Pakenham,[13] and myself with others, had ridden a few hours before close to their picquets, at the very same place, and instead of firing on us, they

only joked and good humouredly asked us to come across the river; when our men fired they returned the compliment, but our firing was stopped by George immediately.

1 July. Heavy bombardment at night, and we marched from Gallegos [de Arganan] to bivouac in the woods.

Charles wrote a letter to his mother dated Alameda [La Alameda de Gardon], 1 July:

We have left Gallegos [de Arganan] at last, fortunately, or Lord Wellington would have chanced to lose his Light Division. My belief is that the ignorance of the French general as to our real situation saved us, but we are now comparatively secure. The siege of [Ciudad] Rodrigo is very distressing, but Lord Wellington is resolved to give no help; very wisely. He is a much better general than I suspected him to be; that is, he has profited from his former errors. That he made them no one can doubt who hears the conversation of the army. He is not popular, less so even than supposed. However, he will not commit himself again, and that is comfort for those in England. My brother William took a violent passion for Don Julian Sanchez the guerilla, but has been a little cooled by the latter having, the day before yesterday, put to death one hundred and sixty Frenchmen, to sixty of whom he had at first given quarter! The don fights with lances, which was the first attraction I believe: he is a bold partisan, but it is to be feared very bloody. One of his men told me, if they caught Ney, they meant to cut him into lengths! beginning at his foot! Ney in return has promised to hang Julian and his men, when he catches them, and has already partially performed his promise: charming warfare and mild!

We shall stay here until Ciudad [Rodrigo] is taken, and then probably the French will move on Hill and Lord Wellington at the same time. It is said the latter makes no secret of his intention to quit Portugal, and that he thinks it will be soon; but don't give me as authority, it may be only rumour. Meantime be satisfied he is not the rash man he was, or Ciudad [Rodrigo] would ere this have been relieved: it might have been for they could not stand an attack from us, and my persuasion is that the siege was little more than a battle-trap for his lordship, which he has not been caught in. Having asked for more leave, Lord Wellington has given me permission to wait for an answer, which he says will be a reprimand and an order to go home – don't care for the first, the last must be obeyed. I have seen a little skirmishing, but being ill mounted have kept aloof, except with the infantry; for amongst the men of feet, if my nag is hurt I am still as good as my neighbours. With the cavalry there is little to learn and I don't wish to be taken again.

Charles continued with his journal:

2 July. Our bivouac beautiful, like a *fête champêtre*[14] rather than an outpost close to an enemy; the baggage got into confusion. Why do we remain in this exposed situation? Why is this fine division risked? If the enemy was entrerprizing [sic] we should be cut to pieces. We are not five thousand, including Carrera's force of fifteen hundred Spaniards, and twelve hundred are Portuguese. The French have twenty-five thousand, and forty thousand more within a day's march; yet we have the impudence to stay close to them: we shall be attacked some morning and lose many men.

4 July. The French drove in our cavalry this morning. Krauchenberg[15] of the 1st Hussars charged them at a small bridge; he invited Captain Belli[16] of the 16th to join in the charge, but he would not, though he had a squadron and the other only thirty men! The French were heavily cannonaded at the bridge by Hew Ross[17] and we retired skirmishing across the Das Casas stream to a new position, near Fort Conception [Concepcion], which is to be blown up. Elder's[18] Portuguese fired on our hussars! [Ciudad] Rodrigo fights well via Herrasti![19] I fear Almeida won't do as much, yet Cox[20] is a soldier I think.

Action of Barquilla, 11 July 1810
George also wrote on this incident:

Upon the fall of the fortress of Ciudad Rodrigo we retreated towards Almeida, the frontier fortress of Portugal. One day a French captain of infantry with about one hundred and fifty or perhaps two hundred men was charged, by order of General Craufurd, by several squadrons of our cavalry, but without effect; for no impression was made upon his small force, as he reserved his fire till the cavalry were almost touching the points of his men's bayonets, and then poured a heavy fire upon them, which frightened the horses so much that it was impossible for the men to force them on, and they turned off and galloped away. This was repeated once or twice, and in the last charge made by the 14th Light Dragoons their commanding officer, poor Colonel Talbot, fell dead on the bayonets of the enemy. General Craufurd then ordered a gun to be brought to bear upon this detachment of the French, and at the same time, sent some riflemen down to drive them off, which had the desired effect; and this small intrepid band made good its retreat and escaped, after having behaved most gallantly and withstood the charges of several hundreds of our dragoons. The officer commanding had proved himself as skilful as he was brave, and every man who witnessed his conduct was delighted to see him escape. The fault was not in our cavalry, but in General Craufurd, who upon seeing that the first charge of the dragoons made no impression, should have instantly sent a party of infantry, who would have settled the affair at once, and saved the life of a gallant young officer of great promise, as well as the lives of the poor soldiers who fell a useless sacrifice to his obstinacy.

11 July. Last night Craufurd laid a scheme for catching a rat and caught a Tartar![21] He marched with twelve hundred infantry and eight hundred horse to waylay one hundred and twenty French infantry and thirty dragoons, and the latter were taken; but the infantry resisted the cavalry charge, and repulsed Craufurd with a loss of thirty-two troopers and poor Colonel Talbot,[22] the French marching off without the loss of a man! Had they been asked they would have laid down their arms; but Craufurd cruelly tried to cut up a handful of brave men and they thrashed him. Talbot was one of our best cavalry officers, yet the loss is less than the disgrace.

15 July. I went with a flag of truce to Gallegos [de Arganan], was blindfolded and taken to Loison's quarters. None of my French acquaintances there. Loison[23] offered a large bet that Lord Wellington would not fight to relieve Almeida; is this a quiz, or do they mean to besiege that place? I was not blindfolded coming back but made to gallop at full speed. Loison is a savage-looking fellow, yet was very civil and much pleased with the brave conduct of the company which beat off our cavalry. We did not allow that we had many men, or that we were beat, but honestly avowed our admiration of his people …The 50th have been removed from Hastings to make room for militia.[24] Our men's recovery of strength, by sea-bathing, is of no moment than compared with the wish of some militia colonel to bathe his wife and children. Perhaps the soldiers are better dead, as England has such a large army! …

Rodrigo[25] surrendered the evening before Colonel Talbot was killed. Old Andreas Herrasti made a vigorous defence, and Loison told me the town was lost destroyed by the bombardment. The French committed no excesses, even the Spaniards allow this. Almeida is preparing for a siege and poor Hewitt is not in great spirits at being a prisoner.[26] His fate is inevitable unless he gets killed; but to be a prisoner now is nothing, as exchanges are permitted; he will only have to return by France instead of the Bay of

Biscay …16 July, Junça. Came here this morning: the cavalry have left Val de Mula [Vale da Mula], and we are now safe from a surprise, and being surrounded, which at Val de Mula [Vale da Mula] was not the case, as the enemy has twelve regiments of cavalry, and on our flank and rear was an open plain. Why do we not get on the other side of the Coa? Why not blow up Fort Conception [Concepcion]? The enemy might have that fort by a rapid movement now, if they were aware of our having dismantled it; our safety has certainly been owing to the enemy's ignorance of our true situation. Went to Almeida and find that Cox is decidedly not vigorous in preparing for a siege, for he gave me a bad breakfast. He cannot fight well on burned bread and bad coffee.

Charles was now becoming very critical of the poor showing of General Robert Craufurd:

21 July. At daybreak the French drove in our outpost, and Fort Conception [Concepcion] was blown up, the shock great, the destruction complete. The powder was put in the casemates in barrels, not filled up like a regular mine and furnished a proof that the latter is not a necessary trouble in every instance; a barrel of powder slung under a bridge will destroy the arch unless a very strong one. This was well done, and our cavalry retreated through Val de Mula [Vale da Mula], skirmishing till near Almeida, about two and a half miles; we lost seven or eight horses and two men wounded, and made one charge with our skirmishers, neither able in conception nor bold in execution, doing no honour to general or men. After that a more ridiculous attempt was made with half a squadron. I saw that Craufurd's ignorance of cavalry disheartened the men; some of whom got near broken ground whence the French could in safety fire on them at twenty yards' distance. They were afraid to regain their own ground when Craufurd ordered them, whereupon I galloped up and called to them to follow, and they did so, and we drove the French back receiving a sharp fire. English troops must always be led, but they will certainly follow their officers, who will generally be as certainly ready to lead. Altogether we had much firing today and little danger. Craufurd does not please me as a general.

The Action on the Coa, 24 July 1810
Charles wrote extensively on the Action on the Coa and was severely critical of General Craufurd:

24 July. At daybreak our picquets were attacked. The French threw forward some infantry among the rocks and were met by two companies of the 95th Rifles. In about two hours the enemy increased in numbers, our cavalry retired, the riflemen and Captain Campbell's company[27] of the 52nd covering their retreat till we reached the guns, when a cannonade opened on both sides, but the enemy soon pushed men down both flanks, and our guns fell back. At this time, we could count fifteen strong squadrons of French cavalry in line, besides detached parties and skirmishers, which may be reckoned at five more, altogether about three thousand cavalry. Their infantry we estimated at ten thousand, and they had the power of bringing up thirty thousand if they pleased.

When our guns retired, the light troops kept firing until we got close to Almeida, and a gun was fired from near a tower,[28] 800 yards from that town: a subaltern and some men of the 52nd occupied the tower, and our cavalry and artillery were drawn up in line behind. At this time the enemy closed on our infantry, and the action there began by the dislodging of Campbell's company and the riflemen from the enclosures. I was ordered to tell Colonel Barclay[29] to fall back from the plain and regain the enclosures behind him, which he did, and the fire became very heavy. Barclay's horse was killed, mine was wounded and threw me, but I remounted and rejoined Craufurd, who then sent me to tell the 52nd, 43rd and 95th to maintain the enclosures until he got the cavalry and guns over the Coa, leaving two pieces to cover the retreat. I gave Barclay and Major Macleod,[30] and Colonel Beckwith,[31] these orders. But they were all hotly engaged and could no longer keep their ground, lest the enemy should turn their flanks and reach the bridge before them.

I had great difficulty to return and joined the 43rd, where I found Campbell wounded, and fearing he would be taken, gave him my mare, making the best of my own way on foot through the vineyards. The fire was hot and the ground very difficult for us, but much easier for the enemy, because we made passages for ourselves and thus made them for the French also; this caused the 43rd and 95th to lose many men. I think we retired too fast in this part; it was owing to the murderous position which kept us in fear of being cut off from the bridge; but we were thus driven in among our cavalry, and the French cavalry got up to the 95th and made some prisoners.

Now we formed in rear of the cavalry on the main road, and went down towards the bridge, firing the whole way. On arriving there, Brigade Major Rowan[32] called to the Rifles and Portuguese Cazadores [Caçadores], and part of the 43rd, to charge up a hill and to retain it, while I rode by order of Colonel Beckwith to draw off the 52nd Regiment, then nearly a mile up the river on the right: the French were trying to push between them and us, and they would have done so had they been in force enough, and that Rowan's charge had not checked them.

I had little hope of reaching the 52nd alive but escaped though a dragoon horse I had caught and mounted was shot in the leg just as I reached Barclay, and at the same moment his cap was shot off. However, the 43rd effected their junction, passed the bridge and took the right of our position beyond the river, down to the edge of which my brother George's company was pushed, and from thence kept up a strong fire. The 52nd were followed over the bridge by the 43rd and 95th and Cazadores [Caçadores], covered by three companies of the 43rd, Dalyels,[33] Lloyd's, and my brother William's, and the French pushed down to the bridge and a cannonade commenced from both sides of the river. The bridge was defended by the 43rd and riflemen, with a long and murderous skirmish, destructive as it was useless, by which many men and officers lost their lives and many were wounded; amongst the latter my brother William. Finally this ceased, and the bloody business closed with as much honour for the officers and men as disgrace for Craufurd's generalship. His errors were conspicuous, and the most prominent shall be noted for my own teaching:

1st. He fought knowing he must retreat from an overwhelming force and having no object in fighting.

2nd. He occupied a position a mile in front of the bridge; thus voluntarily imposing on himself the most difficult operation in war, viz, passing a defile in face of a superior enemy, and in the confusion of a retreat! The result might have been destruction, it was a great loss.

3rd. He detained the cavalry and guns in a position where they could not act till the infantry were beaten back on them; thus he risked the destruction of three; for the defile became choked, and had the French charged down the road, there would have been a bloody scene. This was so evident that I rode up to my brother William and asked him to form a square with his company to resist cavalry; the idea had already struck him, and Major Macleod and Captain Patrickson[34] also; it was general.

4th. The position was amongst vineyards, with walls averaging nine feet high, and he ought to have thrown down enough to open communications to the rear: the want of this caused our chief loss, for while we were pulling down, the enemy were firing and followed our paths.

5th. He sent no guns over to defend the passage and cover the retreat until after the troops had commenced retiring; had one gun broke down, or the horses been killed on the bridge, the troops would have been delayed and exposed to a destructive fire from the heights around, while in the mass of confusion.

6th. He suffered the 52nd to be nearly cut off and never sent them an order to retire, after having given them one to defend their post obstinately. His small division was therefore disjointed and nearly paralyzed by extension.

7th. His retreat over the bridge was confused, though every officer and soldier was cool and ready to execute any order, and there was no excuse to hurry.

8th. When the passage of the bridge was made, he left no man to defend it; and had I not halted some who were going up to join their Colours, the bridge would have been for a quarter of an hour without being enfiladed or exposed to a single musket shot. This was afterwards rectified, but the 43rd were placed in a most exposed position, when a few breastworks previously made would have covered them.

9th. He made our guns fire at the enemy's guns instead of their men. In short there seemed a kind of infatuation upon him, and nothing but the excellence of his men and officers saved the division; and as it was, the rains, which had swelled the river and destroyed the many fords, saved him from a repetition of the Franciscan convent at Buenos Ayres![35]

Charles wrote a letter home dated 25 July with the news:

All safe beloved mother, but William is wounded in the hip. I hate to deceive on such a subject and tell you his wound in my belief is nothing, the ball passed through without injuring the bone; he neither suffers much pain, nor is unable to walk, which if the bone was hurt he could not do.[36] It has been a severe action and our loss great; but as yet we know nothing certain, being all fatigue and wet, for rain poured in torrents all the time; it must rain twice as much ere it washes Craufurd clean for fighting at all. Five hundred killed and wounded will probably be not much above our loss,[37] which chiefly fell on the 43rd; they have had thirteen officers killed or wounded; amongst the latter Tom Lloyd who has a bad clink on the head. Colonel Hull[38] only joined the evening before, took the command and was killed. The action was on the banks of the Coa at the bridge near Almeida, and it should not have been fought at all. Now bless you dear mother, be glad you have got off so well with three sons in the fight. There will be no more fighting, as Almeida is beleaguered.

On 24 July 1840, he recorded a few further thoughts:

This day thirty years, I slept sound and happy on a rock, with my feet to a fire, on a Portuguese mountain. Having come away from the bridge about twelve at night with General Craufurd, Rowan and others, I reached the 52nd bivouac about one in the morning, wet to the skin, rain having fallen in torrents. George and his company were on an immense plate rock; the rain was over, they had a good fire and a supper of beefsteaks with tea. I had not eaten that day, except a bit of bread George gave me during the fight and being tired, starved, anxious about William's wound and depressed at our having fought so uselessly, throwing away lives so recklessly, I stripped and the soldiers, who were then dry and had supped, took one my shirt, another my coat and so on to dry them. I sat meanwhile naked, like a wild Indian, on the warm rock. It was very pleasant, drinking warm tea and eating steaks half raw, taken off the poor beast which had drawn our baggage all day! One cannot be sentimental about bullocks on such occasions.

Reverting to his journal at Celorico [da Beira], some concerns had apparently been raised regarding his exchange and subsequent release from parole:

Tom Lloyd has been teazing [sic] my life out with his concatenations of events,[39] which have he shews, in due course and of necessity, made a hole in his head, because Charles of Spain's head was without a hole for brains. Lo! Again a flag of truce has just come in from Ney with compliments, to know why Monsieur le Major Napier is serving and if he has been exchanged? Ney evidently has not got my letter given to Loison; but Lord Wellington, who is very kind to me on all occasions, has again sent a flag of truce with a copy and one of two things must happen. Either Monsieur le Major will be considered as fairly exchanged and all will be well; or Le Duc d'Echingen [Ney] will judge Monsieur le Major too precious an article to be resigned for two Enseignes des Vaisseaux and therefore not exchanged, in which case he must proceed forthwith to Ingleterra. It is said there is an order to destroy all the mills around; if so we are certainly going to retreat and probably towards Coimbra.

George also wrote on this action in great detail:

In a day or two we retreated towards the river Coa, which is a rapid river that runs behind the Portuguese frontier and the fortress of Almeida. During all this period I was suffering much from ague, which had continued for many months; still I never missed a day's duty or was a day absent from my company, which was very foolish, for had I gone to the rear and remained a few weeks in hospital, I most probably would have recovered and been well and strong all the rest of the campaign; but the truth is, that to be obliged to go to the rear was what I never would consent to.

One night, while in the neighbourhood of Almeida, I was very ill. It rained in torrents; the field where we bivouacked was newly ploughed, making it perfect mud, so that it was impossible to lie down. I suffered so much from a burning fever that the doctor and my brother Charles who was with me, thought I would die. At last morning came; I was a little better, when suddenly we heard firing in our front and in a short time we understood the enemy were advancing with their cavalry. This went on till at last our picquets were driven in, with a good deal of slaughter on our side and a general and fierce attack made upon the brigade, particularly the 43rd and Rifle corps, by the whole of Marshal Ney's corps of near twenty thousand men. We were not much above four thousand including all arms, and as the whole of the British army except ourselves, was several leagues in our rear on the other side of the river at Celerico [da Beira], we could have no support; and moreover Lord Wellington had left General Craufurd merely to watch the enemy's motions and give him every information, while he had positively forbidden him to commit himself by any engagement, but to retreat, ... Craufurd however, let his vanity get the better of his judgment and delayed so long that at last the enemy made a sudden attack, and it was with the utmost difficulty that the brigade made good its retreat over the bridge; indeed, some of the picquets were obliged to make the best of their way towards Almeida and so got protection from the guns of the fortress, and moving down behind the town, crossed the river in the dusk of the evening as well as they could by swimming, and so joined us during the night. As soon as the regiments had passed the bridge, the 43rd, which was the last regiment, and the Rifle corps were formed on the end of the bridge and on the ground and heights which commanded the passage, which was long and narrow; the artillery was so placed upon the high ground as to sweep the enemy's end of the bridge should they make the attempt to pass it. The 52nd Regiment was sent more to the right, in order to throw a flank fire upon the enemy and also to be in reserve to support the other two regiments or cover their retreat, according to circumstances. I was detached with my company to the right, close upon the edge of the river, to defend a part that was fordable. In a short time, the enemy moved down a heavy column of infantry to force the passage over the bridge, but were received so steadily and gallantly by the 43rd and Rifle Regiments, that after three desperate attempts, and pushing better than half-way across, they gave up the point with great loss both in killed and wounded. We also suffered severely, my brother William was wounded in the hip in the last attack and effort to gain the bridge; his colonel and several other officers were killed. Where I was the French only came half-way down to the bank of the river from the opposite height, and then a fine dashing fellow, a French Staff officer, rode down just opposite my position to try if the river was fordable at that part. Not liking to fire at a single man I called out to him and made signs that he must go back; but he would not, and being determined to try it, he dashed fearlessly into the water! It was then necessary to fire at him and instantly both man and horse fell dead, and their corpses floated down the stream! ... the enemy being repulsed at all points the firing ceased, and as soon as it was completely dark the brigade moved silently off and pursued its retreat upon Celerico [da Beira].

Unfortunately, we do not have William's memories of the action, but George recalls that Charles went with him and found their wounded brother:

The French did not immediately follow us, and when we halted and formed our bivouac, Charles and I went into Celerico [da Beira] to see what had become of our brother William and our friend Captain Lloyd, of the 43rd, who had likewise received a wound ...When we arrived at Celerico [da Beira], we found them not dangerously but severely wounded and settled in the Spanish General Alava's quarters, who was then aide de camp to Lord Wellington.[40] He had seen these two English officers brought into the town on a bullock car, dreadfully jolted and a burning sun blazing over their heads; and although the place was headquarters and full of British officers of every description, all of whom had good, comfortable quarters and were idling about, not a soul offered to take them in or to go and look for a house for them, and they lay in the cart for many hours without shade or water or any notice taken of them. Not even did a surgeon go near them; and as Lord Wellington and his Staff were away in front, they did not see them ... William and his friend, General Alava, seeing the neglect with which they were treated, went and offered them his house, and there every comfort he had was given to them.

The army continued to retreat towards Lisbon, George was the only one of the brothers to record a few words on this retreat:

> In the course of a short time the army retreated towards Busaco. As our brigade formed the rear-guard we were continually in conflict with the enemy's advance, but as we generally kept at a respectable distance from each other, but few men were killed and wounded and two or three officers at most. Every night I suffered from fever or ague during this retreat; but what is very curious, as showing the effect the mind has upon the body, the moment we engaged with the enemy the ague left me and I was quite strong and able to do my duty and go through my day's work as well as any officer in the regiment, without the least feeling of illness or weakness; but when we halted at night I lost all energy and was as suffering and miserable a wretch as can well be conceived.

Battle of Busaco
Wellington had identified a position on Busaco ridge where he would make a stand. George wrote extensively of his own and Charles' experiences. George, Charles was shot in the face was struck by a ball on the hip near the end of the battle but was not seriously wounded:

> At length we arrived at the heights of Busaco, a range of mountains very high and in parts very steep and difficult of access. There was a convent of the order of La Trappe [Trappists] on the top, but some distance in the rear of the position. At this convent, Lord Wellington took up his quarters and disposed his army in position to fight a battle if the enemy had the boldness, indeed I might say the temerity to attack him. General Hill's corps was on our right, the 3rd (General Picton's) Division and the 1st Division were in the centre, the Light Brigade on their left and General Cole with the 4th Division, quite on the left flank of the whole. The Portuguese regular troops were mixed with our divisions, and a second line was formed of the Militia and armed peasantry. I should suppose the whole force under the Duke of Wellington was about sixty-five or seventy thousand men,[41] and the position itself was by nature as strong as possible; so that it appeared to all of us that Marshal Massena would never attempt to carry it; and if he did make the attempt, we were perfectly certain he would be driven back and repulsed with great slaughter. We remained in position one day, during which time the various divisions and brigades were employed in getting everything in order, so that when the enemy did come on, he should have enough of it. The morning of the second day we

perceived a movement in the enemy's camp, which was on the heights opposite us, a small stream running through the valley which divided the armies. We judged their force to be nearly equal to ours, certainly Massena could not have had less than sixty thousand men in his camp,[42] so that about one hundred and thirty thousand men were going to have a fierce and bloody struggle with each other; the forces of the two armies nearly equal in point of numbers, but not so in composition, as the enemy's was composed of the finest soldiers of France, none of whom that could not count many years of hard-fought campaigns and had gained numerous victories, and in various countries; in short, a finer army or better appointed could not be well conceived, and at its head was Marshal Massena ... Our army was, on the contrary, composed of bad and inexperienced troops as well as good and experienced ones, for Lord Wellington had not above thirty thousand real soldiers, the rest were raw and undisciplined Militia, who had never seen a shot fired or an enemy in battle array before; so that upon the British soldiers he depended for the successful issue of the fight, and gloriously did they prove themselves worthy of his confidence. The French had now formed their columns and were moving steadily and gallantly down to the valley below in three bodies, meaning to attack and penetrate our line at three different points, viz. the right, centre, and left, where our division (for we had been formed into two brigades, having had two Portuguese regiments incorporated with us, under the command of Colonels Beckwith Rifle Corps, and Barclay 52nd Regiment) was stationed on the steepest part of the mountain. We were retired a few yards from the brow of the hill, so that our line was concealed from the view of the enemy as they advanced up the heights, and our skirmishers retired, keeping up a constant and well-directed running fire upon them; and the brigade of horse artillery under Captain Hugh [Hew] Ross threw such a heavy fire of shrapnel shells and so quick, that their column, which consisted of about eight thousand men, was put into a good deal of confusion and lost great numbers before it arrived at a ledge of ground just under the brow of the hill, where they halted a few moments to take breath, the head of the column being exactly fronting my company, which was the right company of our brigade, and joining the left company of the 43rd, where my brother William was with his company. General Craufurd himself stood on the brow of the hill watching every movement of the attacking column, and when all our skirmishers had passed by and joined their respective corps, and the head of the enemy's column was within a very few yards of him, he turned round, came up to the 52nd and called out, *'Now, 52nd, revenge the death of Sir John Moore! Charge, charge! Huzza!'* and waving his hat in the air he was answered by a shout that appalled the enemy, and in one instant the brow of the hill bristled with two thousand British bayonets wielded by steady English hands, which soon buried them in the bodies of the fiery Gaul! My company met the head of the French column and immediately calling to my men to form column of sections in order to give more force to our rush, we dashed forward; and as I was by this movement in front of my men a yard or two, a French soldier made a plunge at me with his bayonet and at the same time his musket going off, I received the contents just under my hip and fell. At the same instant the French fired upon my front section, consisting of about nine men in the front rank, all of whom fell, four of them dead, the rest wounded, so that most probably by my being a little advanced in front my life was saved, as the men killed were exactly those nearest to me. Poor Colonel Barclay also received a severe wound (of which he afterwards died in England). I got upon my legs immediately again and pursued the enemy down the hill, for by this time they had been completely repulsed and were running away as fast as their legs could carry them. William and his friend Captain Lloyd, who were upon my right, seeing that the French were still in column and in great confusion from the unexpected suddenness of the charge and the shout which accompanied it, had wheeled up their companies by the left, and thus flanked the French column and poured a well directed fire right into them. Major Arbuthnott [Arbuthnot], who was on my left, did the same with the remaining companies of the 52nd, so that the enemy was beset on both flanks of his column and as you may suppose, the slaughter was great. We kept firing and bayoneting till we reached the bottom and the enemy passed the brook and fell back upon their main body, which moved down to support them and cover their retreat. All this was done in a very short time; that is, it was not above twenty minutes from the charge till the French were driven from the top to the bottom of the mountain like a parcel of sheep. I really did not think it was possible for such a column to be so completely destroyed in a few minutes as that was, particularly after witnessing how gallantly they moved up under a destructive fire from the artillery and a constant galling one from our sharpshooters. We took some prisoners, and among them General Simon,[43] a gallant officer, but a bad and a dishonourable man, who afterwards broke his parole of honour. He was horribly wounded in the face, his jaw being broken and almost hanging down on his chest. Just as myself and another officer came to him, a soldier was going to put his bayonet into him, which we prevented and sent him a prisoner to the general. As I went down the hill following the enemy, I saw seven or eight French officers lying wounded.

One of them as I passed caught hold of my little silver canteen and implored me to stop and give him a drink, but much as it pained me to refuse, I could not do it, being in full pursuit of the enemy, and it was impossible to stop for an instant. This may be thought hard hearted, but in war we often do and must do many harsh and unfeeling things. Had I stopped to give him a drink I must have done so for the others, and then I should have been the last at the bottom of the hill instead of one of the first in pursuit of the enemy ... When we got to the bottom, where a small stream ran between us and the enemy's position, by general consent we all mingled together searching for the wounded. During this cessation of fighting, we spoke to each other as though we were the greatest friends and without the least animosity or angry feeling! One poor German officer in the French army came to make inquiries respecting his brother, who was in our service in the 60th Regiment, which was at that time composed principally of foreigners, and upon looking about he found him dead, the poor fellow having been killed.[44] Very soon Lord Wellington, finding we remained as he thought too long below, ordered the bugles to sound the retreat, and the French general having done the same, off scampered the soldiers of each army and returned to their several positions like a parcel of schoolboys called in from play by their master.

I was so stiff by this time that I had difficulty in walking up the hill again and was obliged to get Mr Winterbottom,[45] the Adjutant of the regiment, to help me up. When I arrived at the top, I understood that my brother Charles was severely wounded in the face while attending Lord Wellington during the battle and that he was gone, or rather carried, to the rear, attended by our cousin Captain Charles Napier of the [Royal] Navy, who had been with us for some weeks as an amateur, not having a ship at that time and being too active and enterprising a fellow to remain at home idle waiting for one. He had gone out with me the evening before the battle to skirmish a little with the French pickets, as General Craufurd thought they had advanced rather closer to the foot of our position than was right, so I was ordered to move down and push them a little farther off. Charles Napier our cousin would take a little white pony I had, to ride with us, notwithstanding I told him it was very foolish for most certainly he would get hit, being the only person on horseback. But he chose to go his own way and in less than half an hour he got shot in the calf of the leg, but very slightly; and I was delighted at it, the obstinate dog, he deserved it well! However, he was very good humoured and laughed as much as anyone at his own folly.[46] William had escaped being wounded in the battle and he and I were very glad to find ourselves side by side again.

George wrote further on the aftermath of the battle:

> In about half an hour after we returned to our position, the whole army was under arms and Lord Wellington rode along the line receiving a cheer from every regiment as he passed. While in the act of doing this, I am sorry to say the French general did a most unhandsome thing, and that was to make one of his batteries fire at Lord Wellington as he rode along accompanied by his Staff! This was shameful and cowardly, because Marshal Massena knew (the thing was too evident for him not to know) that he was only reviewing and thanking his troops for their bravery and he should have prevented any such act. Had Marshal Soult or Marshal Ney been the general in command of the French army they would have scorned such an act. We remained the rest of that day and the one following in the position, expecting a fresh attack from the enemy; but Marshal Massena had enough of it and the second day after the action our army silently moved off before daybreak on the road to Coimbra, leaving our fires and pickets, the latter retreating also as soon as daylight came. Our division as usual formed the rear guard and as we were passing by the Convent of La Trappe General Craufurd ordered me to post myself in the garden of it, which overlooked the late position of the army and commanded the road by which the troops were retiring, and there to remain and defend it as long as I had a man left! This I should have done, for I was determined to keep my post if I lived as long as I had a cartridge left to load with; but as no enemy appeared I had no opportunity of showing what good stuff an English company of light infantry was made of. It was ascertained in about an hour that the enemy had moved off also and were marching by another road to Coimbra, which they expected to reach before us and so cut off the British army, or at least a large portion of it, from the retreat to the Lines.

Lord Wellington wrote to Lady Sarah Napier:

> Coimbra, 30 September, 1810
> My dear Madam,
> I am concerned to be again the channel of conveying to you, intelligence of a distressing nature; but you received the last which I communicated to you in a manner so becoming yourself, that I have less reluctance in writing to you than I had on the former occasion, although the cause is more disastrous. The army was engaged with the enemy on the 27th and your sons Charles and George were wounded. I saw the former after he

was wounded, and he was well and in good spirits, although he had a severe but not a dangerous wound in the jaw. George is wounded in the hip but very slightly, and both are doing well. You will see the account of the action in which the troops were engaged, and I hope it will be some consolation to you to reflect that your sons received their wounds on an occasion in which the British troops behaved so well. Ever my dear Madam, your most faithful and obedient humble servant, Wellington.

Charles wrote to his mother a few days later to reassure her of his survival:

Pombal, 1 October I am wounded dear mother; the ball passed along the cheek bone and lodged in the upper jaw, from which it was extracted with great pain to me, although with less mischief than was expected, as it had not passed through the palate. You never saw so ugly a thief as I am; but melancholy subjects must be avoided, the wound is not dangerous …

Charles wrote of his memories of the battle thirty years later:

27 September 1840
Anniversary of Busaco, in which I was shot through the stem[47] and George through the stern; that was burning the family candle at both ends. I was on horseback and the shot stunned me; black shadows came across my eyes, my sight went, I reeled in the saddle and fell. My cousin Charles [Napier] picked me up and then the blood gushed from where the ball had entered; it was supposed to have lodged in my brain and that I was a slain man. I could not see or speak, but heard *'Poor Napier! After all his wounds he is gone at last.'* I felt obliged by this regret, but hoped they would not bury me, being still all alive and bent upon living. The observation made me uneasy though, for when a fellow shows no life, they are sometimes on a field of battle over quick in burying him: so with a tight twist I intimated; alive, but not merry. Four soldiers of the Guards carried me in a blanket to the convent of Busaco by Wellington's orders. He was close to me when I was hit but rode away at the moment and was returning as they bore me off.
'Who is that?' he said.
To answer was not possible, but my hat was pulled off and waved to him and he ordered them to take me to his quarters. Going there we met a clever surgeon (Fitzpatrick of the artillery[48]) and General Alava. Setting me on the grass, he and another surgeon worked, and it was very disagreeable work it was; for the ball was imbedded in the bone and pull as they would, it could not be extracted, though they cut open my cheek for three inches. At last,

one put his thumb in my mouth and pushed, while the other plucked and away it came, tearing innumerable splinters of bone with it. I did not call out, but it was very painful. Poor Alava could not look on and turned his back. I still suffer enough from the wound now, thirty years after!

Charles continued to note the progress of his wound in his journal:

24 October. My wounds are nearly closed, but a swelling in the face and stiff jaw require care and confinement. To be so near well without joining my regiment worries me; but the doctor says stuff, *'get well first, get well'*. His chief objection is fear of cold fixing the stiff jaw, and as even now it is difficult to eat, fatigue could not be borne.

7 November. As to my sufferings, there were none after pulling out the ball; so that matter is settled. Perhaps the use of my choppers will never be regained, and stiff jaws are a bore, but only painful at dinner; so at grace I put a prayer for the fellow who shot me. My surgeon, a shrewd little Scotchman, calls me a fool for thinking of joining [the army] …20 November. My jaws are coming right, but the doctor won't let me move, which is wise. My desire is to join in the pursuit, the French will be touched up now, yet there will be no general action, which consoles George and me much …

In November, Charles wrote with some bitterness of his treatment:

I had to shift for myself after the first half hour and went alone to Coimbra. They were not inattentive to me, but do not by writing thanks, make them think me under an obligation to them; they only did what they would have been brutes not to have done, ie looked to the carrying a wounded man off, when near him. Black Charles indeed, like a true sailor was active as possible, and personally assisted in carrying me … I like Harry Fox[49] and Charles Napier[50] the better for not staying with me and would not have thanked them if they had; I should have attributed it to dislike of returning fire. My uneasiness was great lest George and William should come, though only five hundred yards off, yet I felt almost sure they would not; at the Coa I left William with the first surgeon and went back.

George also wrote of the continued retreat:
We arrived some hours sooner than the French at Coimbra, from which Lord Wellington had ordered all the inhabitants to withdraw and carry all their property and provisions with them; but as they had unfortunately

delayed doing this till we were actually on the march through the town, the hurry, fright and confusion were beyond description, and I never witnessed so heart-rending a scene! Beautiful women and young children, the aged, the decrepit, the sick, the poor, the rich, nobles and peasants, all in one dense mass of misery, wretchedness and confusion; some barefoot, others crying, women tearing their hair with loud lamentations and calling on every saint in the calendar, many of them running to the officers for protection and food, the weather bad and all drenched with rain. And to crown all, when we who were the last of the troops were passing by the prison, which was also the madhouse, the unfortunate inmates, prisoners and maniacs, were all at the grated windows seeing the whole population of the city driven before us through the gate, and these unfortunate wretched creatures all locked in, and a fire having broken out in some houses close by them which they with reason expected every moment to communicate with the prison, and that they must all perish in the flames! The British officers and soldiers could not stand this sight, and we soon broke open the gates and let them all loose; the maniac, the murderer and the thief were turned adrift without a moment's hesitation or an instant's thought, by which many a villain of the deepest dye was again let loose upon society and escaped the punishment due to his crimes. But what else was to be done? We had no time to make inquiries, their keepers or jailers had left them, the flames were fast approaching and the enemy entering the town! If we did wrong, it was from motives of humanity and under circumstances that those only who were present can appreciate, and I feel confident that no man of feeling could for one moment blame us ...

About the third day's march, I was so ill and stiff with my wound that I could no longer sit my horse and was forced to get into a cart and make the best of my way to Lisbon, in the progress of which one cold, dark, rainy night, the Portuguese driver decamped and left his cart and myself sticking in the mud. Seeing a light at some distance I got out of the cart and made my way to it, but was so exhausted with pain and illness (having the ague also) that I sank down perfectly done up at the door of the house from whence the light had proceeded. And luckily for me, this was the quarter of my friend Sir Lowry Cole,[51] commanding the 4th Division, who, upon being informed that a wounded officer was at his door instantly came out, had me carried in, gave me his own bed, had a surgeon sent for to dress my wound (the same who afterwards cut off my arm) and then sent me a good dinner; after which I fell asleep, and awoke next morning at daybreak quite refreshed and able to get on with General Cole's staff to the Lines, where I took my leave of my kind friend the general, whose kindness to me I can never forget or cease to be most grateful for as long as I live. But I am not a solitary instance of Sir Lowry Cole's kindness and generosity, for he never would permit officer or private soldier to want anything that he had, or that it was in his power to procure for him; and though a hot-tempered man, he is as kind and generous as he is brave, and a more truly gallant, enterprising soldier never breathed.

From the Lines I went to Lisbon, which was so crammed with troops, sick and wounded soldiers, commissaries and their clerks, all the skulkers and riffraff of the army, besides thousands of Portuguese driven in from the country towns, that it was hardly possible to get a place to lodge in. But good luck attended me here also, for by accident I found the house where my brother Charles was quartered and who had arrived some days before, having suffered much from the pain of his wound (which was very severe) and the great neglect of the medical men, who seemed to have troubled themselves very little about him or any of the wounded, being more anxious to take care of themselves than to perform their duty to the sick and wounded. But I must say that those medical men whom, unfortunately for him, he came under, were all young men just arrived from England, many of them both idle and ignorant; and from the circumstance of the army being on the retreat and closely followed by the enemy, these young surgeons had nobody to give them orders or teach them their duty as military men, so that they were completely left to themselves, which is some excuse for their conduct.

George went on to describe finding Charles in Lisbon, their slow recuperation and many distractions:

I found Charles in bed very ill, his face so dreadfully swollen that I could neither see eyes nor nose, and having only heard that '*he was dreadfully wounded in the face*', when I beheld him this horrid looking figure, I really thought his nose had been shot off! And as you are aware what a fine long one he has, you can easily imagine how swollen his face must have been to hide it! The ball had entered on one side of his nose and passing through had lodged in the jawbone of the opposite side, from whence it was abstracted with much difficulty, great part of the jaw coming away with it as well as several teeth. During this long and painful operation he never uttered a word or winced while under the surgeon's hands who performed the operation, and who told me he never saw a man who bore pain so patiently and manfully …

The French lady in whose house I found my brother was a very kind, excellent, clever, dirty, snuffy little old woman, who insisted on my taking up my quarters in her house, and she was as kind to us as possible then and ever afterwards. Her name was Madame Frannalette; her husband had been a merchant, but was dead, and because she was a Frenchwoman the Portuguese government was distrustful of her and treated her very harshly in many instances, but being French her gaiety was incessant, whether ill-treated or well-treated, *toujours gaie*.[52] In this house we gradually recovered from our wounds, and used to be merry and happy enough, having many friends who came to see us and often dined with us, particularly when business or duty brought any of our brother officers into Lisbon they were sure to come to us.

Opposite to our lodgings were some very pretty young ladies whom we wished to get acquainted with, but as their friends did not much like the English officers, these girls told us across the street (which was very high and exceedingly narrow) that if we wished to visit them we must get across the street from our window [&] in at theirs (as we would not be allowed to go in by the street door) and then they would be happy to entertain us and give us some tea and coffee. Now in saying this jokingly, these young ladies never had an idea that we would attempt such a thing, as our windows were in the third storey and at least thirty or forty feet from the ground; but they forgot they had young Englishmen to deal with, so as soon as it was dusk and the people walking in the street below could not readily distinguish us, we procured some very long planks, and tying them together so as to reach the opposite window we rested one end on theirs and fastening the other firmly on our own we ran across and jumped into their room to their utter astonishment; however as we had performed our part they very graciously and most good-humouredly performed theirs by giving us coffee and cake, and we had a merry evening, laughing and talking bad Portuguese, to the amusement of the young ladies. However, we were requested not to perform the same feat again, to which we assented upon condition that we should be permitted to repeat our visit in a proper manner through the doorway and up the stairs, which being agreed upon we often paid a visit and were introduced to their parents and friends and found other young ladies invited to meet us …

About this time a very great friend of ours, Captain Packenham of the Navy,[53] who always used to be of our parties to the young ladies, was appointed to a ship and came to dine with us, and in talking over his going home to join his ship he said, *'Well, I care not where I am sent so that it is not to cruise in Lough Swilly Bay*[54] *on the Irish Coast, for if I go there*

I am sure I shall be lost.' We of course laughed at him, but I never shall forget with what a serious and melancholy expression of countenance he held to his opinion. When he arrived in England he found the ship was ordered to the very place he dreaded and in a few weeks after her arrival in the bay a storm arose and she went down and not a soul left to tell the melancholy tale! His body was drifted ashore and buried with hundreds of his unfortunate crew. Poor Packenham! a gayer or more kindhearted fellow never wore a blue coat.

Advance to Santarem

George was able to return to duty soon after the army left the Lines in pursuit of Massena's army, which had retired to a strong defensive position at Santarem:

> In consequence of the French not finding provisions or the towns inhabited as they expected, it was with the utmost difficulty that Marshal Massena could support his army in front of the Lines for some weeks, and he was at last forced to retreat to the town and district of Santarem, where he took up a strong position and fortified his camp, being obliged in his turn to act upon the defensive, for Lord Wellington immediately followed him and took up a position opposite the enemy's front ...
>
> At this time I went to rejoin my regiment, which was in advance, quartered in some of the villages in front of the enemy's position of Santarem, our right resting on the Tagus with a small stream in our front, rather deep, beyond which was a marshy plain. There were two bridges over this little river, with a long causeway leading from one of them, over which was the road to Santarem. These two bridges were about half a mile or less from each other, and a company was posted at each to watch them, with orders that should the enemy attempt to force the passage, to fire the mines and blow up the bridges, as everything was prepared for that purpose by the engineers. My company was posted at the lower one on the right, which was not that over which the great road passed, but there was a private road which led through the marsh to the enemy's position. One night, between twelve and one o'clock, I was visiting my sentinels and posts in order to be sure all was quiet before I lay down to sleep, when suddenly I heard a shot, then another, and the noise of men as if coming down on our post. It was so pitch dark I could see nothing, and I was just going to blow up the bridge when I thought I would first venture a little way beyond on the enemy's side and listen if I could hear the noise of men marching and be quite satisfied before I set fire to the mine. My company was drawn up in three minutes across our end of the bridge and I went

over to the other side with two or three men, and placing our ears to the ground we listened attentively for a few minutes, when I felt assured there was no enemy approaching; and therefore bringing up an officer and ten men, I ordered him to remain there, and if the enemy should advance upon him to fire and instantly retreat as hard as he and his men could run across the bridge, as I should be ready the instant he passed to blow it up. While I was giving the orders we heard several more shots from the left near the other bridge, but I perceived by the flash that they came from our side of the stream; and we also saw and heard many splashes of water, as if people were crossing the river; and at that moment a sergeant came to tell me that the Brunswick Oels Corps (which was principally composed of deserters and French soldiers, who had enlisted into that regiment rather than remain in the Spanish hulks at Cadiz, where they had been cruelly treated by the Spaniards) was deserting, and that I was to fire upon them and take as many prisoners as I could. I therefore sent some of my men on one side and some on the other, and we soon found these poor fellows swimming across. We were obliged to fire at some of them who had got over and were getting off to the enemy, and a great number were killed. However, as soon as daylight came, the greatest part were taken, and the rest returned to their quarters. Next day Lord Wellington ordered seventeen (I think) of them to be tried, all of whom were sentenced to be shot as deserters to the enemy; but he only executed five of them,[55] and these, being Frenchmen, were much to be pitied, as they were taken prisoners at the time of Dupont's surrender,[56] and if the Spaniards had not refused most shamefully to put the terms of capitulation into execution these unfortunate men would have been sent back to France. The British Government did all in its power to get the soldiers of Dupont's army released from their horrible confinement and treatment, but to no purpose; and, as a last resort, they offered to take them into our service if they would enlist, which they immediately did, as by that means they became British soldiers and were claimed by our government as such. These men were sent to the different foreign regiments in our service, and a considerable number came out and joined the Brunswick Oels Corps, then in the Light Division.[57] Being close to the position of their countrymen, and every day seeing their former regiments and comrades within almost speaking distance of them, they were unable to resist the temptation of crossing the little river and being in half an hour among their countrymen, and once more wearing the tricolour cockade and fighting under their national flag. When led out for execution they requested not to be tied to the stakes, and one of them, who had been a '*sous-officier*'[58] in his own service, addressed his comrades who were drawn up to witness the execution, saying *'I know that by the laws of the service I am now in I deserve death, because desertion to the enemy is so punished in the English army; but I have been brought up in different notions, therefore it is no moral crime upon my part, who am not an Englishman but a German (Alsace). I have no fear of death and am prepared to enter the presence of my Maker, being unconscious of having offended Him. I was compelled to enter the British service in order to escape the cruelty of the Spaniards, who had unlawfully kept me a prisoner contrary to the capitulation, and can it be wondered at, or can it be considered a crime that, when opposite my own countrymen and in daily sight of my old comrades, I should try to join them and once more fight under the colours of France? No, comrades! You who know me will consider me guiltless, and, like me, glory in death! When the English bullets have penetrated my breast, dip my handkerchief in my blood and distribute it among you as a relic of my devotion to France.'* He then knelt down with the others in front of his grave, which in a military execution is always dug ready to receive the body of the culprit, and on the word being given to the party to fire, he and his unfortunate companions fell, but not dead (which sometimes happens, though very rarely), and he rose again and would have addressed the soldiers, had not a fresh party instantly stepped close up to these poor fellows and put a period to their existence by blowing out their brains ... When he was dead those whom he addressed ran forward and tearing off the handkerchiefs with which the poor victim's eyes had been bound, pressed them to the wounds, and when all wet with the blood of their dead comrade, tore them in pieces and distributed them among one another. We all lamented the fate of these poor brave fellows at the time, and thought it was a very harsh thing to shoot them; but upon consideration I do not see how Lord Wellington could well have pardoned them, desertion among the foreign troops in our service having reached a considerable height, and it was only a few days before that Lord Wellington had pardoned several of them and issued an order stating his determination not to pardon in future any soldier caught attempting to desert to the enemy, no matter what his previous character might have been; and he warned all the foreign soldiers particularly that they must not expect any mercy, for they would be invariably shot in twenty-four hours after they were taken.

William wrote home in January 1811, betraying a fear that the French may succeed and also a dislike for his career in the army. He clearly missed his friends:

Quinta de Fonte Voa, January 1811

My dear Mother,

The sentiments that caused you to undergo the pain of that dreadful operation on your eye are the original causes also that give to Charles his intrepidity and his ambition of honourable fame, to George his impetuosity and supreme contempt for everything that is not noble and belonging to the character of a soldier. You may smile at my saying George is impetuous, but your smile will cease when I tell you that at Busaco he attempted to break the head of the French column with his own hand and when shot in the attempt, continued on the ground to wave his sword and shout to his men to go on. You feel rejoiced that people of acknowledged merit take notice of your sons, and you attribute it to their own merit; you yourself are the original cause of that friendship. Many officers are as brave and have more talents than us without meeting with the same attention ...

I do not think there will be much fighting here, rather that we shall be obliged to leave the country from want of provisions ourselves, strange as it may appear ... The nature of war is misery. Thus, I am condemned to a profession I dislike by religion, honour, and necessity ... I had two friends who could well have supplied me with sentiments of pleasure to reconcile me to my situation, but Lloyd has left the regiment and Macleod,[59] whom I love as my friend and admire as the facsimile of General Moore's character, is gone home; I am afraid merely to give his poor father the task of putting him [in] the grave. With these considerations and with the thought that if I fall I do it with honour for my country that I fall the way my father would have wished and like Moore, that my name will be respected, will you not allow that I have reason to say death may be a gain? Do not imagine from this that I will expose myself more than my duty requires; notwithstanding reason is on my side, I feel the command of God to live as strong as ever, and I tremble in danger as well as my neighbours, but I feel I cannot lose much by the change in the other world. John Ash is in the 95th;[60] I have seen him before; he sends two guineas to his father and mother: pray give it to them out of my money, he has given it to me ...

Chapter 6

The French Retreat into Spain 1811

Wellington's army waited patiently over the winter months as Massena's troops slowly starved around Santarem, but in early March the French eventually began their withdrawal. George described the pursuit of the French:

> I think it was about the 4th of March, at daybreak, that we perceived the enemy had withdrawn his advance pickets, and immediately upon its being reported to Lord Wellington, the whole British army was in movement, pursuing Marshal Massena, who finding himself unable from total want of provisions to maintain himself longer in his position, had commenced his memorable retreat from Portugal …
>
> We followed the enemy closely, being the advanced guard, and everywhere found proofs of the starving condition they were reduced to and the severe privations they must have endured. Certainly Marshal Massena as a general, deserves the greatest credit for having kept his army in position so long under such harassing circumstances and the great discontent that prevailed in his army; but then we must look on the other side also, and see what misery and destruction he caused to those unfortunate inhabitants who did not get away as ordered by Lord Wellington, or who fled into the hills in the false idea that in a few days the French would either be masters of Lisbon, having forced us to embark, or failing in that, would have marched back again to Spain. These wretched people to the amount of thousands, had every article of furniture and food taken from them, and starved by hundreds daily! A French officer who was made prisoner during this retreat, and to whom I had it in my power to be kind, told me that after a few weeks from their first arrival at the Lines an order was given by Massena that every captain must provide his with provisions in the best manner he could, which was generally done as follows. A captain and his company went off into the country, and on coming to a peasant's hut or cabin he demanded provisions, upon which the miserable father and his wife and half-starving children went down on their knees supplicating the officer not to take the miserable pittance they had left for their sole support. But this had no effect, and the father was told that he should be

hung up to a beam; and if he made a sign, that was agreed upon, that he would show where all his provisions were concealed, he would be instantly cut down, but if not there, he would hang till dead. Well, the wretched man, looking at his starving wife and helpless children, would determine on dying rather than tell where the little he had for their existence was hid. He was hung up accordingly, when in a few seconds the natural love of life and the shrieks of his distracted wife and children overcame the resolution to die. He gives the signal, is cut down, recovers his senses and points out, with despair depicted in his haggard countenance, the spot where all he has to keep life in his wife and children is deposited, and he sees the ruthless plunderers depart without sparing him one morsel. But is this all? No! In a few hours afterwards comes a fresh party of soldiers in search of provisions, and finds this unfortunate family nearly exhausted, but will give no credit to their story of what had already taken place some time before, but instantly resort to the same barbarous measure of hanging up the father, who again urged by the hopes of preserving his life a few minutes longer, makes the preconcerted signal. But, alas! when cut down, not being able to produce what has already been the prey of former robbers, is seized by the merciless soldiers and either shot or hanged, with the certainty that his miserable wife and children must perish with hunger. The French officer who told me this, said it had often happened to him to witness such scenes during the stay of Marshal Massena's army opposite our lines, and very fairly said, *'But what could we do? If we did not find the provisions we must have starved ourselves; and you know soldiers will not do that, nor anyone else if he can possibly avoid it by any means.'* He was a good-natured man, and had great pity for the Portuguese nation, and looked upon the war as most abominable and unjust; and he often told me he was heartily tired of war and all its horrid attributes, but that it was not in his power to leave the army and return to France. He had asked leave, but was refused, and seemed very glad to have been taken prisoner, hoping that there might be some chance of getting home.

The pursuit of the enemy army continued and, I think about the third day's march, coming suddenly upon a small party of them we made them prisoners. But judge of our astonishment to find in the person of one of them an Irishman who was a lieutenant in one of our best regiments,[1] and who had deserted a few weeks previously, and was, at the time he was missing from his regiment, supposed to have been made prisoner by some accident. I shall not mention the name of the regiment to which he belonged because he was a disgrace to it, and it was, and is, one of the best in the service. I shall merely say that he belonged to no regiment in the

Light Division. He had been made aide de camp to the French general of division Loison. We very soon delivered him up to the provost marshal, to be taken to Lord Wellington, in hopes he would have had him shot upon the spot; but His Lordship, having made inquiries about him from the officers of his regiment, was inclined to think the miserable man was not right in his senses, having formerly been insane. He therefore sent him a prisoner to England, with a recommendation that he might be permitted to resign his commission without any further inquiry about the matter, in order to spare his friends the pain of his conduct becoming public. This unfortunate man was not a person whose family was of any note or even known in the remotest way to Lord Wellington, so that his merciful and delicate conduct towards him was from pure good feeling and a reluctance to do a harsh thing when he could by any justifiable means avoid it.

One day on our march we found sixty or seventy poor donkeys who had been hamstrung by the French in a shamefully cruel manner, cutting the sinews of the hind legs just above the hocks, and leaving the poor animals to die by inches. Now it might have been necessary to prevent the animals from falling into our hands, but why not have shot them at once, and not maim them in that cruel manner? The same day we passed by a village in a wild place where we found numbers of the inhabitants lying dead of starvation; among them were many little children, others just alive and that was all; and those who were able going down on their knees supplicating a morsel of bread from our soldiers. We were horror struck at this heartrending sight, and as the men were ordered to halt for a few minutes, with one consent they instantly collected from each other what little biscuit they had left, and which they knew was to last them as their only subsistence for two days longer, without the least chance of receiving any more as there was none up with the army; this they distributed to the miserable, starving survivors of this wretched hamlet. I doubt whether those good people who talk of the army as if soldiers were a set of unfeeling, hard-hearted, irreligious brutes, would have done as our soldiers did with truly genuine charity. It is an easy thing to talk about the necessity of charity, but a very different one to put it in execution when you know that by so doing you are depriving yourself of the means of existence, as the soldiers knew they were doing, and did in consequence of this act of charity, go without food for two days and hard worked all the time, and many of them were left behind ill from weakness in consequence.

On arriving at the plain of Redinha which was of large extent, the river running between it and the village, the enemy drew up his forces in order of battle with the river and village in his rear, the road to the village running over a long causeway and narrow bridge. He sent all his baggage to the other side of the village and waited during this operation for us to attack him; but as soon as all was clear the French army commenced moving towards the bridge, leaving Marshal Ney with the rear-guard of about twenty thousand men to keep us in check, which he did most skilfully and gallantly; and although Lord Wellington had nearly his whole force drawn up, he did not think it prudent to do more than advance in line towards the enemy and make a slight attack with the light troops and cavalry and Sir Lowry Cole's Division. So Marshal Ney made good his retreat and took up his position in rear of the village of Redinha, his pickets occupying half the village and ours the other half. It was my friend Captain Mein[2] of the 52nd who commanded our picket; and when all was quiet and his sentinels posted and no fear of any surprise, he asked the captain commanding the enemy's pickets to have some supper with him, which the poor fellow, who had been half-starved for some months, was delighted to accept. So he came to Mein's house, and after a good supper, for we had some sutlers come up to the army, and an hour or two of conversation, it was time for him to go back to his own picket; and he had not been gone above a quarter of an hour when he was ordered to retreat from his post. Our men, perceiving that the French sentinels were withdrawn, gave the alarm and off started Mein with his picket after his friend the French captain, firing at him as hard as he could. You see by this that there is never any personal animosity between soldiers opposed to each other in war, but I daresay it strikes you as very odd that men should shake hands with each other, drink and eat together, laugh and joke and then in a few minutes use every exertion of mind and body to destroy one another. But so it is, and I hope always will be the case. I should hate to fight out of personal malice or revenge, but have no objection to fight for *fun and glory.* During the early part of this day, I received a ball which went through my coat, waistcoat and shirt, and hit me just over the heart, but only made a bruise and razed the skin. The bullet was fired at so great a distance that it was spent, and when I opened my waistcoat and shirt, expecting to find a hole in my body, the ball dropped quite flat, as if it had been struck by a hammer, this was a narrow escape. A little while afterwards I was standing talking to a friend, the Adjutant of the regiment Mr Winterbottom[3] with my hand resting on the pommel of his saddle, when a cannon shot passed between us and, as he poor fellow thought, only grazed his thigh; but when we came to examine it, the shot had done him more injury than he expected, and he was laid up in hospital with that wound six or seven months and suffered a great deal of pain. He, Winterbottom, had risen from the rank of private soldier in my company by his excellent and gallant conduct upon all occasions, and never for one instant did he fail in his duty. One of the clearest headed, coolest, and bravest men I ever saw in action, and the best Adjutant in the army, either in the orderly room or the field ...

Combat of Casal Nova, 14 March 1811
George continued:

A day or two after the affair of Redinha we had a hard day's work. About half an hour before daybreak our division was under arms, and while standing in close column, Sir William Erskine,[4] who commanded us during General Craufurd's absence (who had gone to England on leave), came up and asked why we were not in march and following the enemy.

Colonel Ross[5] said because the enemy were *not* gone, but were within cannon shot of us at that very moment, for the captains of the pickets, [Captain William] Napier 43rd, and [Captain Joseph] Dobbs 52nd, had patrolled up to their sentinels a short time before, and reported that the enemy was still in position. This did not satisfy Sir William Erskine, who kept blustering and swearing it was all nonsense and that the captains of the pickets knew nothing about the matter, and that there was not a man of them there. Just as he spoke the fog, which had been very dense, cleared away a little and bang came a shot from a twelve-pounder which struck the head of our column and made a lane through it killing and wounding many men; immediately a second and third, and then commenced a regular cannonade. Still the wise Sir William was sure it could be nothing but a single gun or two and a picket of the enemy and desired Colonel Ross to send my company to drive them in on the flank, at the same time sending an aide de camp to point out to me where I was to go to. We proceeded a short distance into some vine fields in a little bottom or valley upon the left flank of our column, the mist being very heavy, and just as we reached the bottom whiz came a few shots from some of the enemy close to us but whom we saw not. One of these shots went through my cap just grazing my forehead. I turned round to pick up my cap and to ask the aide de camp a question, when I saw him just putting spurs to his horse to gallop off back to his worthy general, as he thought it quite unnecessary to remain any longer! He was a young man just come out, and I dare say knew no better; but have no doubt he learned his duty before he was much older or had the prudence to go home as I never saw or heard of the young gentleman afterwards. I pushed forward immediately and had just leaped with the men over a low wall into a narrow road and was almost instantly charged by a squadron of dragoons which was waiting for us behind some trees. However, by this time it was broad daylight and the mist nearly dispersed; so perceiving what it was and seeing the French officer commanding the squadron at its head, I had just time to form up half a dozen file and giving the gentlemen a volley, down came the officer and a few of his men and horses, upon which the rest galloped off and I instantly made my company leap over the opposite wall into a vineyard where I knew I was safe from their cavalry; and forming a line of skirmishers, I advanced towards a French brigade which was drawn up at some distance in my front. However, they sent forward a cloud of sharpshooters to oppose me, and in a few minutes the action became very sharp. I continued advancing, but very slowly, for they were quadruple my strength; which my commanding officer, who was following with the regiment perceiving, sent several other companies to my support, and ere long we were four hundred strong, under Major Stewart, of the Rifle Corps.[6] We then made a grand push and drove the enemy from vineyard to vineyard, constantly advancing and keeping up a hot fire, the whole Light Division supporting us. At this time poor Major Stewart received a shot through his body, several other officers were also wounded and the command again devolved upon me.

It was now about midday, and as my men had nearly expended all their ammunition, I was giving some directions to my lieutenant, Gifford[7] he was a few steps before me, and I had just turned round when I saw some Frenchmen, who were concealed among the bushes, start up, and as poor Gifford's back was turned towards them while he was receiving orders from me, the muzzles of their muskets were within two or three yards of his head, when they fired and he fell! I rushed forward, caught him up in my arms, when to my horror his head fell back and his brains literally splashed on the ground! My excellent and valued friend was a corpse! The back of his skull was blown off! Some of my men who saw the whole thing at the same instant dashing forward, plunged their bayonets into the Frenchmen's bodies and revenged the death of their officer. I laid his body gently on the ground; the soldiers wrapped it up in his cloak, and under a heavy fire from the enemy dug a grave in the sandy soil, and in this rough but glorious sepulchre were deposited the remains of Theophilus Gifford, as honourable, generous, gallant and guileless a soldier as ever the fate of war cut off in the prime of youth, health and spirits! The soldiers then fired a volley over his grave, which volley carried death to some brave fellows in the enemy's ranks, and thus in the space of a quarter of an hour finished the life and funeral of my friend!

As soon as I got my men supplied with fresh ammunition, I moved forward with all the companies under my command, my brother William being my second as he was next senior officer. We drove the enemy from hill to hill with great slaughter, and about three o'clock, while leading on my men to charge a strong body of French which was a few yards before me, and which I thought I might be able to take prisoners, I received a shot in my right wrist which completely shattered it and forced me to go to the rear, as I was also very much fatigued, having been incessantly engaged with the enemy from three o'clock in the morning to past three o'clock in the day. To show that it was pretty hot work, I need only mention that I went into action with sixty-six soldiers, three sergeants and three subalterns, and I lost one officer, one sergeant, and ten or twelve soldiers killed; myself, two sergeants and about fifteen or sixteen wounded, so that of my original number nearly half were killed and wounded. As I went to the rear I saw some men carrying an officer in a blanket who seemed badly wounded, and when I came up to them I found it was my brother William, who had received a shot in the back while giving orders to his company. I and everyone who saw him thought it was a mortal wound, but it proved otherwise thank God! Although from the circumstance of his never being able to get the ball extracted, he often suffers considerable pain from it.

We were obliged to lie down under the shade of a tree at the roadside, waiting till the columns had passed, as the rest of the army was marching to the support of the Light Division. While waiting under this tree, who should come up but our brother Charles, who was with his regiment, having joined from Lisbon that morning although his wound in the face was not quite healed. He was sorry to find us both wounded so severely and was himself suffering from weakness and want of food, as he had not been able to get anything to eat for the last two days and had been continually on horseback pushing on to join the army, being one of those who never remained behind when the troops were advancing unless forced to do so by wounds and sickness, and not even then unless in so weak a state as to preclude his sitting on his horse. While waiting with us under the tree, one of his own officers came up and said, *'Major, here is our surgeon, who is very clever at taking off an extremity; if you like him to try his hand on your brother's arm he will do it elegantly,'* upon which Charles swore that if the little doctor came near me he would shoot him! I laughed immoderately at Charles' rage and assured him he need not be afraid for I would not let anyone take it off…

As soon as the road was pretty well clear, we bid Charles goodbye and proceeded to the town of Condeixa [-a-Nova], William carried in his blanket and I walking alongside of him. On our road we were joined by several other officers, all wounded and ten or a dozen of us went into the only house we could find habitable, as the enemy the moment they left a town set fire to it in all directions to prevent us as they said from finding any shelter ...When we got a little settled upstairs, we were all examined by the surgeons, and on probing William's wound they told me they feared it might prove mortal; mine they said would be very tedious and most probably I should lose the use of several of my fingers. Poor Major Stewart died that night holding my hand; and he blamed an officer high in rank as the cause of his death, this person having said something to him in the execution of his duty which made Stewart gallop forward, when he was immediately shot by the enemy. The conduct of that officer was quite unwarrantable, but as he is also gone I shall not mention his name, but merely say he never had the character of a brave man while in our division,[8] notwithstanding he said that which caused the death of as fine, enterprising and gallant a soldier as ever faced the enemy. ... Lord March[9] came to see us that night, and to say that Lord Wellington had written to my mother to inform her of our being wounded, and that he was well satisfied with our conduct on that day. This was most kind and considerate of him, who was commander in chief of the army and had scarcely time to eat! His time and thoughts were fully occupied, yet he found a moment to do a kind act which he knew would highly gratify my mother and ease her mind about her son's wounds. Lord March also showed us every kindness possible; he had ridden that evening twenty miles to see us and returned to headquarters after a few hours' stay with us ...

This same night another officer came to see us with whom at that time we were totally unacquainted. This officer was marching with his regiment, the 4th Dragoons, through the town and hearing there were several wounded officers in a house without much to eat or drink, he came up to us and said he had brought all the provisions he had with him and requested our acceptance of them; and he would not hear of our leaving him a morsel for himself; and wishing us a speedy cure, he went after his regiment leaving bread, wine, tea and sugar &c. This officer's name was Light.[10] Of course, this was a kindness never to be forgotten, and we have ever since been on terms of great intimacy with him. It is a great pity he quitted the army, as he had highly distinguished himself and was a great favourite with Lord Wellington, who had promoted him for his conduct[11]...

My servant came and told me that John Dunn,[12] an Irishman whom I had enlisted several years before, wished to see me. When he came into the room he immediately said: *'Och, captain, but I'm come to you and your brother is after the wounds. Didn't I see you knocked over by the bloody Frenchmen's shot? and sure I thought you was kilt. But myself knew you wouldn't be plaised if I didn't folly on after the villains, so I was afeard to go pick you up when ye was kilt, long life to you! But I pursued the inimy as long as I was able, and sure I couldn't do more; and now I'm come to see how your honour, long life to you agin.'* I shook hands with him and said, *'But, John, you seem wounded yourself; why is your arm tied up?' 'Och, nothing at all to prevent me coming to see your honour, and your honour's brother lying there, Captain William, long life to him! I hope he's not dead.'* Upon insisting to know if he was wounded, at last he replied, *'Why sure it's nothing, only me arrum was cut off a few hours ago below the elbow joint, and I couldn't come till the anguish was over a bit. But now I'm here, and thank God your honour's arrum is not cut off, for it's mighty cruel work; by Jasus, I'd rather be shot twinty times, though the doctor tould me he did it asy too, long life to his honour! I'm sure he didn't mean to hurt me all he could help.'* I then asked him for his brother, who was also a recruit of mine and in the company, and an uncommonly fine, handsome soldier as ever stepped, and who was a particular favourite of mine. He hesitated a few moments, and heaving a convulsive sob said; *'I seed him shot through the heart alongside wid me just as I got the shot myself,'* and he looked up piteously in my face and said, *'Oh, John dear, my poor mother! And sure I couldn't look at him again for the life of me, my heart was broke, and I came away to the rare. But, captain, he died like a soldier, as your honour would wish him to die, and sure that's enough. He had your favour whilst he lived, God be with him, he's gone now.'* After this anecdote who will dare to say private soldiers have no feelings? By Heavens! it makes my anger rise and my blood boil to hear people talk of soldiers as if they were a different race of beings from themselves …

William also recorded his memories of Casal Nova:

When I arrived at a certain round hill under fire, which I judged a good point of support, I halted four companies to watch our flanks, and with the two others hastily descended a deep ravine on my right to join the left of the 52nd, whose charging shout I had just heard on that side, though an intervening ridge prevented my seeing them. Unfortunately for me, this charge was partial; a momentary effort to extricate the regiment from a dangerous crisis. Thus, with two companies I suddenly found myself in the midst of the enemy, but I arrived just in time to save Captain Dobbs' 52nd and two men who were cut off from their regiment. The French were gathering fast about us, we could scarcely retreat and Dobbs agreed with me that boldness would be our best chance; so we called upon the men to follow and jumping over a wall which had given us cover, charged the enemy with a shout which sent the nearest back. But then occurred the most painful event that ever happened to me. Only the two men of the 52nd followed us and we four arrived unsupported at a second wall, close to a considerable body of French, who rallied and began to close upon us. Their fire was very violent, but the wall gave cover. I was however, stung by the backwardness of my men and told Dobbs I would save him or lose my life by bringing up the two companies; he entreated me not, saying I could not make two paces from the wall and live. Yet I did go back to the first wall, escaped the fire and reproaching the men, gave them the word again and returned to Dobbs, who was now upon the point of being taken; but again I returned alone! The soldiers had indeed crossed the wall in their front, but kept edging away to the right to avoid the heavy fire. Being now maddened by this second failure, I made another attempt, but I had not made ten paces when a shot struck my spine and the enemy very ungenerously continued to fire at me when I was down. I escaped death by dragging myself by my hands; for my lower extremities were paralysed, towards a small heap of stones which was in the midst of the field and thus covering my head and shoulders. Not less than twenty shots struck this heap. However, Captain Lloyd and my own company and some of the 52nd, came up at that moment and the French were driven away.

The excuses for the soldiers were;

1st That I had not made allowance for their exertions in climbing from the ravine up the hillside with their heavy packs and they were very much blown.

2nd Their own captains had not been with them for a long time and they were commanded by two lieutenants, remarkable for their harsh, vulgar, tyrannical dispositions and very dull bad officers withal; and one of them exhibited on this occasion such miserable cowardice as would be incredible if I had not witnessed it. I am sure he ordered the men not to advance and I saw him leading them the second time to the right. This man was lying down with his face on the ground; I called to him, reproached him, bade him remember his uniform; nothing would stir him; until losing all patience I threw a large stone at his head. This made him get up, but when he got over the wall he was wild, his eyes staring and his hands spread out. He was a duellist and had wounded one of the officers some time before. I would have broke him, but before I recovered my wound sufficiently to join, he had received a cannon shot in the leg and died at the old, desolate melancholy mill below Sabugal.[13] Everything combined to render death appalling, yet he showed no weakness. Such is human nature and so hard it is to form correct opinions of character!

As mentioned by George, Wellington found time to write to Lady Sarah Napier again:

16 March 1811
My dear Madam,
I am sorry to have to inform you that your two sons were again wounded in an action with the enemy the day before yesterday, but neither of them, I hope seriously. William is wounded in the back, and this is supposed to be only a flesh-wound;[14] George in the right arm, which is broken. Both are doing well and will I hope soon recover to return to their duty. Your Ladyship has so often received accounts of the same description with that which I am now writing to you, and your feelings on the subject are so just and proper, that it is needless to trouble you farther. Your sons are brave fellows and an honour to the army; and I hope that God will preserve them to you and their country. Ever my dear Madam, your most faithful humble servant, Wellington.

Charles had set out to rejoin the army just as news of the French retreat from Santarem arrived. He maintained his journal of his progress:

8 January 1811. My wound will always be inconvenient, having broken the gristle of my snout inside, one nostril has but little passage left, so my fate is to be always a snuffler, for the doctors say it will never be better. My surgeon is a good one, yet in truth little is due to them for recovery; nature and Charles Napier, that is me myself, saved me. There needed to have been no lump in the snout, had they used the spunge [sic] plug in time, and my wish was for it, but they said no! The jaw might have been set also; but in truth they were afraid of touching me, lest they should bring on inflammation. What a passion the devil must be in at being so often baulked! However, it must please him to see what an ugly saint these clinks have made me! General Kellerman[15] was thirty-two at the battle of Vimiera and had thirty-two wounds! My share is six in two years, hem! Kellerman takes the prize …

6 March. Rode to Mafra. After Loures mountainous, crossed Monte Chica, which is fortified and very strong from its precipitous features. Thence to Mafra, where the heights are strong and covered with works.

The confidence inspired by these Lines of Wellington must necessarily be great; but the danger to be feared is, that they must be defended in a great measure by the Ordenanza[16] who are mere peasants; or by militia who are not [much] better. Now regular troops, however confident at first, would be dismayed a seeing a French column penetrating where the works were deemed impregnable; consternation would then ensue, especially with the Portuguese troops. All lines have this drawback. A soldier who trusts to his firelock alone never despairs while he can use it; but he ever puts too much faith in works, and on seeing them forced thinks all is lost. However, I only speak of what might occur if these lines were assailed by an army equal to the contest, and Lord Wellington says Massena's army is not so; and of that there is little doubt, or Massena would have attacked ...

8 March. Just heard of the French retreat, which I conclude is to seek subsistence in a country not yet exhausted north of the Mondego and perhaps to draw Lord Wellington from his lines, and then attack him in rear with the army now besieging Badajoz. My wound is still open but I am off to join.

10 March. Reached Villa Franca [Vila Franca de Xira], five leagues; passed the plain where Junot was wounded.

12 and 13 March. Rode all night and having made ninety-two miles reached the army between Redinha and Condeixa [-a-Nova]. This distance was done, with only three hours' halt at Tom Napier's quarters[17] who gave me a positive[ly] bad but comparative[ly] good dinner. My poor horse had 2 lbs of Indian corn, on which he performed his severe journey in twenty-two hours, including the three hour's halt!

14 March. A sharp affair between the Light Division and the enemy's rear-guard this day. We lost four hundred killed and wounded here and at Redinha. My two brothers commanded the companies chiefly engaged[18] and are both severely wounded: the ignorance and imprudence of Sir William Erskine said to have been conspicuous; and Colonel Drummond[19] is not extolled for military qualities.

15 March. Great want of provisions. Moved to Foz D'Aronce [Foz de Arouce]. At the end of the march, part of the Light Division was engaged sharply.

16 to 21 March. Continued our route, enemy in full retreat.

22 March. Rode over the mountains to Coimbra to see George and William. Passed Ponte Murcella [Ponte de Mucela] and saw Busaco at a distance.

This Murcella [Mucela] is strong, the position finest on the left bank, but the ford and bridge best defended on the right bank. The ground on the left is very high, yet does not command the bridge like that on the right bank, which though much lower is close and precipitous; the bridge is blown up, the town burnt.

Charles wrote an undated letter to his cousin, Lady Emily Berkeley, from Ponte de Murcella [Mucela]:

My brothers are at Condeixa. George was yesterday in great pain, not otherwise ill; William so much better as to be up; this is nearly proof positive that his inwards have not been injured by the ball and the wound is therefore not dangerous … The French have destroyed two arches of this bridge and our light troops were warmly engaged last night; but we have no chance of a general action, which I am sorry for; my mother will probably not regret it so much. My brothers' wounds will I think, confine them a long time, for though it may be confidently said they are not dangerous, they are very bad clinks. George's poor subaltern, Lieutenant Gifford was killed; his conduct was the admiration of everyone; and that is the only consolation. George is so affected by his loss that it hurts his wound. Our skirmishers were retiring when the gallant young man was killed; my brother missed him, looked back and saw him on the ground, a hundred yards behind. Four Frenchmen were plundering him, but George, sabre in hand, dashed back singly, beat the four men from their plunder, took his friend's bleeding corpse in his arms and bore it off from the midst of his enemies. The company buried him on the spot with their bayonets, under a tremendous fire, gave three cheers and again attacked; never was a soldier's death finer, or his burial more honourable! Gifford was so bravely conspicuous that the French officers called out many times, kill that officer. At last they succeeded, but we had shot for shot, they lost four hundred men.

Charles also wrote to his mother:

Camp at Moita, 21 March.
Both the wounded men are better mother. I make no apologies for the dirt of this note; for flead, bugged, centipeded, beetled, lizarded and earwigged, cleanliness is known to me only by name. Moreover, a furze bush makes a bad table for writing on and a worse chair, when breeches are nearly worn out with glory. Oh! oh! We have very little food, which forced us to halt;

Massena has thus got two days' start, but he is pursued by the cavalry and Light Division. We shall be dispersed in cantonments on the frontier, as Lord Wellington cannot I think, muster men enough to follow into Spain, and probably more troops will be sent to the Alentejo. Celorico [da Beira] again will be tiresome, but we are of Spencer's Division, and it is to be feared will become headquarter pets, as the Guards belong to us, and are favourites of His Lordship; deservedly so.[20] The Light Division are also great favourites and most deservedly so. Lord Wellington has particularly thanked them and is going to give three sergeants of the 43rd, 52nd and Rifles, each a commission for their conduct in the late pursuit of Massena.[21] Neither poor Blanco[22] nor myself are much troubled with bile now. A hundred miles, with only three hours' rest and hardly a bite to eat, did he carry me coming up to the army, and my fear was it would kill him; but that was better than being too late for the action expected at Condeixa [-a-Nova]; he did not even tire! He is the strongest horse ever backed. Still, he thinks a bivouac the worst amusement in the world, as he gets nothing but heath and hard riding. I kiss and coax him, but it don't make up for no oats. He is the most delightful animal that ever was, but thinks being admired by the Lisbon ladies with a full stomach, better than my affection.[23]

He continued the letter over the next few days:

Coimbra, 23 March.
Says I to Blanco yesterday, *Suppose we walk over the mountains old boy and see the other boys*; no sooner said than done. William will be at his duty in two months, but he ought not for six; he suffers little pain and runs about in a go-cart like a child. As to George he suffers acute and constant pain and cannot sleep without opium: however the surgeons are positive he will not lose his hand and think he will have the use of the two fore fingers and thumb if not of all. Are we cats that we live and bear such wounds? But now having told you dear mother exactly the facts as usual, adieu; this is enough after a ride forty miles over the most rugged mountains in Portugal. Poor Blanco almost gives up the ghost.

24 March.
This country is ravaged by fire and sword, we get nothing for love or money, but pass through deserted tracks, the only symptoms of former habitations being the burned walls of villages and dead bodies. What a change in six months; England how little do you know of war! A dollar has been given

for some biscuit; and two complete days and most part of a third I went without food: the boys at Coimbra stuffed me, for there they have plenty. We have also got a dinner here this day and having been again two days without one, I must make haste or it will be gone; we get no bread and the hard biscuit bothers my wounded jaw when there is not time for it to soak.

Charles recommenced his journal:

23 March. Returning from Coimbra lost my way on the heath at night and slept at the bivouac of the Chasseurs Britanique. Reached St Romao [Sao Romao] the 26th the village burnt. Cea [Seia] the same. The fine palace of the Bishop of Guarda's[24] brother, Don Bernardo, quite destroyed. Massena has used fire and sword with an unsparing hand. Numbers of peasants' bodies seen, many had been bayonetted, others shot; some were very old men, some were women! I did not think French gallantry would have suffered this; but Massena is an Italian.[25]

28 March, San Payo [Sao Paio]. Paid a visit to my old patron. At his former amusement, cracking vermin, on whom he seemed to revenge the wrongs of his country. This village has escaped better; in this very house six months ago, stood with me, George and Gifford; now George is sadly wounded and the amiable Gifford dead! Are these the pleasures of war; does glory repay these losses and pains?

30 March. In a delightful village. Colonel Stewart and a Portuguese are trying to cheat each other about a beautiful goat; Caledonia is too much for Lusitania!

2 April. Marched to the village of Muselha [Macainhas de Baixo?], enemy close.

3 April. The Light Division engaged near Sabugal, suffered much but beat a whole corps d'armée and took a howitzer. Colonel Beckwith's conduct said to have been in a great measure the cause of such an extraordinary success; the fact is the French cannot stomach a British attack. Picton's Division was slightly engaged towards the close. The three fighting regiments were the 43rd, 52nd and 95th.

4 April, Ungera [Urgueira]. We arrived last night, wet, tired and no cover; cursing Portugal and Portuguese names, and Frenchmen, and English generals, and Quartermaster Generals, fools and rogues, commissaries and medicos. The baggage of young Soult,[26] who commands Regnier's cavalry,[27] has been taken, and in it a book with copies of all his letters to Regnier

[Reynier], previous to Massena's penetrating Portugal. In one he says, *The English are at Ponte Murcella [Mucela] and Viseu and generally supposed to be preparing for embarkation; they will immediately begin their retreat.* I did not see the letter, but this idea of our weakness is the only way to account for Massena's attack at Busaco, where he learned to his cost we were not ready to embark. He it is, that flies and we have this day been exactly one month in pursuit of him. Where will this interesting campaign close and how? I can hardly think the French mean to re-enter Portugal, or they would not have destroyed the country so dreadfully. There was a horrible instance of brutality in this village; the French say it was the Italians.[28] Massena is an Italian.

5 April, Nave. The French left this village yesterday, followed by the Light Division. On our march we passed the field of battle where the light division fought Regnier [Reynier] on the 3rd. The ground was a gentle slope and open, but this I think always good for us: the French stand fire for ever behind walls, but don't like close quarters. Dead horses and men were still unburied near a low wall, where the French cavalry charged our skirmishers and were driven back with great loss by the 43rd Regiment.

6 April, Alfayates [Alfaiates]. We are making a flank movement to our left to force the enemy at Almeida. This must produce a general action or make Massena let go his hold of Portugal, leaving Lord Wellington master of the kingdom he has so skilfully [sic] and boldly defended. His whole conduct has been able: errors may have been committed, all generals commit errors, but this successful campaign renders him one of the first of his time. I regret that Buonaparte was not here in person; but perhaps it is better as it is; had he been here things would perhaps have been different. I can't help wishing for a general action near Almeida; the ground is perfectly open, and when that is the case our army is sure of victory. Our cavalry can then act and though less numerous, is so superior that the combat would probably be in our favour. A total defeat of the French would put Ciudad Rodrigo into our hands and effectually stop a second invasion of Portugal for a long time. It would also save the Spaniards if anything can rouse their energies: perhaps it is too late but still worth trial.

Charles also wrote to his mother this day:

Alfayates [Alfaiates], 6 April.
No long agreeable letter, or even a civil one for you dear mother, civility is indeed a useless thing when one has neither food, nor drink, nor sleep.

We have now, for one month, been up at three am marching at four and halting at seven o'clock at night, when we eat all we can get, from shoe soles to bread and butter. Writing is not agreeable and done only to tell you how George and William are. The last is well now and a Brigade Major; and as George writes better with his left than his right hand, he may do his own letters. You may rejoice at these fortunate recoveries from two as ugly wounds as could be, short of mortal ones. They are living well, we are on biscuits full of maggots, and though not a bad soldier, hang me if I can relish maggots. We suffer much in point of food, but the French are nearly cleared out of the country. Our late movement was to force the enemy from Almeida by turning their position there; they have run and the garrison of Almeida will blow that place up. Meanwhile our life for the last month has not been an easy one for a convalescent, yet I have worked through well, except a little rheumatism in the jaws: a splinter of bone protrudes still from the jaw, but very slowly. The first week, cold and sleeping out at night and severe riding made the wound bleed at the nose, but now all is right. Blanco is starving and curls his nose into a thousand wrinkles, cursing Buonaparte; there! my biscuit has run away on maggots' legs. We found many *Moniteurs*[29] in the French camps and one had an account of Busaco, with this passage, *Le major Napier, dejà blessé à Corogne, reçu un coup de feu dans la figure*. [Major Napier, already wounded at Corunna, received a shot in the face.]

George wrote of William and their wounds and of his own slow recuperation:

In a few days William's wound took a favourable turn and we all proceeded in a wagon to the city of Coimbra, where by this time the hospitals were established; and as it was not exactly in the line of retreat the French took, all the houses were untouched and the inhabitants were daily returning to it, so that before we got there many houses were occupied and all the colleges and monasteries filled rapidly with students and priests. Here we were treated kindly and had as much comfort as we could wish or expect and were skilfully and feelingly attended to by our own medical officers, who were indefatigable in their endeavours to make every officer and soldier under their care as comfortable as they could …

A few days after we were settled at Coimbra our brother Charles got leave to come and see how we were getting on. He found William walking about convalescent; but my wound, from the bone being so shattered, had taken a bad turn and I suffered very much. We gave him plenty to eat and drink, which was a great treat to him poor fellow, for he had been on short allowance ever since we parted. The next day he was obliged to be off, and having seen us and his mind being relieved he joined his regiment in much better health and spirits.

Coimbra was at this time made a depot for the army, and an officer appointed commandant, whose duty it was to look after all the hospitals, the sick and wounded, as well as all the civil departments; to see that all recruits and reinforcements for the army were properly kept in order and equipped, ready to march at a moment's warning to join their respective corps &c; and as often as a body of men were dismissed from hospital as fit for duty, he appointed such officers as were also recovered to command them and march with them to the army. It is a very troublesome and arduous duty that of commandant and a difficult thing to find a good one, because the best officers do not like to accept it (though double pay) as it keeps them in the rear and out of action; but it is of essential consequence to have a good one and quite impossible to do without them.

About a month after we had been at Coimbra, William being sufficiently recovered though his wound was not healed, re-joined the division and was appointed Brigade Major to the second brigade under Colonel Beckwith, who is one of the best general officers in the field that I know of. He is never at a loss, always cool and particularly skillful [sic] at penetrating the intentions of the enemy, and always ready to oppose him in the very nick of time; and as to his gallantry, no man was more conspicuous for intrepid conduct …

George was lucky to survive an attempted robbery:

About three weeks after William left me, I had been sitting up late in a room adjoining my bedroom and trying to write with my left hand and to mend pens, but being fatigued I left the lamp burning and my penknife on the table and went to bed, hanging up my watch and sword over my pillow. About an hour or two afterwards I awoke, thinking I heard a noise in the room, and listening attentively I heard something which I supposed was a rat; but as the lamp was gone out in the other room and it was quite dark, I could not distinguish anything. In a few minutes I distinctly heard a noise as if my clothes were being dragged about. I then was certain someone was in the room and stealing my things, so I got up softly and taking down my sword, which was in a steel scabbard, I went gently to the door, listened very attentively, but could hear no sound and was on the point of returning to bed, when I thought I would just cross the other room and try if the passage door was open. In doing this I suddenly came in contact with a man, who instantly seized me round the waist and made every effort to throw me down. Thinking he was a Portuguese, I expected every moment to have a stiletto plunged into my body, well knowing that a Portuguese thief would not come unprepared for assassination in case of discovery. I struggled hard with the fellow and recollecting that I had left one of the windows open which was very high from the ground I attempted, as well as I was able, with only one hand (the other being bound up and the bones not knit together again) to get him with his back against it, so that I could then throw him out into the street, which would have settled him forever. But in this, from weakness I failed. I then made an effort to approach the table, where I had left the penknife open, with which I might stab him before he stabbed me; but I had not strength to push him along and finding that he had not made any attempt to kill me, I began to suspect that he must be an English soldier, and therefore struck at him with the hilt of my sword in the face and calling to him said that if he would speak I would let him go. But speak he would not, and suddenly as if recollecting himself, he seized my wounded arm in his teeth, and gave me such pain by tearing at it, that I let go my sword, and being exhausted by so long a struggle, I had no more power, and the fellow immediately picked it up, drew it out of the scabbard and began cutting at me as well as he could in the dark. However, I got under the table and by that means avoided his blows. Finding he could do nothing more and that by this time a medical officer, who lodged opposite me, was up and alarmed by my calling out for assistance, he cut open a glass door with my sword, which opened into a balcony and from thence let himself down into the street and got off just as my servant came into the room, who immediately ran to the window and levelled his musket at him, but it missed fire and my friend escaped. As soon as we got a light, we found he had removed my trunk and all my clothes into the passage and had everything piled up ready to carry off. When I went to my bed, I found the rascal had taken my gold watch, which I was very much vexed at, as it was an old family one, given me by poor William Craig before he died. I never could trace this robbery, or get the least clue to the perpetrator of it; and indeed, I was very glad of it, for had I found him out he would have been hanged, and as he certainly had no intention of doing me any bodily harm when he first entered my room, I should never have felt comfortable if he had been hung. The struggling and the laceration of the wound by his teeth, in my weak state, brought on fever and I was laid up in bed for some weeks after and my recovery much retarded and I was prevented joining my regiment as soon as I had hoped to have done.

The French Retreat into Spain 1811

In another letter Charles wrote of the army's frustrations over Almeida:

29 April.
Under arms all day, because four or five poor devils of French battalions came from Ciudad Rodrigo to get food, perhaps to throw supplies into Almeida. Seventeen hours under arms for these ill-mannered knaves, who certainly came because it was post day. We shall be under arms again at there in the morning, being cruelly afraid of letting your friend Brennier [Brenier] feed.[30]

Charles continued his journal:

Albergaria [La Alberguería de Argañán], 9 to 16 May. This is my third entrance into Spain and the cleanliness of the inhabitants is most striking on leaving Portuguese filth. Almeida still holds out and Massena is said to have reached Salamanca; yet I think, a threat to storm Almeida and put the garrison to the sword would make it surrender.

17 May. How able we are in the art of war! Our army surrounds Almeida, the French are many marches from us, we thought we had blockaded the fortress and daily expected its surrender from want of food. Now we hear that two days ago a convoy got into the place, it being on a plain, and we having plenty of cavalry, artillery, infantry and means of all kinds! The French are our masters in war as to all but courage and bodily strength.

18 May. The convoy got into Ciudad Rodrigo, not Almeida, and a reinforcement also, in face of the wonderful Sir William Erskine, who is the laughingstock of the army, and particularly of the Light Division. In the south also we are exposing ourselves. A squadron of the 13th Light Dragoons under a major, has been surprised and the whole made prisoners in the Alemtejo. What a pity our fine cavalry should have such officers as this, and others I know of; however we have good ones in training. It is said heavy artillery is coming from Oporto to besiege Almeida; I hope this is true, the more work more glory. Lord Wellington is off to the Alemtejo, as Beresford has got in a fright and says, *cock a doodle do*, I don't know what to do.

19 May. All majors in the action of Barrosa[31] are made brevet lieutenant colonels for their conduct. This is owing to their being brave and their general not afraid to say so; nor selfish enough to take all reward and leave those who saved him to shift for themselves. Had Moore lived, or had

Graham or Lord Wellington commanded at Corunna, I should have been now a lieutenant colonel for two years' standing, instead of a major of five. General Hope neither gave my regiment deserved credit, nor mentioned me. Of 480 privates and 23 officers, my regiment had 150 of the first and 10 of the last killed and wounded, total 160. This was as hard fighting as Barrosa; yet I am kept from promotion, because old David Dundas[32] was jealous of Moore's glory … But I must be patient for, the commander in chief entertains the highest opinion of your meritorious services! I have the Military Secretary's[33] word for this; yet I don't believe it to be more true than that I have the highest opinion of the commander in chief's meritorious services.

Almeida still holds out. I wish Lord Wellington would give me 60 scaling ladders and 200 volunteers with a supporting column and the British standard should fly in Almeida in two hours without losing 50 men. The ditch is dry and not deep, the garrison is weak and British volunteers are irresistible; they would be on the rampart in fifteen minutes. Once there the devil would not get them off again, and I should be a lieutenant colonel, or lie in the ditch of the place.

In a letter written by Charles at this period, the Barrosa issue still clearly wrankled:

Albergaria [La Alberguería de Argañán], undated.
… Almeida will not surrender, Brennier [Brenier] refuses. All the majors got brevet rank for Barrosa. Acheson[34] is two years younger than me, and if they refuse me now my resignation shall go into David Dundas; for this is insult added to injustice, and I will have justice or quit the service. I will write to him plainly, careless of a court-martial! for which indeed I wish, that the matter may become public. My intent is to have promotion or a trial and if both are refused, appeal to the [Prince] Regent; if he supports Dundas, resign; exit in a rage.

Charles wrote to his mother following the Battle of Fuentes de Oñoro:

7 May. Moonlight. Dearest mother, William and I are quite well and the French it is thought, will not try another general action again. We lost a good many men on the 5th. I was lucky, for we were many hours in a severe fire, and my bridle was hit by a grapeshot. We are in mad spirits and long to fight again, but Massena is not inclined. The 50th lost only a few more than thirty men by the cannonade; but we were obliged to be quiet all the time and had no French lives in return. Remember now dearest

mother, that fight more or no more fight, a hundred thousand men are in the pickling tub with William and myself; it was our turn to escape and we did so. This was proper and though the fire of grape and shells was very heavy, I made it a point of honour not to be hit.

8 May. The French are satisfied with the fillip we gave them on the 5th and are retiring. We shall move close to Almeida, where poor Brennier [Brenier] has been firing and blustering in vain, he can't get out! he can't get out!

14 May. On the 2nd instant came a sudden order to march. We crossed the Turon River and bivouacked at Nava d'Aver [Nave de Haver], the French army being in sight; at least they were distinctly seen. At daybreak we found our army assembled, stretching from Nava [Nave de Haver] to Fort Conception [Concepcion]. Our division formed the right of the line. The two armies manoeuvred, the enemy to gain Almeida, the allies to cover it, and night brought both on to the plains about the villages of Villa Formosa [Vilar Formoso] and Fuentes Onoro [Fuentes de Oñoro], extending to Almeida, which lay in the rear of our line on the left. Headquarters were at Villa Formosa [Vilar Formoso], about the centre of our line. Two armies thus drawn up on a plain, each from thirty to thirty-five thousand strong, was a most beautiful sight; but the next day's sun was to shine on the graves of thousands who then beheld it set! No man knew his fate, but each anxiously awaited it in the coming combat, which all believed inevitable, and to be one of the bloodiest ever fought; one in which defeat to either side must be destruction.

Our right was on Nava d'Aver [Nave de Haver]; our centre advanced to Fuentes Onoro [Fuentes de Oñoro]; our left stretched to Fort Conception [Concepcion]. There was much skirmishing at Fuentes this day, yet it ended towards night. We nearly lost some guns in the morning, but the enemy's cavalry fought shy and lost their advantage by timidity. At night I was sent out with the picquets, and never did I see any worse posted or more negligently; but there was no choice for me but to obey orders and keep good watch. On the 4th slight skirmishing at Fuentes [de] Onoro. On the 5th at daybreak fighting began in the village of Fuentes and soon after a bloody contest was sustained there. The enemy then turned our right flank with his cavalry, nearly *en potence*,[35] our cavalry keeping as they could in front; we lost many men, so did the enemy. Then a heavy cannonade opened and continued in the centre for five hours, with smart skirmishing so close as to knock down many in the line, which also suffered severely from grape shells and roundshots: our guns however beat those of the enemy out of the field. Thus closed the Battle of Fuentes [de] Onoro, the

5th of May; a battle in which our loss was eighteen hundred, that of the enemy greater; both far short of what was expected, as everyone thought we should have had a severe general action. Massena certainly drew out his army with the intention of saving Almeida and driving us into the Coa. Lord Wellington out-manoeuvred him and covered Almeida, present in so formidable a line of battle as to oblige the Prince of Esling [sic] to give up his project. He retired covered by his cavalry, on the 7th or 8th, after which our army was ordered into surrounding cantonments. Our brigade marched first off the position, playing the *British Grenadiers*, which was a little like dunghill cock-crowing, but the men like it.

Charles wrote home to his mother:

Albergaria [-a-Velha], 20 May.
You will hear of Almeida being blown up, and that your friend Brennier [Brenier] gave us the slip.[36] Who is to blame we don't know, nor the particulars. Yesterday I went there. Never was there a more complete blow up; the achievement has been brilliant and marks Brennier [Brenier] forever. Our generals, or whoever is in fault ought to be shot; the whole army is disgraced. Lord Wellington must feel it deeply. To have all his operations for securing the town against a large army succeed, to see that army defeated and retire and then to have the generals under him let the garrison out! It is enough to break his heart. England will begin to see that our generals are [idiots?]. Take Lord Wellington away and we are general-less. It is said Sir William Erskine[37] is to blame and next to him General Campbell.[38] On my ride to see Almeida after the blow up, I passed the field where the two armies had fought and saw such a multitude of eagles, vultures and kites eating the carcases [sic] of man and beast, that I congratulated myself on not making a side dish at their feast; they would have gained little additional good by it and to me it would have been a great inconvenience. So gorged they were, they could hardly fly and I hunted some on Blanco, but he did not half like their looks, thinking they might take to live flesh for a change.

Lord Wellington is again gone to the Alemtejo, to prevent disasters arising in the south from Marshal Beresford's blunders.[39] In short, when Lord Wellington is in the south, we in the north grow frightened lest the French should advance; and when he is here, things go wrong in the south. He has to fly back and forward ... and does the journey in five days: hard work this for body and mind.[40] So Sir David is at last turned out! The Duke of York's advent will however do Napiers no good, and indeed Old Davy going to pot is luck enough for ten years.

Charles was now off on a particular service as an 'Exploring officer':

Talavera [la] Real, 10 June.
I am dear mother on a particular service; my post will likely be about Medellin. If you don't hear from me be not uneasy; for taking no baggage, means of writing may not be found. This mission displeases me. My duty will be to get information of the enemy, but I will not go near him to risk being taken. Not being a spy, no danger but great responsibility, which I don't like; be sure however of my keeping within safe bounds not having the least desire to be taken in a ridiculous way, and my orders are not to risk anything. I have only a new coat and a greatcoat; the rest was designed for smart days; but lest the Spaniards should think me a spy, I wear my blazing uniform and so wear it out; Blanco and I are like meteors; we cannot go near the French and so I send Spanish. This however will only last the siege [of Badajoz] and is because an active, intelligent officer was required. What a bore to be so clever!

Charles had written to the Prince Regent to complain of the unfair treatment he had suffered, by which junior majors had been promoted over him. He was pleased to advise his mother that he was now to be promoted by exchange. He also wrote of the severe fever he had contracted.

19 July 1811
Dearest mother read the following:
'Sir, I am directed by the commander in chief to acquaint you, that previous to the receipt of yours of the 27th ultimo, His Royal Highness, bearing in mind your claims, had recommended you for a lieutenant colonelcy in the 102nd Regiment and the state of discipline in that corps requires that you should join it without loss of time, H Torrens'

I am better, a little, and have not had delirium the last two fits, otherwise no change; nor is any expected until home and quiet restore me; but if the voyage don't send away the fits I must shift about for new air. The doctor says three months will recover me after the fits go; I say he is wrong and Bellarmin being thus confuted,[41] I shall act on my own opinion. Lord March is well, yet requires two months of home for complete restoration, though he has had but three fits: I have had six weeks, that is twenty-one fits.

Charles then sailed home, taking a few months' leave at home before joining the 102nd Foot in Guernsey in January 1812. The second siege of Badajoz ended without success on 10 June 1811; William had also contracted a severe fever and was effectively ordered by Wellington to return to Lisbon with his brother to get well. He was then given leave to return to England with Charles and the two brothers were home for Christmas. In that same July George wrote of a number of changes in his battalion and he considered joining the Portuguese army to gain his lieutenant colonelcy but was dissuaded:

> Before I left Coimbra I received a letter from Lord Wellington's Military Secretary, to inform me that His Lordship had recommended me as well as my brother William for the brevet rank of major in the army in consequence of our conduct, and particularly on the day we were last wounded. This was a pleasing communication, as I had been a captain eight years and began to fear I never should be promoted, although I never was a moment absent from my duty except when disabled by wounds. When I joined the army the Light Division was on the march towards the south. I wished at that period very much to be allowed to enter the Portuguese service as a lieutenant colonel commanding a regiment, and therefore I asked Lord Wellington's permission to make application to Marshal Beresford to appoint me to the command of a light infantry regiment, as the Portuguese army was under the command of the marshal. Lord Wellington granted my request and accordingly I went to Marshal Beresford, who received me very kindly, said he would appoint me with pleasure to a light infantry regiment which happened to be vacant at that very time. I was delighted at this and went off to get my things ready &c, but I found that our general (Craufurd), having heard of my application to enter the Portuguese army, had gone to Lord Wellington and represented that he had been at great pains to make good field officers in the Light Division, and that if he was to be deprived of them in this way the division would be ruined; and as he was pleased to say I was one of his best officers he positively refused to let me go out of his division. He would have been content if the marshal would appoint me to one of the Portuguese light regiments in his own division which was commanded by a Portuguese colonel whom Craufurd did not like; but this was out of the question, and Lord Wellington therefore acquiesced in General Craufurd's demand that I should remain where I was. This was very annoying to me, but from the flattering manner General Craufurd had spoken of me to the commander in chief, I could not be angry; and indeed I think he was right not to permit those officers who had been constantly serving with him and formed under his own directions in the finest division in the army, to be taken from him just as their long experience had made them more valuable to him.

Lord Wellington sent for me the next day and told me he was very sorry for my disappointment but that he hoped it would be made up to me by his informing me I was made major of the 52nd Regiment,[42] and although I actually [now] belonged to the second battalion, which was in England, I should remain on service with the first battalion. This put me in such good spirits that I cared very little about going into the Portuguese service. I went however, to inform Marshal Beresford and to thank him for his kindness. He was not very well pleased with General Craufurd and expressed himself in pretty strong terms on the occasion …

About this time my friend General Ross,[43] then lieutenant colonel commanding the 52nd Regiment (poor Colonel Barclay[44] having died of his wounds), was about to leave the regiment and go home. He sent for me one morning and told me he wished I would go to General Hill's corps and see my friend Colonel Colborne, who commanded the 66th Regiment, and tell him that he would exchange regiments with him if he liked, as he thought by so doing he would do the greatest service to the 52nd, as he well knew the high opinion Sir John Moore had of him and that his great abilities and character pointed him out as the best person to be in command of the regiment … The morning of the day Ross left us he divided his watch, chain and seals among his greatest friends. The watch, which is the gold one I wear, he gave to me and it has ever since been my constant companion and will be to the hour of my death. It had belonged also to poor Captain Powis (a brother of Lord Lilford)[45] who was killed at Badajos [Badajoz].

Colonel Colborne soon joined us;[46] and taking the command of the 52nd, it fought under his superintendence many a battle, stormed many a town and distinguished itself by its perfect discipline and steady, cool intrepidity as much as any regiment ever yet did in any army in the world, thus proving that the system of discipline acquired under Sir John Moore and Colonel Kenneth Mackenzie had infused such zeal and spirit into both officers and soldiers that few regiments equaled, and none ever surpassed it!

Chapter 7
Ciudad Rodrigo, Badajoz and Salamanca 1812

William did not return to Portugal until April 1812, therefore only George was at the siege of Ciudad Rodrigo. Meanwhile, Charles had sailed to Guernsey to take command of the 102nd. George wrote extensively on his experiences at the siege:

> We were continually moving about till 8 January 1812, when we broke ground before the fortress of Ciudad Rodrigo, one of the frontier towns on the north of Portugal and from which we had retreated to the Lines about a year and a half before.

Attack on the San Francisco Redoubt

> There was a small fort outside the works of the town, with a small party to defend it. Two companies of each of the regiments of the Light Division[1] were ordered to attack it as soon as it was night. I volunteered to command this party, but Lord Wellington said whoever was the first field officer for duty should command, and as Colonel Colborne was the first he got it. The colonel formed his party, and gave his orders so explicitly and so clearly, made every officer understand what he was to do, that no mistake could possibly be made. The consequence was that in twenty minutes from the time he moved to the attack the fort was stormed and carried. The watchword of *'England and St. George'* was heard shouted loud and strong, and re-echoed by the division, which was under arms, and in a few moments came a report from Colonel Colborne that every man in the fort was either killed, wounded, or prisoner. We lost a few men and some officers wounded, among whom was my friend Captain Mein, who was shot through the thigh and was sent to the rear to hospital and recovered soon enough to be at the siege of Badajoz, where he was again wounded in the assault, shot through the other thigh.

The Siege

> After the fort was taken, we immediately pushed forward some sharpshooters to keep up a fire and [to] mislead the enemy, while the engineers commenced

marking out the parallels, &c. The ground being soft, the great thing was to work hard with the spade, and very soon the trenches were began. Each division took [turns of] twenty-four hours in the trenches, and upon being relieved the next day marched back to its cantonments. Our division had a river to pass, both going to and returning from the trenches, and as it was very frosty weather and sometimes sleet and snow, we found it terribly cold going through the water above our knees and sometimes up to the waist.[2] And when going for the twenty-four hours of duty in the trenches it was hard work, for we were not allowed any fire all night, the men and officers cooking their provisions before they went, so that our clothes used to freeze on us and we became so stiff and cold that we were forced to drink lots of brandy to keep us warm inside at all events. About three weeks before the assault of the town I was field officer of the trenches and was standing with some men who were digging a trench, when a thirteen-inch shell from the town fell in the midst of us. I called to the men to lie down flat on the ground, as by that means most probably few if any, would receive injury. The men knowing this, instantly obeyed orders and lay flat except one of them, an Irishman and an old Marine, but a most worthless, drunken dog, who ran up to the shell, the fuze of which was still burning and striking it a blow with his spade knocked it out, and taking the immense shell in his hands came and presented it to me saying, *'There she is for you now, your honour. By Jasus, she'll do you no harm, since I knocked the life out of the cratur.'* I never saw a cooler thing and of course was *obliged* to give him a dollar and leave to get drunk if he got safe home to the cantonments. He told me he had often done the same thing in Egypt, where he had served under Abercrombie.[3] The same night I was standing talking to Colborne near a battery which we were finishing, when bounce came a shell among us, and before we had time to lie down, burst with a proper crack, killed two poor fellows, wounded several, one of whom had both legs taken off close to the hip. I received a severe bruise and scrape, but, although I was knocked down by it, [received] no further injury. It struck me on the top of the shoulder, but luckily it was the top of the shell which fell on me after having been blown up into the air and lost its force. The next day, as I thought from all I saw and heard from the engineers that ere long the breaches would be practicable, I went to General Craufurd and asked him as a favour that he would allow me to command the storming party of the Light Division whenever the commander in chief determined on making the assault. This he promised, and on 19 January 1812, we received orders to move from our cantonments and march to the trenches.

Storm of Ciudad Rodrigo

About a mile from the town, we halted and General Craufurd desired me to get one hundred volunteers from each British regiment in the division, with proportionate officers and non-commissioned officers, to form them up in front of the division and take the command of them in order to lead the assault. I went to three regiments, viz, the 43rd, 52nd and Rifle Corps, and said, *'soldiers, I have the honour to be appointed to the command of the storming party which is to lead the Light Division to the assault of the small breach. I want one hundred volunteers from each regiment; those who will go with me come forward.'* Instantly there rushed out nearly half the division, and we were obliged to take them at chance. I then formed them in companies of one hundred men each, Captain Ferguson[4] commanding the 43rd, Captain Jones[5] the 52nd (this officer afterwards volunteered to be of the storming party at Badajoz, and was killed after behaving most gloriously; he received fifteen balls through his body!), Captain Mitchel[6] commanded the Rifles. These were preceded by what is called the *Forlorn hope*, consisting of twenty-five men, two sergeants and one subaltern, a lieutenant, because if he survives he gets a company. The officer who commanded in this instance was a great friend of mine, a very excellent gallant officer, Lieutenant Gurwood,[7] of the 52nd. As soon as all was formed, we marched at the head of the division in high spirits and determined that nothing should stop us from carrying the breach. I felt that I was on the point of fulfilling my old motto, *'Death or glory.'* I knew if I failed it must be my own fault, as I had at my back three hundred British bayonets, wielded by as able hands and stout *'hearts of oak'* as ever faced the enemy! that I had only to lead, to give the word, and all would be carried by British steel, let the opposition be ever so great. If I fell, I should fall as I wished; if I lived, most probably promotion, certainly glory, the soldier's greatest prize would be my reward; and above all, I knew I should receive the approbation of the commander of the army Lord Wellington. When it was nearly dark in the evening, the Light Division was formed behind the old convent on the outside of the town, nearly opposite the small breach. While waiting here for orders, I told a friend of mine, the Assistant Surgeon of the 52nd, Mr Walker,[8] that I had an idea I should lose my arm, and, if so I hoped he would perform the operation of taking it off. A few minutes after Lord Wellington sent for Colonel Colborne and myself, and pointing out as well as the light would permit, the spot where the foot of the breach was, he said to me, *'Now do you understand the way you are to lead, so as to arrive at the breach without noise or confusion?'* I answered, and we then went back to the regiment;

and just before I moved on, some Staff officer present said, *'Why, your men are not loaded; why do you not make them load?'* I replied, *'Because if we do not do the business with the bayonet, without firing, we shall not be able to do it at all, so I shall not load.'* I heard Lord Wellington, who was close by say, *'Let him alone; let him go his own way.'* The 3rd Portuguese Regiment of Caçadores, under Colonel Elder,[9] was to carry bags filled with long dry grass, in order, by throwing them into the ditch, to prevent any accident as we leaped down into it, as it was deep and thus prevent the jump from being so great. The signal of attack of both breaches (there was a large breach at another part of the fortress attacked by the 3rd Division, under General Picton) being made, and the 3rd Caçadores not having arrived with the bags of grass (owing to some want of proper orders, as neither Colonel Elder nor his excellent regiment were likely to neglect any duty; and I am sure the blame rested elsewhere, for George Elder was always ready for any service; no man has distinguished himself more), I gave the order to move forward, cautioning the officers and men to be silent, and once having gained the breach, to wheel right and left, and clear the parapet on each side, in order to effect which without confusion my party was in double column of sections, the 43rd on the right, the 52nd on the left, Lieutenant Gurwood in advance a few yards with the forlorn hope. We soon came to the ditch and immediately jumping in, we rushed forward to the *faussebraie*,[10] and having clambered up we proceeded towards the breach. But Lieutenant Gurwood and party having, owing to the darkness of the night, gone too much to the left, was employed in placing ladders on the un-breached face of the bastion, when he got a shot in the head; but immediately recovering his feet he came up to me, and at that moment the engineer, or Captain Staveley of the Staff Corps,[11] I cannot recollect which, called out, *'You are wrong; this way to the right is the breach;'* and Captain Ferguson, myself, Gurwood and the rest of the officers and such men as were nearest the engineer officer, rushed on and we all mounted the breach together, the enemy pouring a heavy fire on us. When about two-thirds up, I received a grape shot which smashed my elbow and great part of my [right] arm; and on falling, the men who thought I was killed, checked for a few moments and forgetting they were not loaded commenced snapping their muskets. I immediately called out *'Recollect you are not loaded; push on with the bayonet.'* Upon this the whole gave a loud *'hurrah,'* and driving all before them, carried the breach and wheeling as I had given orders to the right and left soon drove off the enemy; and a part of the stormers under Captain Ferguson rushed down upon the enemy where they were defending the large breach, and commencing a flank fire upon them, soon drove them from their defences and thus opened the way for the 3rd Division to enter the town. Lieutenant Gurwood, who had pushed into the town, followed the garrison to the citadel, where the Governor surrendered, and delivering his sword to Gurwood, the latter made him prisoner and took him to Lord Wellington, who immediately desired Lieutenant Gurwood to keep the Governor's sword as a mark of his approbation.

During all this time the troops of the Light Division kept pouring into the place through the breach and I kept cheering them on as well as I could, but I got terribly bruised and trampled upon in the confusion and darkness. However, very soon *'Victory! England for ever!'* was shouted by thousands and then I knew all was right, and I waited patiently in the breach till all had passed, when I heard my name called several times, and upon answering, the Prince of Orange,[12] Lord March, and Lord Fitzroy Somerset came up to me, and the Prince taking off his sash (which I [still] have) they tied up my arm, and with the help of a sergeant and some men I got down and proceeded to the old ruined convent, where I found numbers wounded and the surgeon very busy with his knife. I learned here that General Craufurd was mortally wounded and I saw General Vandeleur,[13] who commanded our brigade, sitting on a stone waiting to be dressed, having been wounded in the shoulder. He is a fine, honourable, kind-hearted, gallant soldier and an excellent man. I never knew him say or do a harsh thing to any human being. No man can or ought to be more respected than he is.

It soon came to my turn to have my arm amputated, and I then reminded my friend Walker, who was there, of his promise to me a few hours before and begged he would be so good as to perform the operation; but he told me he could not, as there was a Staff Surgeon present, whose rank being higher, it was necessary he should do it, so Staff Surgeon Guthrie[14] cut it off. However, for want of light and from the number of amputations he had already performed and other circumstances, his instruments were blunted, so it was a long time before the thing was finished, at least twenty minutes, and the pain was great. I then thanked him for his kindness, having sworn at him like a trooper while he was at it, to his great amusement, and I proceeded to find some place to lie down and rest, and after wandering and stumbling about the suburbs for upwards of an hour, I saw a light in a house, and on entering I found it full of soldiers and a good fire blazing in the kitchen. As I went towards the fire, I saw a figure wrapped up in a cloak sitting in the corner of the chimney place apparently in great pain. Upon nearer inspection I found this was my friend John Colborne, who had received a severe wound in the shoulder. Upon asking me if I was wounded, I showed him the stump of my arm, which so affected him poor fellow, that he burst into tears. He was in such horrid pain, his spirits were quite sunk and he could not stand the sight of my loss. How often afterwards did he wish *his* arm had been taken off, for the sufferings he went through for two years afterwards were very great. His arm was broken close up to the joint of the shoulder, which, and the scapula itself were split. The ball remained in the joint for two years, when at last it was taken out and then he recovered, but [still] has a stiff joint. Never did any man suffer more patiently than he did. But it was Colborne and that is sufficient, there being no suffering in human life which he would not endure if necessary, either for his country or his friends.

Wellington wrote to George's mother again:

Gallegos, 20 January [1812]
My dear Madam,
I am sorry to tell you that your son George was again wounded in the right arm, so badly last night in the storm of Ciudad Rodrigo as to make it necessary to amputate it above the elbow. He however, bore the operation remarkably well and I have seen him this morning quite well, free from pain & fever and enjoying highly his success before he received his wound. When he did receive it, he only desired that I might be told that he had led his men to the top of the breach before he had fallen. Having *such* sons, I am aware that you expect to hear of these misfortunes, which I have had more than once to communicate to you & notwithstanding your affection for them, you have a spirit & notion of the value of the distinction which they are daily acquiring for themselves by their gallantry and good conduct, that their misfortunes do not make so great an impression on you. Under these circumstances, I perform the task I have taken upon myself with less reluctance, hoping at the same time, that this will be the last occasion on which I shall have to address you on such a subject, and that your brave sons will be spared to you. Although the last was the most serious, it was not the only wound which George received during the siege of Ciudad Rodrigo, he was hit by the splinter of a shell in the shoulder on the 16th. Ever my dear Madam, your most faithful humble servant Wellington.

His friend Lord March wrote to his mother:

Gallegos, 21 January 1812
My dear Lady Sarah,
I am very sorry to have to tell you that George has had his arm amputated, in consequence of a musket shot he received at the top of the breach of

Ciudad Rodrigo. It has been done just above the elbow of the right arm and both Robb[15] and Maling[16] of the 52nd desire me to say that he is going on as well as possible. He suffers very little pain and is in high spirits. He volunteered, leading 300 volunteers of the Light Division and with them entered the small breach, everybody in the army admires his gallantry and I trust they cannot refuse to make him a lieutenant colonel. His friend Gurwood of the 52nd led the *Forlorn hope* and they were the two first in the place. I will let you know how he is by the next mail, but at the same time I am convinced it will be a favourable account. He wanted to write to you, but I told him I would. He is coming here to my quarters and I will take every care of him. Believe me ever your affectionate March.

PS ½ past five o'clock 21 January – I am just returned from seeing George who is going on very well, he sends his love to you all.

Charles Stewart[17] wrote to his Aunt Louisa:

Gallegos, 21 January 1812
My dear Lady Louisa[18]
Little did I imagine when I last addressed you, I should as soon have to communicate afflicting intelligence, but the gallant spirits of those Napiers lead them ever in the foremost rank to danger, and honour is sure to be their just reward. George Napier commanding 300 as brave followers as himself, stormed one of the breaches in the wall of the town and sad to relate received a wound in his right arm which has been since amputated & he is doing as well as possible. His conduct equalled that of his brother Charles [at Corunna], to surpass it would be hard, but the gallantry of the Napiers is as proverbial in the army as the fame of our chief. God of his mercy be praised we have not George to deplore as we once had (as we all thought) his brother. Alas, our victory has been attended with some cruel losses, General McKinnon[19] is irreparable and I have scarce a hope of my poor friend Craufurd. I write to you my dear Lady Louisa rather than Louisa[20] or any of the family to break this intelligence to dear Lady Sarah. God Almighty bless you. Believe me ever most affectionately Charles Stewart.

March also wrote to William:

Gallegos 21 January 1812
My dear William,
Ciudad Rodrigo was stormed on Sunday evening, George volunteered leading the men from the Light Division which was to storm the small

breach, 300 as fine fellows as ever moved from the Light Division went with him and he and his friend Gurwood who led the *Forlorn Hope*, were the two first up the breach. Though it is one of the finest things that have been done yet, we have to regret that George received a musket shot through the elbow. The consequence is that his right arm was amputated just above the elbow. He bore it very well and is doing as well as possible, suffers little pain and is in high spirits. Of course he will go home to learn to use his other arm. He is coming here to live in my house. Craufurd and Vandeleur are wounded, the former it is said will die. Poor General McKinnon [Mackinnon] was killed. I will not bore you any further as you will see the dispatches which Gordon[21] takes home. Pray write or get somebody to write to Charles [in Guernsey] to tell him that I hope George will soon be a lieutenant colonel as he deserves better than anyone in the army. Believe me ever yours March.

George continues his account:

I cannot leave the subject of Ciudad Rodrigo without mentioning the death of one of my greatest friends and companions, Captain Joseph Dobbs, who was killed upon the ramparts. Never fell a braver soldier in the flower of youth, beloved and regretted by all who knew him. He was open, generous and warm-hearted, enthusiastic in his profession, and just sufficiently romantic to make him enter into any project with spirit and ardour. An Irishman, like them he was gay and cheerful, with a spirit of honour marked by the most scrupulous integrity. When his purse was full, it was open to all and shared with his comrades; when empty, he only regretted it because he was thus deprived of the power of giving to all round him; but being empty, his high and independent spirit would make him submit to any personal deprivation rather than be under pecuniary obligations to any man. Such was my lamented friend Joe Dobbs. Arduous in his professional duties, honourable in his dealings with all men, generous, kind and cheerful with his comrades, high spirited and daring, he met a soldier's glorious death while in the act of cheering his men to victory.

As soon as I could get a bed I went into it, but sleep was impossible, for the pain increased and the inflammation got so high that in a couple of hours I was quite delirious, and remained so for the next twenty-four hours, after which I fell asleep and began gradually to get better. In the room above me was General Craufurd dying from a wound, the shot having passed through his arm, entered his chest and lodged in his lungs. He suffered dreadfully, his moans were very distressing to me, and more particularly so in consequence of his daily, nay I may almost say hourly, sending down messages to me to know how I was, and to express his approval of my conduct, and his regret that he should never see me again. I never shall forget this; I should be, what I am not, an unfeeling brute if I did! Indeed, General Craufurd was always kind to me and ready to do me a service when in his power. In a day or two he breathed his last, and thus a period was put to his long, faithful, and I may add, brilliant services in many instances, for although he was a most unpopular man, every officer in the Light Division must acknowledge that by his unwearied and active exertions of mind and body, that division was brought to a state of discipline and knowledge of the duties of light troops which never was equaled by any division in the British army, or surpassed by any division of the French army ...

To give a sketch of General Craufurd's character is neither an easy nor a pleasant task, as truth compels me to acknowledge he had many and grave faults. Brilliant as some of the traits of his character were, and notwithstanding the good and generous feelings which often burst forth like a bright gleam of sunshine from behind a dark and heavy cloud, still there was a sullenness which seemed to brood in his inmost soul and generate passions which knew no bounds. As a general commanding a division of light troops of all arms, Craufurd certainly excelled ... He was seldom deceived in the strength of the enemy's outposts, for he reconnoitred them with the eye of one who knew his business well; and although in some few instances he got into scrapes, it was more through vanity than anything else, as he was so vain of the division he commanded, that he really had persuaded himself he might oppose it to any number of the enemy; and when once in action he was obstinately bent upon holding his ground at any risk, and in the heat of the battle often let his temper get the better of his judgment. The action with Marshal Ney's corps at the Coa was a proof of this ... I believe the first impulse of General Craufurd's heart was kindness, but as he never made any attempt to control his passions the least opposition made that kindness vanish, and in its stead violence, harshness and hatred ruled his feelings in spite of himself.

As Lord Wellington had positively ordered that every wounded officer should be removed from the town to a village about thirteen miles from Ciudad Rodrigo, it was necessary as I was the only officer still remaining there, that I should be carried in a blanket by eight or ten men as I was too ill to bear a cart. The troops being all drawn up to receive the body of General Craufurd, I had to pass through them and as I went through my own regiment I was greeted by many a kind look and exclamation of approbation and pity from the men who had so gallantly supported me in the assault. Nothing is so sweet, so soothing to a wounded officer as the homely expressions of approval and admiration which he receives from the soldiers. You may perhaps, laugh at it, but it made me cry with pleasure and joy to find myself among the *men*, and to see their rough, weather-beaten countenances look at me with every expression of kindly feeling. I could read their thoughts, and it made me ready to jump out of the 'brancard'[22] with enthusiasm. The day was intensely hot, although the month of February, and by the time I arrived at my journey's end my poor bearers and myself were completely knocked up. I was so ill and delirious that night, that the surgeons thought I should have died. A few days restored my strength, but what most contributed to my recovery was a visit from Lord Wellington, who brought me the English newspapers; told me my battalion (the 2nd of the 52nd) was ordered home and that I should go also and see my mother; that he was highly pleased with my conduct and had in consequence recommended me for the medal which would be struck upon the occasion, and also for the rank of lieutenant colonel.[23]

About three weeks after the loss of my arm I commenced my journey towards Lisbon. The first day I left my room I mounted my horse and rode sixteen miles in a hot sun, and in a few days arrived at Coimbra, where I found my friend Colonel Colborne in bed suffering dreadful pain from his wound, while comparatively, I was not suffering anything. Here we stayed some time, till Colborne was able to travel by easy journeys to Lisbon. When we arrived there he was so ill and weak that it was impossible he could undergo the fatigue of the voyage, so I embarked in the *Agincourt* 74, commanded by Captain Kent,[24] and after being sick and miserable for upwards of six weeks, I landed at Plymouth and proceeded to London to my mother's house, where, you may be sure, I was most affectionately received.

As George was making his way home, William was returning to the front, having married Caroline Amelia, daughter of General the Honourable Henry Fox, in February 1812. William appears to have previously been only an infrequent correspondent, but he now eagerly picked up the pen to his wife at least weekly. However, his arrival in Lisbon coincided with the storming of the Fortress of Badajoz and news of the death of his greatest friend, which clearly shook his intention to continue as a soldier:

Lisbon, 17 April 1812
My dearest Caroline,
Macleod is dead and I am grovelling in misery and wretchedness; temples ache with the painful images that are passing before me. He was the best

and will be the last of my friends, for I cannot endure the torture that I feel again, and where can I find another like him? ... I had buoyed myself up with the hope of meeting him, and now I must weep over his grave. Farewell my dearest Caroline.

PS George sailed two days ago, take care of him.

Alfayates [Alfaiates], 23 April 1812
My dearest Caroline,
I wrote by the *Latona* frigate[25] from Lisbon, and as I was in great agony of mind at the time, you must not let anybody see it nor let it hurt your own spirits. I arrived late last night at Sabugal where I found headquarters. I am exceedingly tired from riding 200 miles post in the country saddles, without a stop and am therefore going to stay this day with Lord March, who has been as usual as good natured as it is possible to be. My regiment is only 4 leagues from here. I shall take the command of them tomorrow, as the only field officer not wounded or killed is gone home sick of fever.[26] Everybody says I am the most fortunate of men to have the command of such a regiment; for my part, I only find that the recollection of Macleod comes with more bitterness to my mind. What comfort or pleasure can I have in filling the place that belonged to him! ... My poor Charles [Macleod]! If I could have seen him once before he was killed or been with him when he fell ... I saw poor Colborne in Lisbon very ill indeed and in great pain, part of his epaulette was coming away from the wound and he was in hopes of having less pain after. I bought his horses and as McDonald[27] had not money for one, as he said, you make keep the £160 I gave you for yourself; I having been obliged to draw upon Mr Drummond to that amount to pay for them. Bless you my Caroline, your affectionate husband W Napier.

William wrote of the death of his great friend Macleod, with details he must have gleaned from the other officers of the regiment. He was also fully engaged in restoring the discipline of his battalion, but found time to write a string of letters to his wife:

La Encina,[28] 29 April 1812
My dearest Caroline,
... You will have seen by the dispatch how highly Lord Wellington thought of Macleod's courage and abilities and yet he only knew half his worth. The storm was dreadful; for three hours and a half the Light Division were in the ditch and on the breach in close order, exposed to the fire

of 4,000 men at 20 yards from them, while artillery from the flanks and shells, stones, fireballs, and beams, were poured upon them incessantly, and yet not one man left his post, or for a moment gave up their efforts to tear away the obstacles that were laid across the breach; every officer and man has received two or three wounds each; those that are returned are amputations or body wounds. My poor friend was struck down from the breach twice before he was killed, once with a stone, once with a bayonet wound in the head; nevertheless he persevered in his attempts until a shot went through his right breast and finished his career in the only manner that was worthy of his life. I have 520 or more men left in the regiment, but the plundering after the town was taken, and the death or wounds of almost all their officers (only 7 being with the regiment fit for duty), has so disorganised them for a time, that I have been forced the two first days of my command to punish three of them by that most infamous manner of flogging, which is now doubly so from the gallantry of their conduct at the storm; but robbery and insolence to their officers are crimes not possible to be forgiven. Cheer up your own spirits, my Caroline and write to me much about yourself; it will go farther than any other thing to dispel the gloomy prospects and thoughts that torment me now. Your affectionate husband William.

La Encina, 1 May 1812
My dearest Caroline,
This letter will be very old by the time you read it as it goes by Captain, rather Major Duffy of my regiment,[29] who is extremely attached to your family and who is a very intimate friend of mine, he will give you some trinkets from me, as I have left them entirely to his choice, I cannot answer for their beauty ... You will find in this packet a little handkerchief, preserve it my Caroline with the greatest care, it is the only present (I have remaining) out of many that my poor Charles Macleod gave me and if the memory of the kindest and dearest friend your William ever had can stamp a value upon it, you will preserve it for me until I see you again; ... Give my love to all my brothers and sisters and still believe me my dearest Caroline, your very affectionate husband W Napier

NB Duffy will give you [a] batch of papers for Bunbury's amusement,[30] they are Phillipon's orders during the siege.

William wrote of regimental intentions to pay for a memorial to Macleod, but he also wrote of his loneliness, being among strangers, knowing few of his officers:

La Encina, 4 May 1812
My dear Caroline,
I have been so occupied by the misery of losing Macleod, that I have not attended sufficiently I fear to the lowness of spirits which you described to me in your letter, nor have I expressed myself as I feel for the tenderness you display in your expressions of love for me; but be assured, my Caroline, that they are not lost upon me; ... The business of the regiment is of such an imperious nature that in spite of my disinclination I am obliged to give my mind to it for some hours of the day, and this has in some measure calmed my spirits. The officers have a mind to erect a monument in Westminster Abbey to Macleod,[31] but are not aware of the expense being within their means: pray ask Bunbury what it might be done for. If it can be done, how dear to me will be the place, doubly dear from the tyes [sic] of sorrow and of joy ... The Commodore kept us so close to the land, that we were on the third day embayed in the groyn near Corunna and remained there beating about for six days while a fair wind blew out at sea. During the gale we lost all our topgallant masts at one crash and one man fell from the main topgallant masthead onto the deck, crushing a soldier under him and I fear that they both died soon after I left the ship. We had also a man overboard, who was picked up with some difficulty and in the nick of time. My horse *Tamerlane* was sold for £67 and was very near dying; poor beast! ... My roan mare I found at Lisbon completely done up, and my servant, not Feagan,[32] (who by the bye has not arrived with my baggage) burnt my dressing-case the first day I arrived at the regiment. It is not rendered useless however ... How dreadful it is to find in one half-year that I am deprived of so many friends as I have been, left the regiment full in officers and men, and now I stand almost alone; but one officer whom I know is left. Both the young boys that I had in my company are desperately wounded.[33] I was very proud of them, and they have not disgraced their captain, poor little fellows; their courage and fortitude surpassed that of much older men; but I am sick of the wretchedness that every report brings in. The poor fellows are dying fast of their wounds, both officers and men, and I fear we have not yet heard the worst ... Yours ever W Napier

La Encina, 13 May 1812
My dearest Caroline,
Your letters are the comfort of my life and I look as anxiously for them, ... for I am a stern animal as a commanding officer (although I trust not an inhuman one) and the pleasure of unbending from my dignity, to talk nonsense with you, is greater than you can imagine. ... When I desired you

my love to ask Bunbury about the expense of a monument at Westminster Abbey, I meant the fees of the place, but if you could find out what a figure in marble, about 3 feet high would cost by a good sculptor I wish you very much so to do. I must now bid you adieu my dearest wife as the post is called for much sooner than I expected. Your very affectionate WN

La Encina, 19 May 1812
My dearest Caroline,
… I am at present very much distressed about the conduct of Mr Hull's son, a captain in our regiment[34] who has acted like a swindler and a fool, cheating everybody he could and married to his mistress, a woman of the most abandoned character. I care not for him, but for his good old father and his mother and sisters, who are as amicable people as I know anywhere. The fellow has not the spirit to shoot himself and I have the painful business of breaking it to his father. I have spoken to Lord Wellington, who very kindly has consented to recommend him to be allowed to sell his lieutenancy, which will nearly cover his deficiencies and save the disgrace of a publick [sic] trial to his family. You express a wish to know about my Staff employment; I have none, having given it up in order to assume the command of the regiment; when I am superseded in that command I will go upon the Staff if they will put me with the Light Division, otherwise my sweetest Caroline I will go home to you … five junior officers have obtained rank above me for their services even in the short time that I was away; and yet I do not think that they were more capable, at least they did not prove so when I was present; but a soldier's life is one of hard striving; if your foot slips you fall inevitably. I have just got an order to enlist 100 men from the Spaniards into the regiment. This I think is the fairest prospect we have yet had of succeeding in the Peninsula, that is if it is followed up on a great scale … Tell George that the mutiny at Ciudad stopt [sic] of itself, and I believe they were paid … The bridge of Alcantara is repaired, but that speaks two ways, and this recruiting of Spaniards may alter the designs Lord Wellington had before. I think it very likely that he may endeavour to cripple Marmont in the north, so as to prevent him from undertaking anything against Ciudad Rodrigo while we find it necessary to move southward; but everything must be conjecture, as the present movements are evidently with an intention to deceive the enemy to the real object … I bid you adieu yours most affectionately. W Napier

I had a bad fit of the ague two days ago, but by dint of bark I have chased it away.

It is clear that William was struggling with his command, being horrified by the state of insubordination within both his battalion and indeed the entire Light Division:

La Encina, 26 May 1812
My dearest Caroline,
Since I wrote last to you we have made no move of any kind. You have of course heard before this of General Hill's business at Almaraz[35] ... Major Duffy will have arrived in London before you get this, and will have given you the trinkets, from the description he sends [of] one of them I should think they were vulgar enough except the chains, I have not much opinion of his taste. The lieutenant colonel[36] of the 3rd Caçadores having been reported dead (which turned out false), the officer who commanded them paid me a visit with the next eldest officer to request I would apply to enter the Portuguese service and ask for this regiment. This was very flattering to me, but I declined it without any hesitation for many reasons, the most prominent of which was that it left me a most indeterminate time to look forward to seeing you, and if that was not the case, I cannot reconcile myself perfectly to the idea of fighting for any country but my own; besides which, I am perfectly dead to all the feelings of glory that I used to have; and so little pleasure do I find in command of troops, but if the Duke would allow me to sell my commission I should go ... You will easily understand this when I tell you that the barbarity of our soldiers extended to that pitch that they would not for two days carry off the wounded men at the foot of the walls, our *own men*!!! They also stripped them naked, the officers as well as the men who were wounded; I do not mean our regiment in particular, the 95th were the worst. The town was dreadfully plundered and the inhabitants murdered of all ages and sexes. The French were the only people to whom they gave quarter, out of a spirit of honour not humanity. They even killed one another. Such is war, ... Your most affectionate William.

William could finally write in hope of movement:

La Encina, 8 June 1812
My dearest Caroline,
... We expect to move in a day or two, as the whole army is concentrating about this place and the stores have been collecting to a great extent. I think that Marmont had certainly better look about him, or we shall be disagreeable. It will be curious if Lord W[ellington] should make the same

manoeuvre that General Moore did 3 years ago upon the line of French communication in the north. Your affectionate husband, William Napier.

PS Tell George I got his letter and [am] immensely thankful for it, I think he is a little in love with you and I cannot blame him. I am not sure where my brother [Charles] is, give my love to everybody and believe me once again my best love, your affectionate William.

4 miles in front of Salamanca, 18 June 1812
My precious Caroline,
We have been on the advance *for the last 7 days*: what we are going to do I cannot *tell*; some say going to Paris, some to Madrid; some to *Hell*; I think, as far as we can and then we shall come back again. Tell George we had a slight skirmish of cavalry 6 miles from Salamanca; the French evacuated the town, save about eight hundred who are in very strong forts near the bridge.[37] The ground was broke before them last night, I believe with trifling loss, but have not heard. The 6th Division carry on the operations; I think 3 days will finish them. I hear that a general combination of Sicilians, Spaniards and English,[38] are the means we are to use for the expulsion of the French, which nevertheless will not take place, at least I think so. I have been very well since we marched, which I was not before by any means. Pray tell Major Duffy when you see him that the butchers shot poor '*Jim*' the horse I bought from him; he however is not dead; the farrier says he will die, I say not. I am sorry for him, as he was long the property of poor Charles Macleod, which gave him an interest with me, besides being an excellent horse ... Again bless you my sweetest Caro, your affectionate husband ever W Napier.

Parada Rueblias [Parada de Rubiales], 29 June 1812
My dearest Caroline,
There was no post left the army last week which will satisfy you about the lapse in the dates of my letters. Since I wrote last, we have been constantly in position within cannon-shot of the French army under Marmont. There have been several skirmishing affairs along the line & some manoeuvring. The forts in Salamanca have taken 11 days, and one unsuccessful assault by the 6th Division, in which General Bowes[39] behaved most gallantly and was killed. The loss has been severe I believe, for the extent of the operation and the 6th Division are generally abused as cowards in the Army. I think Marmont had about 35,000 infantry, for which I am laughed at by most people, who say he had only 20,000; I believe Lord Wellington thought as I did, as he did not attack him, which he might have done.

Marmont crost [sic] the River Tormes with 9 or 10,000 men and threatened our communications, but was stopped by 2 divisions sent for that purpose; his view appeared to be to induce Lord Wellington to pass the river with his whole army, in which case Marmont would have taken up the line of the Tormes, which is very strong; Lord W[ellington] was not a young bird, after the *forts* fell the French retired and we have made a march of 4 leagues after them. The news of their retreat is various; some say they have divided, part for Madrid, part for Toro; but George, for whom this is intended, will see best and most from the despatch ... By the bye so is the Army and the abuse of the French, who are certainly great scoundrels, as certainly as that the English are as great. General Moore was the only general who knew how to make good men & good soldiers in *themselves* ...

P.S. ... Tell George I am second in command of the brigade and likely to continue so.[40]

Rueda, 7 July 1812
My dearest Caroline,
You are a good little girl for taking so much trouble about the monument and a clever little one too ... I know Westmacott's brother in the Staff Corps[41] very well and I am obliged to him for the interest he takes in it. George's sword is one of 5,000 presents he has made me, so much for his veracity ... With respect to us, General Graham[42] is going home with sore eyes and I believe old age. Lord W[ellington] has astonished everybody, and most people here abuse him; I confess it appears to me not only without reason, but contrary to reason to do so. He has had several opportunities of fighting with great advantage, which he has declined and has not even prest [sic] the enemy in his retreat. I think his object is to force the enemy to cede territory to him, in which he succeeds and also to inspire the Spaniards with confidence in the strength of his army and the greatness of his enemy. Were he once to fight this would all vanish, because the French army by acting on less extensive lines than they do at present, would again be able to show a force superior in number to himself, and he would have to retreat as usual after a victory; besides which, any movement from Madrid upon the road leading through Placentia [Plasencia] or Avila would threaten his communications and oblige him to return much quicker than would be convenient with the train of wounded &c, which he would have after a battle ... God bless you my precious Caroline, your affectionate husband Lt Colonel Napier.[43]

Rueda, 9 July 1812

My dearest Caroline,

... Major Burg[44] Lord Wellington's adc, puts this letter up with the despatches which go off this night, although not the regular post-day for the army; he is a good fellow for his pains and I am a good fellow for taking advantage, or rather not taking advantage of what formerly would have been an excuse I'd have been too happy to have jumped at ...

Most earnestly do I hope that Charles will get Gifford[45] to exchange with him; for my own part, I would sooner almost quit the army than go to garrison the Bermudas;[46] not from fear of the climate, but from the knowledge that you are among people whose whole soul is given up to their more than luxurious appetites, whose enjoyments are founded on cruelty and whose principles will every moment shock the feelings of a man of honour; while any abhorrence he expresses of them will engage him in quarrels or expose him to derision. Do not think this a picture at all exaggerated; our regiment was many years in the West Indies and I know the amusements, the principles, the feelings that belong to them ... Lord Wellington does not appear to be anxious to shake Marmont; the latter has been these last 6 days in front of us at Tordesillas, entrenched behind the Duero, seeming to care very little about us ... Goodbye my well-beloved wife, long life and love a thousand years, your loving husband, William.

A short section of William's Journal survives:

15 July. The Light Division marched from Rueda 3 miles to the left, the French marched to Toro from Tordesillas.

16 July. Marched during the night to Castrejon [de Trabancos] to the right and rear of Rueda, the enemy still supposed to be at Toro.

17 July. Got [the] order to march, heat increasing at daybreak towards Rueda, pushing a brigade up to the town.

18 July. Daybreak heard cavalry skirmishing. 4 o'clock marched up the heights in our front, found the French in great force. Heavy cannonade, cavalry lost a good many men, our brigade 4 only. French dragoons made a bold movement and a squadron charged two squadrons of the 11th & 12th our dragoons *ran* away in the most cowardly manner, *saw it myself*. French Army tried to turn the left, Lord Wellington retired, Light Division in contiguous columns towards the Guarena River, the Hussars & 14th Dragoons beat the French cavalry on the left. The two armies marched in

columns within musket shot, heads of the columns abreast of each other cannonading the whole time. Light Division might have been attacked at a great disadvantage just before we crost [sic] the Guarena, but the French declined it. Got info (assertion) French attacked 27th & 40th Regiment with 3 battalions, but were charged and beat.

19 July. The French moved upon our right, we moved also, our brigade put by Sir Stapleton Cotton[47] under the French guns without reason. We got pounded and retired (with the loss of 14 men) by order, men very steady.

20 July. The French again turned our right, we fell back towards Salamanca.

21 July. Kept falling back and crost [sic] the Tormes in the evening near Salamanca, French crost [sic] at Huerta & Alava [Alba de Tormes].

22 July. The French again tried to turn our right, committed a mistake and got licked for it, vide Lord Wellington's dispatch.[48] Light Division very little to do, marched in line against their left, French skirmishers knocked some down, might have done more mischief but were frightened at our imposing appearance. Pack's Brigade wonderfully retired, Sing[49] killed, not certain, brigade behaved well.

Generals Cole wounded in the arm;[50] Leith lost an arm;[51] Beresford shot in the body; Victor Alten in the face; ditto Spry very badly wounded;[52] Sir Stapleton in the back by a Portuguese after the action;[53] Le Marchant killed.[54] I know nothing more.

William wrote home after the victory of Salamanca, but he seems to have been war weary, seeing no end to the death:

Flores de Avila, 25 July
My dearest Caroline,
As I am sure you wished much to hear of a bloody battle and that I should be at least wounded if not killed, this is to let you know that in the latter part you have met with a disappointment. Our division had little to do; the regiment has only had 18 men wounded and two officers, of whom I am not one. Lord Wellington has beaten Marmont with the loss of near 5,000 men prisoners, 4,000 killed & wounded and 16 pieces of cannon, and this is the second day's march in pursuit. Marmont has lost an arm[55] and is otherwise wounded. We have lost 1 general killed[56] and 6 wounded,[57] with 4,000 killed and wounded of the men; 2 eagles are taken.[58] I am sorry to say that *Cole* has been wounded in the arm; Leith has lost an arm. Tom Lloyd commanded the 94th,[59] and I have not heard of his being wounded.

I have not had a letter from you later than the 25th of June. Although we had not as much as we wished of the battle, yet I am much pleased with the conduct of the regiment, which marched in line near two miles under a disagreeable fire from the French skirmishers, with a degree of correctness that I never could persuade them to do on a field day. We should have lost a good many men was it not for the dusk, which prevented them from seeing correctly; great part of the battle was fought after dark. General Pakenham[60] has particularly distinguished himself. For George's information I give you an abstract of our movements, which will be better than bothering you with military affairs; to say the truth it bothers me much. I am really tired of seeing people butchered in a skilful [sic] way, and the more so as I do not perceive how we are to be ultimately successful, but that must be a secret ... Your affectionate husband William Napier.

Aldea Mayor [Aldeamayor de San Martin], 3 August 1812.
My dearest Caroline,
I have been waiting with the greatest impatience to get letters from you ... we having no sort of rest or amusement, long marches, camps without water or wood and the pleasant sight of murdered French, sick and stragglers, and the still more agreeable occupation of proving the truth of Vitellius's observation that '*dead enemies are pleasant perfumes.*'[61] I cannot be pleased with my luck, which by preventing me from having considerable share in the battle has deprived me of the chance of getting the brevet rank of lieutenant colonel. It certainly was not my fault, nor should I have failed in gaining it if we had been engaged ... at all events, I shall have a medal tied to the fourth button of the right side with a blue and red riband of full three inches long.[62] Lloyd is to get a lieutenant colonelcy, whereat I am glad, but then Hearn is arrived at Lisbon to take the command from me, whereat I am sorry. Our loss has been greater than was at first supposed, 5,300. Tell George poor General Ferrey[63] who fought the Light Division at Barba del Puerco, at the Coa and at Busaco, died of his wounds at Olmedo; and the fine spirited Spaniards dug up his body and bruised his head with stones. For the honour of the Light Division I have buried him again in spite of them. Marmont lost his arm and had two or three wounds. The people of Tudela say he died three days ago.[64] He was a brave fellow and a good officer and had the best of the business until the 22nd, when he extended his left wing too much and Lord Wellington seized the opportunity like a hawk.

We have so little communication at present that I really cannot give you any idea what we are going to do; Soult may however insist on our fighting him. When you see Mark, tell him to let you know where Lopez's grand map of Spain,[65] in sheets of provinces, is to be found in London and then if you can get it for that sum give 20 guineas for it; if for less, so much the better; but remember it must be Lopez's, his own and not Tadius. I hope most earnestly that Charles is not gone to the West Indies.

Getaffa [Getafe] near Madrid, 12 August 1812
My dearest Caroline,
… Don't send me anymore [news]papers, as we get them regularly. I had written a long letter to you which was to have [gone] by Major Burg,[66] but charming Mr Feagan lost my fine writing desk and your letter in it, together with my drawings and several curiosities which I had collected for you, a Legion of Honour, &c &c … I shall look after Mr Campbell[67] when arrived, as he does not know anybody in the 2nd Battalion, tolerably & freely. Feagan has also lost my *cocked-up* hat and a few other trifles, and my best English horse is dying of the cholic, a most dangerous complaint in this country …

Madrid, 30 August 1812
My dearest Caroline,
I am much surprised at your saying I missed a packet about the latter end of June; I not only wrote every time the mail went, but once out of the regular post … I perceive upon looking over your letter that it is Bermudas and not as I supposed Barbadoes [sic], where Charles is gone; there is much difference in the climate, although I suppose he will go on to Halifax or Canada … Yours affectionately William Napier.

William complained of inactivity in Madrid, but did not improve things at home by describing his womanising to his wife:

Madrid, 5 September 1812
My dearest Caroline,
Since I last wrote to you we have been quiet, if dancing and other sports can be called quiet. Lord W[ellington] left this three days ago with a division to oppose Marmont's army at Valladolid, which is again in force, I believe 28,000 men. The 3rd and Light Divisions have been left here, and it seems to be the object now to let the latter have nothing to do: it is rather hard that the only period in which this has happened should be the time I command a regiment. I have seen a bullfight, which is really too horrid, although the dexterity of the men who fight is so great as to

leave you in doubt whether it was in earnest or not, and yet 3 horses were killed and nine bulls; it is much more cruel than bull baiting. Since my last letter there has been a great change in the household; the senior Feagan has been turned away and William[68] near dead; he is however now quite well, but rather weak. I have got in place of Feagan, a very handsome young gentleman whom I hope Mrs Holm will not think so outré[69] as Feagan. Some people now look upon me as a reprobate because I sing and laugh as much with pretty women as I used to do before I was married. If I was certain that you would not agree with them, I would say what fools, but as I have a great respect for your opinion; shall wait until I hear your observations upon the subject. The siege of Cadiz they say is raised and there seems to be some ground to believe that the French mean to pass the Ebro, but nothing certain. Maitland[70] has landed at Alicant[e], the worst place he could; and since he has landed he acts like a blockhead. This is a great pity; I am afraid he will get a beating, although he is cautious enough, as he made a forced march of 7 leagues to avoid a French army who were only 150 miles from him ... your very affectionate William.

Madrid, 20 September
My dearest Caroline,
...We have been now a month without a post starting from here, which will account to you for the long time you must have been without a letter from me. ... If Patrickson[71] comes out I will go home, provided that Hearn does not fall sick &c &c.

Madrid, 27 September 1812
My dearest Caroline,
We are still at rest here while the divisions under Lord Wellington are besieging the castle of Burgos; it is very strong, and we have lost 420 men in storming *one* of the outworks, but it will probably fall soon ... I send you a bill in a letter to the Paymaster of the 2nd Battalion for 30 pounds, pay my taylor [sic] and be a good little wife & believe me your very, very affectionate William.

Cox & Greenwood[72] will tell you where the 2nd Battalion is, direct the letter to Francis Fraser Paymaster 2nd Battalion 43rd, wherever they are.

Madrid, 12 October 1812
My dearest Caroline,
... I am at this moment preparing to hand over the command of the regiment to Daniel Hearn, resigning my glory and my dearer promotion

into his hands and yet I live and am merry, very merry. Have you seen Marmont's despatch? It is scientific, modest and true to the utmost extent; and is methinks, a hard hit upon the French despatches in general. Burgos goes on ill, very ill, and doubts are entertained if it will ever fall.

Alcala [de Henares], 25 October 1812
My dearest Caroline,
I believe that I told you Stanhope left all the writing paper in Lisbon; and as they have not given us any money these three months, I could not buy any in Madrid. What a long excuse for such small paper! ... Hearn is at last arrived and I believe that Patrickson is at Corunna, in which case I have no doubt that I shall be ordered home when the latter arrives at the regiment. Soult has been making some demonstrations near us, which is the cause of our present move. Burgos has cost us *3,000* men, and I am afraid there is little chance of its falling at all, certainly not without a farther loss of at least two thousand more; all the assaults latterly have failed; either from cowardice or the impossibility of the attempts, bad faults on both sides, it is now a sort of blockade under Pack. Lord Wellington has moved forward under the idea of fighting Massena, who is said to command Marmont's army now. In the meantime, the Spaniards do nothing in the way of exerting themselves; they voted three months back 50,000 men and they have not at this day taken the census of the villages from whence the men are to be drawn. The government is abhorred and with the greatest reason; each night from 20 to 30 poor people are taken up in Madrid & put into the Retiro.[73] No trial takes place, nobody knows what becomes of them; their estates are confiscated & their families driven to die of famine in the streets. Nothing but the presence of the British army prevents an insurrection and I am certain that if we were to set up for ourselves, the people would willingly and instantly join us & declare Lord Wellington King of Spain ... It is an unfortunate country, cursed with a thousand ills, and in all the thousand there is none so bad or so cursed as the guerillas that are so much admired in England, happy, stupid, credulous England! I cannot describe to you the grief of the people when the English left Madrid. We had fed numbers of them by subscription and they said *'Now we shall starve, and worse than starving, we shall have the dreadful guerillas again.'* This was the language not of the poor alone but of every class of people ... Lord Wellington has a great force under him, a month of fine weather and a head that I believe is not overmarked by any Cabeça[74] in the Peninsula. The greatest fault he has committed is in endeavouring to

take Burgos without means and it is the worse as he might have had ample means for [the] asking. Adieu my angel, your most loving W Napier.

[La] Caridad Convent, Ciudad Rodrigo, 20 November 1812
My dearest Caroline,
I have very little time to write, but I am in much fear of your hearing bad news of me, a report having spread that I was slain; I am not wounded or sick. We have had a retreat of 68 leagues, bad roads, rainy weather, no provisions and constantly lying out at night. The retreat to say the truth was badly managed, the loss immense, the behaviour of all the army, our division excepted, most shameful. Do not say so however, as there is a party in the army to bring Lord Wellington into disrepute, Gordon[75] at the head of it, his only fault is never trusting his generals. From Salamanca the number of stragglers amounts to at least 5,000 men. We had on the seventeenth marched some hours through woods when we found the French cavalry had cut us off from the other divisions, taking baggage, sick and Sir Edward Paget.[76] We were attacked, formed squares and then found that their infantry were upon us; retreated, leaving four companies under my command to skirmish and cover the retreat over a deep narrow river, under a hill within musket shot; this we did, losing 27 men. I had a shot through my clothes, nothing more on my honour my dear, and I beat a path for Barnard[77] and General Alten [who] were both there directing, although I had the command.[78] We were afterwards cannonaded severely and lost an officer wounded and some men; Ridout [had] his leg off.[79] This is for George, who I am glad to hear is married.[80] Tell him so & also that Dawson[81] is killed, poor fellow! and Fuller badly wounded.[82] Hearn is very ill and I have the command ... Yours my darling for ever, W Napier.

Gallegos [de Arganan], 1 Dec 1812
My dear little Caro,
We are settled in winter quarters ... The sketch you sent me by Bacon is good, and I think will be adopted, that is, without the little genie at top, which is perfectly absurd; the inscription is to be in Lord Wellington's words about him in the dispatch.[83] I am doing a copy for the officers to decide upon which they like; mine is without the boy, which I think will, by being taken away, allow the artist to give more relief and execution to the figure. It must not cost more than £300,[84] although I would pay myself a few more guineas, (if it were necessary to do it correctly) without the officers knowing anything of it. In my next I will let you know more about it. I am in command again; Hearn is sick, but I hope he will not go

home, as that would put an end to my hopes when Patrickson appeared, which he ought to do now, as if he is sick. Despair nought, I am with other officers, suffering very severely in my feet from a fever in them. We are the funniest cripples you ever saw, in uncommon pain, our toes feeling as if they were always out of bed of a cold winter's night, and the foot has all sorts of *ache*s in it. There are no marks and we hobble along like Grimaldi,[85] everybody laughing; for my part I think it a bad joke. Poor Ridout who was so badly wounded, is dead. He bore the amputation with the most admirable fortitude and serenity and two days after died of a gangrene in the *well foot from cold*. We regret him much; he was so inoffensive, so handy, and so willing to do everybody service, that if he did not make very attached particular friends, he certainly left no enemies of any kind. It was astonishing how the recollection of his unoffending manners seized upon everybody during his funeral and people who never thought of him before actually wept then. I always liked him much, poor fellow! Your dearest, most affectionate husband William.

Gallegos [de Arganan], 9 December 1812
My dearest Caroline,
You may thank George's friend Charley Rowan,[86] for not getting letters by the last mail. He chose to go to headquarters and forgot to send notice to the division that the mail went … We are all in winter quarters and have fagged a degree to get drunk, to act plays, to hunt, shoot & play rackets [sic], to dance bolero, to write verses and to damn the *parlevous*[87] until the next campaign. You may perceive the good affect the rackets have on my writing already, one would think the fever was in my hands and not in my feet. I have no chance of getting home, that's of course as Hearn is certainly going home again and I suppose he & Patrickson and Gifford will take it turn-about and keep me here as a scapegoat … Yours my pretty, William.

William, like almost every other officer in the Army, was highly critical of Wellington's complaints regarding the lack of discipline during the recent retreat:

Gallegos [de Arganan], 15 December 1812
My dearest Caroline,
The Peer Wellington has just issued what he calls a circular to the army, in which he obligingly informs them that they are a pack of the greatest knaves and the worst soldiers that he not only ever had to deal with, but worse than any army he ever read of. He was good enough to say that he excepted the Light Division & the Guards, but he makes no exceptions

in writing with regard to the rest of the army. It is true there never was a worse one and moreover they will never get better under him, he does not know how to make a good example. We are inferior to the French in every part, but fighting; apropos King Joseph[88] is an excellent man, as I can prove in a thousand instances of his merit and good nature told me by a prisoner who benefited by his disposition, *escapades I mean* ... The papers are uncommonly diverting about our movements. Wise people! how much they flatter themselves they know about it! Old Gordon's gone home with the character of as great a fool as ever showed his nose on the Staff or elsewhere, Lord Wellington is gone to Cadiz with Lord Fitzroy Somerset only attending him. Apropos, the last is as good as he is clever and nearly as clever as Lord Wellington himself; he will one day be a great man if he lives. As soon as *Junius* is known in England send me an express[89] and do not send any more soap balls, my baggage is already beyond all reasonable dimensions ... I am your affectionate husband W Napier

Gallegos [de Arganan], 27 December 1812
My dear Caroline,
I have not yet heard of the arrival of Patrickson. I hope he has not been drowned in the late gale of wind. I send my servant with Oliver Mayer's[90] letter as you desired, but as the Guards are only 120 miles from here, he has not come back yet so I can't tell if he got it or not, but I dare for today he did. ... The weather is so cold I cannot write any more ... W Napier

We last heard of Charles in Guernsey with his regiment. In July, however, they were ordered to Bermuda. It is clear that Charles was no sailor:

Plymouth, 28 July 1812
Forced in here by stress of weather, and my sea-sickness horrible; with enough to make the pot boil in England, no other country should see my pretty face. Unable to eat, my spirits are low, and six weeks, perhaps two months, of this before me ... *Jonathan*[91] has declared war. We reckon ourselves equal to two frigates; three we should fight hard and even four would have a tug; we have seven hundred men onboard, and my left hand should go to board the *President*[92] and smite Commodore Rogers[93] with my right. I swear now, *Jonathan* lacks a licking and an English line of battleship is the thing to provide the needful. It would however please me more to delve for pratees[94] at home, for an American war is a miserable thing.

He made only a few notes in his journal during the long passage:

[End of July?] While at Plymouth I procured bedding for the men, which idle official rascals had thought quite unnecessary. Whether the Admiralty or Transport Office are in fault is unknown, but the attempt to send five hundred soldiers on a voyage which may last two months, with only the deck to lie on, is shameful.

Charles' new base was not much to his liking:

12 September 1812, Bermudas. This island beautiful to look at, but food and all things but rogues so scarce as to make a miserable quarter.

Chapter 8

The Advance to the Pyrenees 1813

George remained in Britain for almost the whole year, only returning to Spain in January 1814, therefore we only view the Peninsular campaign through the eyes of William:

Gallegos [de Arganan] 6 January 1813
My dearest Caroline,
I have just heard that Patrickson is really arrived at Lisbon at last; as soon as Lord Wellington comes home from Cadiz I will ask for leave. Yours, my dear Caro. W Napier

William returned home in February following the arrival of Patrickson, he therefore missed the advance to Vitoria and the hard fighting in the Pyrenees; but by August he was onboard ship on his way back to Spain, where he would be involved in the push into France.

Plymouth, Sunday 8 August 1813
My dearest Caroline,
… Havelock[1] is a young and very fine lad in the 43rd to whom I once gave *a very severe* lesson, and he has, like a very proper spirited lad, proved by his attention and zeal, that he knew I was right. Please to recollect that Duffy is a *younger* officer than me when you talk of his leaving the army as a help to my getting the command … The horse transport was left at Portsmouth. You may when you have time and money pay my taylor [sic] and tell him *after* you have paid him, that he has made my clothes so ill and treated me in such a manner, that I will change him … A report of the most unfortunate kind has just been propagated here; that Lord Wellington has been taken. I hope to God it is not true, Government could not exert their vigour better than to find the author, if false and punish him. It is too rascally to set any false report of that kind about. God bless you my darling, believe me your most affectionate husband W Napier.

Bellona Transport, 9 August 1813
My dearest Caroline,
The wind is fair, and we are actually under sail. I have no time to write any more. Bless you my darling Caro, your affectionate husband W Napier.

Passage [Pasaia], 19 August 1813
My dearest Caroline,
After a very tedious passage we made this place this morning. I think it is the most romantic beautiful place I almost ever saw, a long narrow arm of the sea, for 4 or 5 miles[2] between very high and nearly perpendicular rocks surmounted by evergreens, and these again overtopped by the Pyrenees. We have heard nothing of our horses, but the regiment is only 6 leagues from this place, still at Vera [Bera]. San Sebastian still holds out; the loss has been severe, and as well as I can judge, it may hold out a month longer; the citadel is uncommonly strong. God bless you my own love, your affectionate husband W Napier.

Camp over Vera [Bera], 24 August 1813
My dearest Caroline,
… Havelock was perfectly right about the plunder and I am happy to say that the story about Madame Gazan and the other ladies is positively denied by all parties. The last battle[3] was very severe; Soult very nearly defeated Lord Wellington, as you may guess, when I tell you that hardly more than one division was actually engaged, or could be so, against fully 50,000 men; in short, for the first 3 or 4 days Soult had the best of it, and nothing but Lord Wellington's extreme activity and courage could have brought [up] sufficient troops to man the ground where the battle was. The position during the 28th was perfectly impregnable, and nothing but the extreme confidence the French always have in themselves, and the increase of that from superior numbers, could have prevailed upon troops to attack it. They are now opposite to us on the French Bas Pyrenees. We on the Bas Spanish side, our picquets touching.

If you wish to know the place, read that book which Bunbury lent me, '*Mémoires du Guerre de la Basses Pyrenées, par le Citoyen B*****.'[4] You will find all the posts described, Vera [Bera], St Estevan [Doneztebe-Santesteban], Orbacete [Orbaizeta], Irun, St [San] Sebastian, St Jean Pied de Port, St Jean de Luz, Echalar [Etxalar] &c. It is very interesting.

There are many desertions from *both* sides. The French it appears, are sending their men into the interior for clothing; they talk strongly of peace and have even given us a sketch of the basis, viz Russia to have Moldavia and Wallachia (this makes me doubt it); Austria to have Salzburg and the Tyrol; Italy to be a separate kingdom under Joseph Bonaparte; Jerome to have Holland; Westphalia to belong to the Confederation of the Rhine; Spain and Portugal to be free; Sicily ours; Malta the Grand Master's; and the West India islands to be given back to France. The French army opposite to us is about 60,000 men, independent of Suchet, and neither Pampeluna [Pamplona] nor San Sebastian are fallen; so that the Speaker lyed [sic] confoundedly when he said that Spain and Portugal were freed by the decisive battle of Vitoria ... your own affectionate William.

William had not been allowed to command the Light Division contingent at the storming of San Sebastian and was considering selling up in a fit of pique!

Camp above Vera [Bera], 2 September 1813
My dearest Caroline,
The posts are very uncertain; do not therefore conclude that I have either forgotten you or got myself hurt. You will have heard before this reaches you that we have had another battle,[5] the 43rd did not fire a shot. I was detached with half the regiment to keep open the communication of the army by Kempt,[6] who is very zealous, but I think very inexperienced, as may be seen by that very order to me. The French army were in possession 2 hours before of the whole road, and I of course passed into the middle of them; 3 companies of the 95th sent on the same errand by another road, supported by two Spanish regiments, were cut [in] upon by a French column. The Spaniards fell back; the 95th pushed on, joined me and left the French to stare between two good things. In the meantime, the French formed several strong columns and marched against me, who like a wise general, put my tail between my legs and ran up a high mountain, where I showed a very pretty front and frightened them away. By this time a general called rain, who I dare say you know is very formidable in mountains, accompanied by Lieutenant Generals Thunder and Lightning, set upon me without mercy for the whole of that day and night without cease, and having no cover of any kind, they did considerable execution before morning. Apropos, the priest of Vera [Bera], being asked how he got on in this valley between the French & us, answered very well, '*Even as Jesus Christ between two robbers.*' The same day a soldier of the 43rd, being asked how long his comrade had been dead, said, '*If he had lived until today, he would have been dead a week.*' I send you back the saddler's bill, from which you must deduct the last charge of 4s 6d for a girth which it appears he never furnished. You must also pay Lingham's bill.

My horses has [sic] arrived, the grey mare crushed in every part of her body by being let to fall between the ship and the boat in disembarking; Lingham took the greatest care of them, I am in some hopes she will recover. Having now said my say about common affairs, I will upon another sheet of paper write to you about affairs of much more importance, in which you must give me your *advice sincerely* and without reference to any feeling of your own, with regard to doing what I wish. If you agree with me on the subject, you must write to *George* and speak to Bunbury upon it, who may be of use to me about it ... I have a strong disposition to leave the army for the following reasons. In the first place I am 28 and only a major, I cannot rise to the head of my profession for want of time. Next, I dislike the scenes I witness so much that nothing but the prospect of arriving at the head of my profession could make me endure it. Next, my health is very bad and getting worse. I am married to you whom I love better than anything else, and I give up your society and endanger your peace and happiness in order to acquire a little, very little, fleeting reputation or a rank, dependent on the whim of Lord Wellington. Certainly nothing ought to make me do this except the necessity of defending my country, but I think the war is not now carried on from any necessity of the kind; it is rather for the purpose of giving power to Lord Liverpool &c, to oppress Ireland which is my country. Lastly, I have been ill used in the following manner. The 5th Division under General Oswald[7] behaved ill, Lord Wellington wrote a letter saying he wanted a hundred men and officers from the Light Division to *lead* the storm of San Sebastian; of course I volunteered to command them. I was accepted, and two hours after put in orders to take the command; but lo! When I arrived at the post appointed I found the command had been taken from me and given to Hunt[8] of the 52nd, a Lieutenant colonel by brevet, and 9 children dependent on him for bread. I went to Pakenham[9] and Lord Wellington upon the spot with the order in my hand; was told it was hard and that I was ill-used, but that it must stand; thus I was cut off from promotion and one of the most splendid opportunities of gaining reputation that could have offered itself. Under all these circumstances I wish to quit the army, and I think for my wounds, for my loss of health and length of service, I am justified in asking leave to sell my majority. I should put it all upon my wounds and want of health of course; as it is not necessary that I should be so explicit to the Duke as to you ... You are my dearest darling love and only yours W Napier.

Vera [Bera], 5 September 1813
My dearest Caroline,
... I hope you have got my long letter about leaving the army; I have been very low-spirited since I wrote it and with reason; I had not then heard of the result of the storming; our loss has been fully 1,600 *there*, if not more. The 43rd gave one officer and 30 men volunteers; 21 including the officer have been killed or wounded. When I thought that I was to have had the command, as I knew the eldest subaltern was old & stupid, I asked a young man of the name of O'Connell[10] (who had led two storming parties before), to volunteer, thinking that I could get him a company. He would not have done so were it not for my sake, and he has been killed, leaving a mother who was supported by what he spared her out of his pay. She has other sons, but it appears from his last words that they are not attentive to her, as he sent a message to one (the eldest) begging him, as his last request that he would be more attentive to his mother. Is this not very painful, and how much it ought to strengthen me in my disposition to quit a service where friendship is a curse and kindness kills. However, I will not pain you any more upon the subject ... There is a Major Marlay[11] here of the stupid kind, Acting Adjutant General, who never lets us know when the post goes, you must of course expect the letters to be uncertain ... There does not appear much chance of entering France, more likely another attack from Soult upon us; he has still 60,000 men independent of *Suchet* ... I hear that Graham says nothing in his dispatch about the volunteers from us and the [1st &] 4th Divisions, this is not fair, but the truth is that they were very *sore* about it. Lord Wellington's letter cannot be got over, General Alten has it in his possession. *'I want 300 men & officers from the Light Division to lead the 5th Division to the attack.'*

Bunbury's friend General Oswald, talked in such an improper and even cowardly manner before the storm that I believe he has *dished* himself in Lord Wellington's opinion. Upon the whole I think I could be content to hear that you were well, without entering into a detail of what you feel, as I am not a nurse or old woman, although I do not like the Army.

Camp, Vera [Bera], 13 September 1813
My dearest Caroline,
... When you write to George, tell him in justification of my abilities as a general (I told him I did not see how Lord Wellington was to cross the Douro this campaign), that I dined with Lord Wellington 3 days ago, and that after dinner he explained to me all his manoeuvres and arrangements for the campaign, and that deceiving the French and passing the Douro,

turning their right by that movement, was the most difficult move he ever made, that it was touch and go, and required more arrangement and more *art* than anything he ever did: had he been one day too late, he must have gone back. He made me laugh much, I asked him it if could have been done by the other flank instead, and after some time considering, he answered me with a great deal of malice, *'No, I'll be damned if my way was not the best.'* He farther said that the French might have made a much better campaign of it, but that they were damned stupid and he was very clever. He was very kind and very glad to see me.

By the bye, Mr Hevey[12] is here and has made the best likeness of him I ever saw, when the print comes out I will subscribe to it. Little Edward Fitzgerald[13] is here. I like him better than I expected. I believe they told lyes [sic] about him. He is very modest and was good natured enough to ride up to the top of one of the Pyrenees to give me Lucy's letter to him, saying you were well at St Anne's Hill. He dined with me, and told me among other matters that he liked me best, because Charles and George were too good and liked beefsteaks as well as pyes [sic], but that I liked good living and girls; further, that he liked command, wished he was colonel, because he would then row the commissary and feed on livers and lights; he has a proper idea of obedience and does not think himself a very great general yet; these are good signs … Yours my darling wife, for ever & day W Napier

Camp of Vera [Bera], 20 September 1813
My dearest Caroline,
… We have a great many reports of battles here, and one French bulletin which says the Allies lost 80,000 men. This of course will be voted a lye [sic] by the good people of London; for my part, I am persuaded that in the main points the French tell the truth, allowing for a little exaggeration in the detail. I have no map of Germany and therefore I cannot give you my opinion of events, particularly from the crude unconnected reports of events that we get. I think however that he will find most trouble from Bernadotte;[14] but if he is able to check him, he will march upon Vienna and endeavour by fright or other means, to draw Austria from the Confederation against him. What a ridiculous figure the account of General Gibbs[15] and his army of 3,000 men makes among the armies there! Oh! the wonderful works of Lords Bathurst and Liverpool! I am very anxious to get your opinion about what I proposed to do in my letter of August; I find myself more inclined than ever to quit the army than ever; to tell you the truth, my health is really so bad, that my life is a perfect burthen

to me; pain and lowness of spirits are my constant companions ... If you agree with me about it, pray ask Bunbury to sound Torrens[16] about giving my leave to *sell* out; otherwise, I cannot quit, as it would be reducing you to a situation of less comfort than I took you from, and that is what I will *not* do. Love me always dearest Caroline and believe me your *most* affectionate husband W Napier.

Camp of Vera [Bera], 21 September 1813
My dearest Caroline,
...We hear a great deal of news from the French. Vandamme[17] seems to have been *dished*, or got *Von-dam* licking. There is a report that Boney has been beaten in person and Marshal Ney killed. I am sorry for the last *part*, but I don't believe any of it; you know I am sceptical upon that subject.

I have had a large swelling about 4 inches below my wound, accompanied with inflammation and some pain; the doctor thinks it is a small part of the ball or backbone coming away; in a few days I shall be better able to tell you. We are tormented here by constant desertion to the enemy and the attendant upon it of shooting those that are caught. You will hardly believe that the calculation of 500 men from the army has been made as the number within these 5 weeks; and what is very strange, the Portuguese go off faster than us ...

Old General Kemmis,[18] who is a fine-spoken man, found a soldier very dirty. *'Take him,'* said he to a sergeant, *'take him and lave*[19] *him in the Tagus.'* Some hours after, *'sergeant, did you do as I ordered you?' 'Yes sir.' 'Where is the culprit, what have you done with him?' 'As your honour ordered me Sir, I left him in the Tagus up to his neck'.* Heaven bless you my little darling Caro, keep yourself well for the sake of your affectionate husband W Napier.

PS The pain in my back continues, the swelling gone, and I don't know what it is.

Camp of Vera [Bera], 1 October 1813
My dearest Caroline,
... Bunbury's military friends don't seem to thrive. Colonel Adam[20] appears to have been *again surprised* and beaten out of a very strong position. Your friend *Lingham* I pardoned and paid his debts, and employed as a horse doctor, but 3 days after he charged me 13 shillings for a blister which I found by enquiry amounted to only *2 shillings*, leaving a profit of 11, this put me out of all patience and I had him tried by a court martial which sentenced him to be flogged and I really think he deserved it.[21] I hope Julia won't break her heart about him. There is some *talk* of our invading France,

but I do not think it can take place so late in the season and with such a force and positions as Soult has in our front; besides Suchet having been victorious in the south is very much against it. Bonaparte appears to have had too many people opposed to him, but that is no reason for supposing that he is ruined, which is *all* the talk *nowadays*. His chances are as follows; he has a better head than any of them, nearly as many troops, and all the fortresses. The enemy have some good heads, a great many bad ones, a great many troops with a better *morale*, but no fortresses; this morale of theirs is likely to evaporate soon, particularly the Austrians.

My chestnut mare has had her leg also crushed by a beam, *most* unsightly, unlikely she will recover but the grey I am afraid never.

I see the papers praise a Mr Cecil Percy very much for bravely shedding his blood at San Sebastian, he being the son of Lord Limerick. I *returned* Mr Percy when I was Brigade Major as a *deserter* from the 95th Regiment, and he was generally thought a coward; what a good scrubbing-brush a *peer* is![22]

8 October 1813
My dearest Caroline,
… About an hour before your letter came we had received an order to attack on the next day at 7 o'clock the position in front of us.[23] I will tell you candidly that I expected we should be cut to pieces, and I believe very few of us thought otherwise; it was however managed perfectly. Great precision, great courage, great luck and great numbers enabled us to carry with little loss an immense mountain, entrenched with abattis, walls, rocks and obstacles of every kind in a space of two hours or less. The 43rd lost few; the 52nd under Colborne, were opposed in the strongest manner and carried everything with the bayonet before them. Our brigade under Kempt had apparently more difficult ground, but by outflanking the enemy we did our business easily; there were fewer troops and less courage opposed to us. Tell George of it; the position was stronger and higher than Busaco 3 times over; in short, if the enemy had put men enough into it, we must have been beat. I need not tell you that I was *not hit*. Old Hearn is a downright coward.

The plains of France lie before us, cultivated, enclosed and rich and beautiful beyond description. The Spaniards, Portuguese and I am sorry to say the British, are exulting in the thoughts of robbing, violating and murdering the unfortunate possessors of what they see before them. Lord Wellington says they *shall not* do it, but Lord W[ellington] only says these things and never prevents the commission of the crimes. General Pakenham is the only hope I have; he is able from his situation and most willing; he has already begun by endeavouring to punish Colonel Halkett[24] for permitting 140 of his men to remain unpunished who had already begun this villainous work; and says he is determined to prevent it if possible, I believe it will be impossible. Kempt I like very much, and he also is full of indignation at such conduct and will be a powerful help. The cause of our country may justify our killing our enemies in battle, but it cannot justify our being *even* spectators of the merciless acts of a licentious army; and well I know there is no cruelty that hell can devise that this army is not capable of and anxious to inflict upon the wretched people below us; but I trust in God that we shall either from policy or principle, find a sufficient number of people in power to prevent it. If it is not prevented, the vengeance for it will keep pace with the crime, and one continued scene of murder will be the consequence ... Never forget that I am your own devoted William.

I enclose you also a paper of the Spaniards to entice the French to desert. I can only remark that they neither pay or feed their own troops; that Russia does not free Poland; that assassination is not [a] virtue; and that the *love of France* is not *very* apparent in *Moreau* or *Bernadotte*; neither does it become a soldier to desert his country under any circumstances. It has had *no effect*.

Camp, French side of Vera [Bera], 17 October 1813
My dearest Caroline,
Since I wrote last to you, we have remained in the same position that we drove the French out of; they are in our front below us, in considerable force and strongly fortified, the weather extremely wet and disagreeable. The French attacked and took a fort from the Spaniards three days ago, which event caused me to be sent to support another batch of Spaniards before the top of La Rhune; and I was again discomfited by General Rain without cover from his fury. It seems to be my fate to remain with the unfortunate right wing of the regiment on the tops of bleak mountains without cover upon rainy nights. The pontoons are gone to the right and we expect an attack will be made by General Hill and his division upon the left of the enemy. Should it succeed, of which there is little doubt, it will most probably give us the line of the Nivelle river and the town of St Jean de Luz, with quiet for the winter. March went home with the despatches ... I would be so happy if I was with you. I do not know if it is an increase of love towards you, or the very great difference I find in the regimental society, that makes me discontented where I am; but certainly from some cause or other I do not feel the same man that I used to do and I am gallant

enough to attribute it to love for you ... General Pakenham has taken my grey mare under his protection, which gives me some hopes of her final recovery ... I have had a very kind letter from George and I enclose you an answer to him: I am your own most affectionate husband W Napier.

General Pakenham makes me now and then think that there are some good men in the world, as you do, that there are some good women. I am sorry to see that Clouet[25] has been wounded and taken prisoner by Bernadotte. If Bunbury can write to anybody about him I hope he will & have written to George about it.

Camp, Puerta do Vera [Bera], 7 November 1813
My dearest Caroline,
... I asked Lord Fitzroy [Somerset] yesterday if Major Mein was to get a lieutenant colonelcy. He said yes, and also that he had spoken to Lord W[ellington] for me, but that Lord W[ellington] thought I would not *like it*, as we had been so little engaged! After being 14 years in the army, having seen 15 engagements of different kinds, receiving two wounds, and being mortified by seeing 9 younger officers[26] in the Light Division alone put over my head, I did not expect to be told that I ought to be ashamed of taking a lieutenant colonelcy; if I ought not to, I must say that the greatest part of headquarters ought therefore to be ashamed to show their faces. For my comfort, I am told I shall certainly have it next engagement. I shall not feel particularly grateful for it then, as by their own account, I shall only then get what is due to me; I thank them much for the care they have of my modesty. I have got my medal[27] and old Hearn is gone sick to England at last, intending to sell out. The command of the regiment is mine again: this is some comfort at least, but it has not altered my opinion the least upon the subject of selling out if I am allowed: nothing can compensate to me for the loss of your society, and I shall always be my own darling Carro's much affectionate husband W Napier.

Battle of the Nivelle, 10 November 1813
William recorded his memories of the battle in a later memoir:

Colonel Hearn having resigned to me the command of the 43rd, I was charged to storm the hogsback ridge of the Petite Rhune mountain, which had been entrenched by six weeks' continuous labour on the part of the enemy. The plan of attack was entirely my own, for General Kempt wished me to attack the rocks with my whole battalion and it was with difficulty I obtained his leave to detach Captain Murchison[28] with two companies

View of the Berlengas Islands, 1810.

View of Alfaiates, 1811.

A Castillian Peasant.

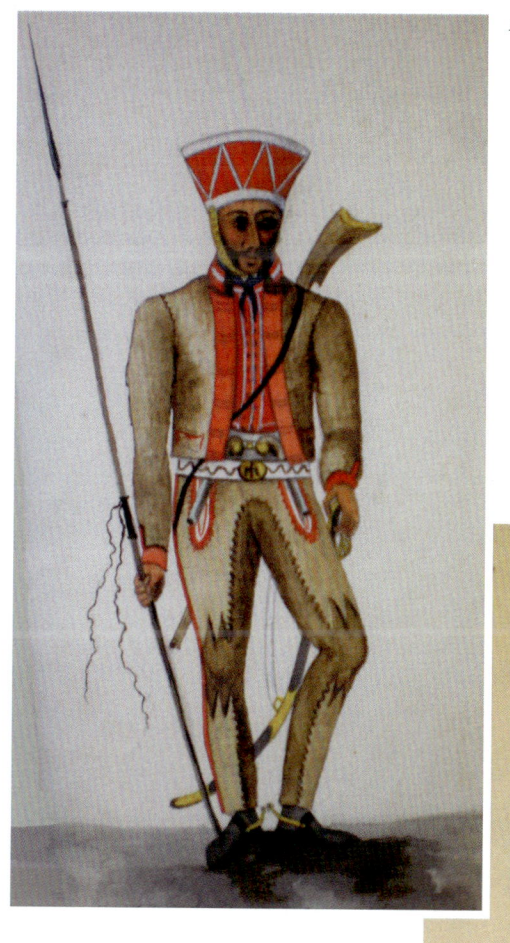

A lancer of Don Julian's.

An inhabitant of Albergaria.

Patrona Criada.

Mikmak Indian.

Busaco Ridge, c.1811.

Village of Albergaria, 1811.

Man of the Grand Canary Islands.

Mikmak squaw.

Squaw and her papouse.

to try the marsh on our left and to keep down if possible, the enemy's fire. A rifle sergeant sent to sound the marsh had assured the general it was impassable, but I was convinced it was not; and so it proved, for Murchison passed it and contributed by his judgement and gallantry very much to the success of the attack; he was mortally wounded at the very moment of victory.

I had a great distance to march on a front line towards the rocks and under fire, before I could gain the narrow entrance between the lower part and the marsh, where only the enemy could be attacked, for in other parts the rocks were 200 feet high. There were two things to be principally looked to; first, not to blow the men by running too soon and thus coming breathless upon the stone castles which had been built up by the enemy and would require great exertions of bodily strength as well as courage to face; this my experience at Casal Nova[29] made me very anxious about; secondly, as the men were sure to be so broken and dispersed by fighting among the rocks and as they would be liable to disasters when they had carried them; for we knew nothing of the nature of the ground nor of the enemy's reserves behind the ridge, it was essential to have our reserves well in hand. In this view I placed four companies under Major Duffy at the distance of 300 yards and with the four remaining companies advanced in person to storm the rocks. I had not however, proceeded above half the distance when the fire became very heavy and at this moment, when I had the greatest difficulty to keep the men from breaking into the charge, the Honourable Captain Gore,[30] adc to General Kempt, who looking down upon us from the heights behind could not see how rugged the ground was, nor judge of our distance, thinking us slow, with the impetuosity of a young Staff officer rode down at full speed and galloped up behind my line, waving his hat and shouting out to charge. The men instantly cheered and ran forward. It was in vain to try and would have been dangerous to stop them and I could only make the best of the matter. I was the first man but one who reached and jumped into the rocks and I was only second because my strength and speed were unequal to contend with the giant who got before me. He was the tallest and most active man in the regiment, and the day before, being sentenced to corporal punishment, I had pardoned him on the occasion of an approaching action. He now repaid me by striving always to place himself between me and the fire of the enemy. His name was Eccles, an Irishman;[31] he died afterwards a sergeant and pensioner on the Irish establishment.

The mischief I had foreseen now arrived; the men were quite blown and fell down in the rocks within a few yards of the first castle, from whence the enemy plied them with a heavy musketry. When they had recovered wind, I advanced against the first castle, leading the way with one man; the enemy fled with the exception of an officer and two of his men; but aided by my own man I scaled the wall. We put the two men to flight and wounded and took the officer, for he fought to the last, standing on the wall and throwing heavy stones at me. One I parried with my sword, but I received a contusion in the thigh from another.

The regiment then carried several castles in succession, the enemy fighting us muzzle to muzzle the whole way, so that many of the men's clothes were scorched all over the front with the fire. This fact Lord Seaton[32] knows, for I showed him my own clothes thus scorched. When I got to their principal place of arms and had only one remaining castle called the *Donjon* to carry, I saw that a breastwork entrenchment and fort below the ridge were still defended by the French and that they were very numerous. I therefore endeavoured to rally my companies, both to make a vigorous assault on the Donjon and to have a body of men in hand, to attack the rear of those defending the entrenchment below. At this moment Sir Andrew Barnard came up to me alone and I explained my intentions to him. While thus employed, Lieutenant Steele,[33] a very quick and brave officer, called out that they were wavering in the Donjon; and as it was very strong and covered by a cleft in the rock fifteen feet deep and only to be turned by one narrow path winding round on a rock on the right, I gave up the notion of rallying the broken men and rushing forward with what I had, carried the Donjon. I now saw the French flying from the entrenchment below also and had an opportunity of cutting them off or driving the greatest part into the hands of the 52nd, who were in the ravines beyond the tableland upon which the French were retreating. I looked for my reserve under Major Duffy, but I was told it was dispersed; I could therefore do no more. How or why my reserve was dispersed, so contrary to my orders and without any apparent necessity, I never could learn.

Nevertheless I had with six companies (my own four and the two under Captain Murchison) stormed the rocks in twenty minutes from the time I first jumped into the lower part; I took about 100 prisoners and the violence of the action may be judged by the loss; 67 men and 11 officers of the 43rd having been killed or wounded and of the 11 officers, four were killed on the spot or died next day of their wounds and two others were so desperately wounded as to be reported killed.[34] I do not think if Lord Wellington had witnessed the action, he would have mentioned it in the dispatches.

A poignant moment involving young Edward Freer apparently occurred the night before this battle:

> Major Napier was stretched on the ground under a large cloak, when young Freer came to him and crept under the cover of his cloak, sobbing as if his heart would break. In his endeavours to soothe and comfort the boy, Napier learnt from him that he was firmly persuaded he should lose his life in the approaching battle and his distress was caused by thinking of his mother and sisters in England.[35]

William wrote home soon after the action, deeply affected at the loss of so many close friends:

> France, Camp 1 league in front of San Pe[e-sur-Nivelle] [12 November 1813]
> My dearest Caroline,
> I am safe after a good deal of hard fighting. This I hope will reach you before the news of the battle and save you the danger of a shock. I am much afraid that some foolish report will reach you, as I had a very narrow escape and it was reported during the action that I was killed. This is all I have to say for myself. Well, I am not; my head is actually turning round with the misery I suffer from the death of so many friends; at the head of these you will see Lloyd;[36] but two really perfect friends, and one year has laid them both in the grave. Of two boys that I have brought up in my company for 4 years, who have been in every action with me, and who were my constant companions, that I looked upon as my younger brothers, one is killed, and the other so dangerously wounded that it is next to impossible that he can serve again. Barnard, for whom I had a very great admiration, and really loved, is also wounded in such a manner that I expect to hear [of] his death every moment.[37] Captain Murchison, another friend and companion of 11 years' standing, with every good quality, died in great agony yesterday from his wounds. What misery, that the very number of my losses have left me hardly a point to fix upon to rest my grief! Poor Lloyd! this is the deepest; but I cannot understand it yet, I must understand that every friend is dead, that five people that I loved and spoke to in health but a few hours back, should be all dead or dying. How little should I feel the value of living longer myself if it were not for you. But there is a sensation for you that I feel keenly above any other feeling, which breaks through that dead horrible sensation that this crush of feeling has caused. God bless you my angel Caroline, pity your unhappy husband, but do not forget that your health and happiness are necessary to his existence. Yours William.

Arcangues, 24 November 1813
My dearest Caroline,
We have had an affair yesterday[38] which has caused me much mortification. We were meant to take possession of a ridge for our outposts, which we did with a loss of less than ten men; but the general that we had [mis]understood what they wanted, and instead of halting us, allowed us to halt ourselves. Some young sanguine officers who are more vain than good, concluded that with 3 or four companies[39] they could drive the whole French army before them; the result was that I have lost 75 men more than I did in the last action; poor Bailey[40] who you will remember dined twice with us, was killed and Hobkirk[41] dangerously wounded and is taken prisoner with a good number of men; another officer also wounded.[42] And I run much risk of being called the cause of the misfortune, as I know that generals sometimes never scruple to tell a lye [sic] to save their own credit. They have already thrown the whole blame upon those officers who went forward, forgetting that they themselves were the original and principal cause of it all[43] from ignorance in not knowing where to stop, or pointing out what they wished to have done to anybody; nay, I believe they did not know that any mischief had been done until they were told of it, for they came smiling up to me as if they had done great things in getting 100 yards of ground with the loss of 3 brave officers and 75 men. I know not what Lord Wellington will say to it, but for my part I will not be abused for other people's faults. God bless you dearest Caroline your affectionate husband W Napier.

Arbonne, France, 27 November 1813
My dearest Caroline,
I wrote to you a hurried letter 3 days ago, when my mind was agitated with the events that had just occurred ... I have heard from Hobkirk, who is not badly wounded and whom I hope we shall be able to get exchanged; he has been as usual very well treated by the French, who I am sorry to say exceed us considerably in their attention to officers who are made prisoner. Torrens flatters me much, but old birds are not to be caught with chaff. I am recommended for a lieutenant colonelcy; and I trust a peace will put an end to all anxiety on that head. Emily's[44] letter I did not answer ... she says that my father & General Moore would not have quitted, or approved of my quitting. I cannot take her word for my father and as for Moore, he was an enthusiast about the Army, I am not ... Yours my darling love for ever William.

Battle of the Nive, 9–13 December 1813

Arbonne, 14 December 1813
My dearest Caroline,
… We have had 5 days of constant fighting, sometimes one wing and sometimes the other, of the army. Nothing decisive has happened, but both sides have suffered considerably; the enemy much the most, but ours is nevertheless I should guess 5,000 men. Tom Napier[45] is hit rather badly, his arm broke near the elbow, not in two, but the bone splintered; he will not lose it however. I hope *I* have not been mistaken, for him. I was *very slightly* wounded in the hip, a ball having grazed against a gravestone in the churchyard and struck me there. I would not return myself for fear of alarming you; but I tell you upon my honour, that it is no more than what I say; so you see I am not so vain as you imagine, having given up that feather in my cap to please the little lady in the straw. My horse was wounded also the day before I was, so you must be so good as to divide your sorrow between us. I must not tell a lye [sic] however; some vanity lyes [sic] the bottom. We Napiers are supposed to be always wounded; now, if I returned myself as such and people afterwards saw me walking about with a wound in the hip, they would say *we* were a damned humbugging set, and that would not do either. After all I do believe I am as vain as my neighbours, and nearly as besotted about the name of Napier as some of my *cousins* can be about the name of Fox.

Pitty 'ittle 'ady will so get well and tell me so, for I don't half like you at present; any more than I do Lord Wellington's dispatch about Petite La Rhune; I don't want to brag, but the best thing done upon the 10 November 1813, was the attack of the 43rd Light Infantry upon the said place, and he has not done us the honour to mention our names, while the only two regiments he has praised are two that were most uncommonly well *beaten* the same day. However, if he gives us a medal for the last five days, and one for the 10th, I shall only want *one* for a cross;[46] and then what a fine wench you will be; only *I bar* giving my cross to the baby to *bite* after the manner of ladies in general, who think nothing *too fine* to put on their little ugly heads, nothing too good to wipe their snotty noses and nothing too valuable to give them to put in their drivelling mouths.

March is come out again; you never told me that he called upon you and saw you. If it was not that you are so ugly that I can trust *him*, I should be very jealous. Goodbye darling, your own William.

18 December 1813
My dearest Caroline,
… Wells will purchase and I shall not get a lieutenant colonelcy *without* purchase, having now sent in my name. This is no matter as I don't want one out of the regiment, but what is matter, is that having in one month asked if I might be allowed to sell commissions which I did not purchase, purely on account of ill health; the next month (being refused), I send in my name to purchase; nothing could be more inconsistent and Torrens naturally concludes that I am not sick at all, indeed I can hardly think that you yourself believe that sickness was the principal cause of my wish to quit. The army and I are not at all surprised to find that Emily viewed it in a false light, send to Greenwood to withdraw my name directly and to say that it was a mistake, as I would not give 6d for a lieutenant colonelcy … Yours affectionately W Napier.

Arbonne, 24 December 1813
My dearest Caroline,
… Poor Tom Napier has lost his arm, his left above the elbow, but is doing as well as possible and is to get the brevet. The dispatch with my recommendation was taken by the French, which accounts for the delay …

George, having gone to Edinburgh and married Frances Dorothea Blencowe who had previously been married to William Freeman, was appointed Deputy Adjutant General in the Yorkshire District, who were quartered at York. George then resumes his memoir:

After remaining at York about eight months, I became effective major in the 1st battalion 52nd Regiment, which battalion being in Spain, it was necessary to join immediately. This was a severe blow to my poor wife, who did not expect to part so soon; but as she loved me with a pure and ardent affection, she was as anxious about my honour and fame as I was myself, and never for one moment let me see or be aware of what misery she endured … although I had received a letter, by the Duke of York's command, from the Adjutant General permitting me to remain upon the Staff at home, as his Royal Highness considered the loss of my arm entitled me to do so. But my wife well knew my sentiments upon that point and how strongly I had censured others for not joining their regiments, so she made up her mind to bear it …

Chapter 9

The Chesapeake Campaign 1813

While William continued to serve in Spain and southern France, albeit with serious reluctance; and George remained in Yorkshire, Charles had proceeded with his regiment to Bermuda, little suspecting that he would very soon be heavily involved in the war against America. However, from his journal, it is clear that his initial concern was maintaining discipline within his regiment:

13 February 1813 The drunkenness of my regiment is beyond endurance. After doing all that was possible to stop it, I warned them that the lash would be used, for drink was killing them, and discipline was subverted. My boast had been that the young ones should never see a bloody back, and the drummers here did not know how to go about it …

He confirmed his concerns in a letter, but also his hopes:

February. All hope of reclaiming my men is not extinct. Severity of punishment and disgracing all when one sins has had an effect, for Pat fears odium for getting his comrades into trouble, more than punishment. He does some moody mischief in his cups, but it is horrible to flog him when you know he is as sorry as possible himself. There are however, always some ruffians who may be flogged with satisfaction. One of the 98th was lately wounded by me with a bayonet and beaten besides, which saved him from a flogging. Before my eyes the ruffian, after beating his wife, gave her a kick which absolutely lifted her from the ground, and then before he could be reached, jumped twice upon her breast with thick shoes, leaping high up to crush her! I laid open his head with a bayonet instead of stabbing him; but that, with another blow, served to make a show to the court and saved his back; however he was cut enough, for any act short of the one he committed. He was so frightened at my striking him down that he conquered his passion; had he struck me I would have killed him on the spot, and even wished he had given me occasion.[1] Had you heard the horrible shrieks of the woman, till her breath was stamped out, and seen the rascal's violence and face, you would have thought, as I did, that her days were numbered. Mr Burke of the 98th was the villain; he was not drunk, she had merely contradicted him. This kind of man it gives me pleasure to flog, and no regiment is without several. There were in the 50th grenadiers two murderers; one of them murdered two wives; his name was Campbell and he deliberately shot the last at Lisbon; how he escaped hanging is inconceivable: the first he strangled in bed. This letter is filled with Paddy's tricks, which I hope to get out of him with as little flogging as possible. Poor fellows, with all their sins they are fine soldiers, and their blood should be kept for better use than being drawn with a cat-o'-nine-tails. I allow them to box, it is the best issue for the rum, and such a parade of black eyes was never before beheld. Oh! Pat thou art a very odd fish, very odd.

He continued in a letter to his mother, with hopes of commanding a commerce raiding force:

May. ... I would prefer fighting Americans with the 102nd, to fighting French with the 50th for a while. What is truly hateful is, sojourning in Bermuda. I would rather fight neither, but stay quiet in England till in better bodily strength for a hard campaign; chance must decide, but for interest America is the game; and if made prisoner there it will not be eternal captivity as in France. This is an inexpressible advantage to me, who shudder at the idea of being taken again by the French. I have doubts as to accepting quarter, so great is my horror. However, always on going into action, my song is, that I shall be as well off as a canary bird, so it is a folly to fret.

To be afloat with a thousand light infantry and two pieces of cannon, and allowed to land where it pleased me and be off again is my wish. A force of that kind might pay itself and save government the expense; not by plunder, which is horrid and leads to every dreadful crime, but by contributions, levied by the magistrates. I would not take a man's purse myself, but would have no objection to make his own magistrate levy a tax and remit it to government. This predatory warfare might easily be practiced, but should be carried on by honest men, who would account honourably to government and never make a shilling for themselves; and who would rigidly preserve discipline, otherwise their men would plunder and commit every enormity. I would not take such a command without unrestricted power to execute on the spot any marauder. On expeditions of this kind there should be but one marauder, the king. He has a right to make the enemy defray the expenses of the war, and it would be delightful to have the Americans paying taxes for us. I am not a hater of Yankees though, they are fine fellows, liars it is said, but so are we. You English wise ones, hold Yankee cheaper than he merits, you take him for a dollar when in truth he is a doubloon. My desire is to have command of the Marines that are coming and of the 102nd, and to land, to sack towns and commit all possible enormities on the coast; how delightful to deserve hell by command! By Jove! I am most amiably disposed to maraud and make money of[f] the Yankees. But dearest, blessed mother, to return to you is the first wish of my heart: when this American war is over I must go home or mad.

Soon after he was celebrating the news that he was to go with such a force:

Sir Sydney Beckwith has just come with a force, to whop the Yankees. I go second in command, and am in most excellent tranquil spirits, having much to do.

In another undated letter, he talked of his officers:

A^2 is a fine young fellow and will make a good soldier; a little of a spoiled child now, and don't like drill so well as the Opera; but you may tell mama that he is going on very well and stands a fair chance of losing the genteel slouch he has at present. He is a very fine lad indeed, and no one is more convinced of that than himself; but I like him because he don't sulk at drill though clearly to him a bore. H^3 grows tall, broad, fat, ruddy, attentive and steady; he is one of the best subalterns in the regiment, makes a point of being seldom in the wrong, and of never admitting it if he is. I make counterpoints, of proving to him that he is in the wrong; which proofs though in black and white before his eyes he always rejects; but then he notes down for himself that he was in the wrong and does right another time which is just what I want. Of a third, who wanted promotion he says K^4 is one of the best officers in the regiment; he is nearly six feet high, is in love and in debt: what greater claims can an ensign have? Of a fourth L^5 is always wrong, but means to be always right, and he will be so at last.

Finally, he was able to confirm his role in another letter:

1 June. Beckwith has divided his force into two brigades, the largest under me; the other under Lieutenant Colonel Williams[6] of the Marines. My fear is that my gents maybe too eager; all young soldiers are dangerous in

that way; but ours will be less so than the Americans, for they are young also and without even theory. My regiment will probably do right, but I must be much with the Marines if we engage and shall have all the anxiety of a lady sending her daughter to court the first time. Very anxious also I am, to ascertain my own force in command of an awkward brigade; for the Marines, being ever onboard ship, are necessarily undrilled and the foreigners[7] under me are duberous [sic]. Fight these last shall, all men will fight when they begin, but delay enables rogues to evaporate. My self-confidence makes me wish for the chief command; yet am I fearful of estimating my powers too high, and much I dislike sacking and burning of towns, it is bad employment for British troops. This authorized, perhaps needful plundering, though to think so is difficult, is very disgusting and I will with my own hand, kill any perpetrator of brutality under my command. Nevertheless, a pair of breeches must be plundered, for mine are worn out and better it will be to take a pair, than shock the Yankee dames by presenting myself as a sans-culotte.[8]

Charles now began a regular campaign journal. His first exploit was, however, a signal failure:

22 June 1813. Last night we got into the boats at twelve o'clock, pulled on shore by moonlight, and landed in tolerable confusion at daybreak without opposition. Craney Island[9] was attacked by a force under Captain Pechel RN[10] but a large creek stopped our progress by land and shoal water stopped the boats by sea. A sharp cannonade from the works on the island cost us seventy-one men, without returning a shot! We lost some boats also and re-embarked in the evening with about as much confusion as at landing. We despise the Yankee too much.

26 June. Last night again landed in rather more confusion than on the 22nd; but with the advance we drove away some Yankees, with [the] loss of a few men ourselves, killing many of them. They were inferior in force and of course were beat at every point and lost their guns &c. They would have been all taken but for the extreme thickness of the wood and our local ignorance. Yankee never shews himself, he keeps in the thickest wood, fires and runs off; he is quite right. Local knowledge is very hard to gain, yet we might gain more than we do. We go on badly, and it is hard to say with whom the blame lies; but I think one of our naval leaders is a little deficient in gumption; he has much hurry and little arrangement. On the night of the 26th we embarked in such a style that a hundred bold fellows would have shot one half of our people.[11]

30 June. I am going on a detached expedition, but with no great hopes of doing anything with such a coadjutor. I am to command the troops and yet am kept in profound ignorance of the object and destination!

[16 July?] Returned from Ocracoke,[12] where we took a 20-gun brig and a schooner of 16 guns.[13] Cockburn[14] is no doubt an active good seaman, but has no idea of military arrangements; and he is so impetuous that he won't give time for others to do for him what he cannot or will not do himself. If he had the conducting of any military operation before an active enemy he would get his people cut to pieces. In landing at Ocracoke we were nearly all drowned; the same in coming off. Luck is a good thing and I have it, but it will very quickly play a chief a trick that will ruin him, if he trusts to it, without providing for its ceasing. Cockburn trusts all to luck and makes no provision for failure; this may do with sailors, but not on shore, where hard fighting avails nothing if not directed by mind, and most accurate calculation. The services are very different. Sailors' business is mechanical, and they have no idea of order and system out of their ships. With them subordination does not really exist; tyranny not discipline is their system, generally speaking; and their habits of life appear to me to contract their ideas and destroy their judgment. I find however more mind, more expansion of ideas in the younger officers of the navy, who have not been long enough in it to suffer from the system. I never perceived that any dependence could be placed in a naval captain's accurately fulfilling his orders; this may perhaps do at sea, but our service could not exist with such loose discipline. My regard for the navy officers in general is very great, they are open-hearted, generous-spirited men; but their life is one calculated to injure the mental powers, and turn them from enlarged views of things, and judgment of human nature, to the minutiae of their profession. A captain rules, and all under him rule by force; no one speaks to, or dare be familiar with him; the terrible confinement of a ship renders this necessary they say.

In the army officers are eternally forced to use their judgment in command, and from habitual familiarity have to support themselves against wit and satire, and even impudence at times. A naval officer has only to enforce manual acts of obedience, and being ever in his ship has no eye to trust to but his own. A regimental commander has to convince those under him that his orders are wise, and to procure obedience to them when he is not present. In fine, a soldier's intellect is always exercised in the study of mankind, and a seaman's in the theory or practice of mechanical operations. A proof of this is, that a thousand soldiers on shipboard can be easily managed by their own officers; but put a thousand sailors on shore and their officers cannot manage them; the moment they can elude despotic sway, away they go into excesses. I have however no intention of saying naval officers are less able men than army officers, the generality of men run very equal; but whatever talents a soldier has are called into constant action, whereas sailors sustain the disadvantage of being compelled to keep theirs dormant, which in the study of mankind is a very bad thing. I have no agreement however with those who think navy officers illiberal and self-interested; my feeling is that they are generally more open and generous than soldiers in moral character; and this in face of the advantage our service has as to mental enlargement, arising from habits incident to their respective professions.

Charles wrote home to his sister of these escapades, but still saw no relief from his incessant seasickness:

HM Ship San Domingo, 23 July 1813 (In the Potomac River)

Here I am just arrived my dearest Emily from my expedition to the coast of North Carolina, which was a foolish business, as there were no troops to oppose our landing and nothing to be gained by landing except a little prize money. I am horribly sick always and long to get back to the 50th, for being a *Marine* officer is detestable when a man is so ill as I am. This day completes *the year* since I sailed from Guernsey and I shall probably spend another birthday on the Atlantic, but nought I won't growl. We have [a] nasty sort of fighting here amongst creeks and bushes and by it we lose many men without a *show* or a good fight for it. We have lost in killed and wounded and missing above one hundred men and three officers & have *had* no *battle*. The Yankee get their show though, for at Hampton we *killed on the spot above 100*, but it is an inglorious sort of warfare and though a thousand times better than Bermuda, is not pleasant to anyone who is seasick. We expect to have one or two attacks on the coast more and then go to Halifax. Baltimore is the great point, but it is very strong I am told and likely to hit hard, besides there are seven thousand men there and we have no force like that. I yet am of opinion, *if we tuck up our sleeves and lay our ears back*, we might thrash them if we can get them out of their cursed trees, so as to get a fair slap at them with the bayonet. They fight very unfairly and fire jagged pieces of iron and every sort of devilment they can, nails, broken pokers, old locks of guns, gun barrels, in short anything they think will do mischief. This is against the laws of nations, but as they do it I will make our men do the same. I don't speak from hearsay because onboard a 20-gun ship we took,[15] *I found* this sort of ammunition regularly *prepared*. This is wrong, for a man *delights* in being killed according to the law of nations. Nothing so pleasant or correct, sent to be *doused*, against all rule is quite offensive, a man don't kick like a gentleman. A 24-pound shot in one's stomach is fine, one dies heroically! But to have a *brass candlestick* for stuffing, with a garnish of *rusty two-penny nails*, makes one die as *ungenteely* as if one had a cholick [sic]! The appearance of the American coast is easily described; one great stretch of *flat land, covered with wood* so thick that nothing can pass except in the cleared lanes between *detached houses*, and along the great roads which are very good. I caught a beautiful little *tarapin* [terrapin] or tortoise for you, but he got away from me, he was like the one Blake the dentist had, only much prettier. The fire-flies are beautiful in a dark night, just like millions of flints striking fire. I have seen them in Portugal but not in such quantities. The mocking-bird is pretty and his notes very sweet when he likes, but any bird near gives the *tune* to him. There are humming-birds, but I have not seen any. There is also in Carolina a bird like a *bat* but covered with beautiful green plumage, I only saw the skin of one. Snakes are abundant and very large some of them. There is a shrub here which makes tea, they call it *Wopong*[16] I think, it is reckoned good for the health, particularly in consumptive cases; if I can get seeds from it, I'll send it to you. We have but little opportunity of seeing the country, as we are in danger from the moment we land till we are off. As to making sketches, it is no use, for if you jump in any bramble bush in the thickest wood, you can find there you have a *complete view* of America; if a dry quagmire is near, with lots of frogs and land crabs you are *made*. The Yankees are wretched shooting animals, imagine *me* more thin (if you can), more yellow (if you can) more wrinkled (if you can) or then stretch me out to as [a] tall man & wring me as one does a wet towel and strike my eyes deep in my head and make me *drawl* out every word & call O's A's as *maartal* for mortal; and *Aye* for *I* and lug in '*Aye Swear*' for I calculate, '*I guess*' I swear. When you manufacture me so, you have your Yankee. We have been using Congreve rockets. They are silly things and frighten us, for they often take a wrong direction and come among their friends. We have thank God sent off the Frenchmen, who are the damndest rascals existing. I had not an opportunity of shooting any of them, which I most wished to do, but hope we may catch one of the men who deserted and if we do I'll invite the soldiers [to] put him out of the world that minute. They really murder without any object on earth but the *pleasure of murdering*. One fellow robbed a poor Yankee and pretended all sorts of anxiety for him; but that it was the custom of war to take what a prisoner had, but that he was sorry for him. When he had coaxed Yankee into confidence of his own safety, he told him to walk on before him, to bring him to the general; the poor wretch obeyed, and the moment he turned his back, he just fired his musket into his brains. This is one of many instances in which there was no end, no object but that of *murder*. They intended to desert in a body. I would rather see one Frenchman shot than ten Americans. It is quite shocking to see men, who speak one's own language brought in wounded; one feels as if they were English peasants and I longed at Hampton when the Frenchmen began firing, to make the 102nd give a volley into them. Everyone feels more inclined to shoot a *Johnny Crapeau* than a Yankee. I am in great hopes we shall go to Canada, for I see we shall do *nothing here*. Our force is ill composed and not capable of doing what our numbers should accomplish, for the Marines though brave and well-appointed are ill disciplined, their life having passed onboard ships, we must understand that on land they are *unmanageable*. You have requested me to give you an instance of the dangers occasioned by awkward troops. At Craney Island my brigade, on which the loss all fell, the other not having been brought up, stood in a road when a battery opened on us, the first shot however enfiladed the road and killed a light infantry sergeant of the 102nd who was with me. I instantly ordered the brigade to file into a wood where the enemy could not strike us, I suspected. The 102nd executed this order instantly and were safe, but the Marines were all in a fuss & could not move for a quarter of an hour, the consequence of which was that the battery threw discharges of grape & round shot into the very thick of them, which wounded and killed 8 or 9 men, without many more who was hurt the whole day, except 2 light infantry sergeants of the 102nd who were hit unavoidably. One is well again, but my favourite one was killed, both his legs being shot off close to his body. Good God! what a horrid sight it was! And to that added to the misery of the news, was that the Yankees kept pelting us at his ease, for not a single shot could we give in return, for we had no guns and were too far for musketry, with a wood between us, and I would have soon got close to them and wipe off scores. Only imagine how pleasant for me to see these poor devils hit & find every exertion to move them out of the fire impossible, from their want of drill and what was of no small consequence to me, expecting to be minus a leg myself every moment; fortunately, the Yankees did not see the powerful effect of his shot and some I conclude *see'd*, though they did not protect us. We therefore ceased fire after the 3rd or fourth discharge, or we should have lost a great number of men. Though the 102nd have been more in fire than any other regiment, we have had only three killed & wounded. Sir John Warren[17] is very civil to me, Pechell also and the whole of the Navy are determined to work well with us, but somehow we have no arrangement. Nothing so regular as a ship, yet the captains when *out* of their ships have no method and will make sad work in landing the boats, all get in confusion & I fear some fine morning we shall get cut up. You can hardly imagine anything more interesting than our landings, it has been done always by moonlight and the numbers of boats all filled with armed men, gliding in silence along the smooth waters, with their arms glittering in the moonshine, the oars just breaking the stillness of night, the dark shade of the woods we are pushing for and the expected danger. Then suddenly, '*Cast off*' the rapid dash of oars instantly begins, with quick '*Hurrah! Hurrah! Hurrah!*' as fast as the rowers pull to shore. Then the soldiers rushing into and through the water altogether has great effect. We have generally two or three miles to row, the boats are tied together and we push quite slow; but when in reach of shot of the shore every boat is cast loose, and they pull furiously with shouts; except the 102nd, *who no shouting has!* I forbid all noise till they can rush on the enemy and then they have leave to give a *deadly screech* and away! away!

There are numbers of officers, of the navy in particular, whose families are American, and their fathers in one or two instances absolutely living in the very towns we are trying to burn. Even Sir Sydney Beckwith has relatives in America; it is certainly a most unnatural war, a sort of bastard rebellion. At Ocracoke I flatter myself, I put a *stop to plunder*, and though I assure you the people were treated *too well*, being paid nearly *double* for everything and the soldiers kept in perfect order, yet I am told I shall be abused in the American papers as a perfect savage, the same way as Sir J[ohn] W[arren] and Admiral Cockburn were. There was one atrocious attempt by a 102nd soldier (I believe) to murder a man. I unfortunately could not detect the villain; but we took all care of the man who was hurt, and the whole of his family and himself were quite grateful to us. We offered to take him on board & cure and set him on shore anywhere he chose, and the Admiral gave him 8 pounds. If we are therefore abused, the Yankee papers are as great liars as the English, greater they cannot be.

Now God bless you my sweetest Emily, I have chatted nonsense enough I think, for whilst you may thank or abuse the *calm weather* which gives me a short respite from sea sickness, give my love to dear Anne who I hope recovers. God bless her & you (you see I do pray sometimes) though a vile buccaneer chieftain, a regular '*Mop trooping Scot*', your affectionate Charles Napier

Tell Aunt I don't bayonet many children out of regard for her. I have (with shame I confess my sins) *kissed* 3 or 4 to quiet them, poor little things, *they* never saw red-coated men and thought the terrible English would cut them up.

Charles returned to his journal:

12 August. We left Kent Island[18] to land near St. Michael's town.[19] There were five hundred men there and a few guns. I wanted to attack the place with the 102nd alone (250 men) to clear them of the Queen's Town[20] business and intending to make them do all with the bayonet; of success I had no doubt, and it would have been a brilliant close to the expedition. We were only four miles from the town, the men were steady and eager, and it might have been done in five hours. I would have attacked three times our number of Yankees with confidence, but Beckwith was resolved to let nothing take place; he would neither let me go with the 102nd and two field-pieces, nor yet with the whole of our force. However, hearing they had a camp of five hundred men four miles on the other side, he placed himself with two battalions of Marines and one gun on the road, and detached me with the 102nd and two companies of Marines to attack it, meaning himself to intercept any attempts to unite with the camp from the town. This supposed camp proved to be a miserable picquet, which fled, and I had still some hopes of a stroke at the town, but he would not consent, though the admiral pressed him strongly. We re-embarked, having landed for no purpose, done nothing, and retired to our ships with the Yankee videttes quietly following, to see us off!

I have never said anything publicly, but am inclined to think that more might have been done in the Chesapeake; but whether doing more would be doing good, is a point to dispute. Taking an extended view of the expedition, as a diversion in favour of Canada, it was a complete one; but it ended too soon or too late:- too late if the troops were to be afterwards sent to Canada for reinforcing Sir George Prevost;[21] too soon if not to go there. With a different arrangement we might have done both. The alarm on the coast might have been kept up with six hundred men, allowing the two Marine battalions to go at first to the lakes; or, if a serious attack had been designed against Norfolk, the Marines might have gone to Halifax, and regulars been drawn thence. Again; leaving Halifax for a time to its militia, the whole military force might have united and have taken Norfolk easily. Our attack on Craney Island was silly. Had Norfolk been decently attacked it would not have resisted ten minutes; had we landed a gun,

Craney was gone; had we attacked at high tide it was gone; still it was the wrong place to attack, we should not have lost more men in striking at the town. But the faults of this expedition sprung from one simple cause; there were three commanders! It was a council of war, and what council of war ever achieved a great exploit?

Had either Sir John Warren, Sir Sydney Beckwith or Admiral Cockburn acted singly and without consultation, we should not have done such foolish things. Sir Sydney wanted neither head, nor heart, nor hand for his business; but he was not free to do what he thought wise, and run sulky when required to do what he deemed silly, which in my opinion made it more silly. He is certainly a very clever fellow, but a very odd fish. I like him, yet do not like to serve under him in his Chesapeake fashion. He ought to have hanged several villains at Little Hampton; had he so done, the Americans would not have complained; but every horror was committed with impunity, rape, murder, pillage; and not a man was punished!

I have learned much on this expedition; how to embark and disembark large bodies in face of an enemy; how useless it is to have more than one commander; how necessary it is that the commanders by sea and land should agree and have one view; finally never to trust Admiral Cockburn. All this has been learned by seeing our faults, for we have done nothing but commit blunders. Nothing was done with method, all was hurry, confusion and long orders. If the Yankees are worth their salt, they will give us a thrashing yet in one of our landings, going as we do like a flock of sheep instead of rowing ashore in lines. I have always thrown myself into the woods with any men that could be first got together, to cover the formation of the others from the boats, which never has been effected under half an hour; and had Jonathan come down to the water's edge or to his waist in it, he would have destroyed half our men; our soldiers themselves grow frightened at the evident want of arrangement. Why not land in order of battle? It was so in Egypt.

Well! whatever horrible acts were done at Hampton they were not done by the 102nd, for they were never let to quit their ranks, and they almost mutinied at my preventing them joining in the sack of that unfortunate town. The Marine artillery behaved like soldiers; they had it in their power to join in the sack and refused. I said to that noble body of men, I cannot watch your conduct, but trust you will not join those miscreants. They called out, *'Colonel we are picked men, we blush for what we see, depend upon us, not a man of the Marine artillery will plunder. We are well paid by His Majesty and we will not disgrace him or ourselves by turning robbers and murderers. Whatever you order we will execute'*. Never in my life have I met soldiers like the Marine artillery. We suffered much fatigue and hardship, but never was seen anything not admirable in these glorious soldiers; should my life extend to antediluvian years,[22] their conduct at Little Hampton will not be forgotten by me.

22 August 1813, *HMS San Domingo*

At last our expedition is over my beloved Emily, except one attack we have to make previous to our going to Halifax and it is one of little danger or use. We are now sailing down the Chesapeake most beautifully. On the 13th we had a touch at the Yankees which I think I told you of. We got into confusion in a thick wood in the night, fired on one another, killing & wounding several of our own folks. How the officers escaped God knows but we did (Beckwith's horse was shot though by a Marine) 7 Yankees were killed and many wounded and so ended our *raid* from Kent Island to Queenstown on the Maine. I rejoice at the expedition being closed for the present as I hope to see my name in the 50th before operations begin again, for reasons which would not be wise to trust to a letter and moreover I really suffer so much at sea that I am very unfit for a *Marine*. The fortnight we were on shore at Kent Island has quite recovered me, I am pretty well as to health, at least I have one satisfaction, I find I can bear any great fatigue and be the better for it and that it is the being at sea that made me so ill and therefore only local illness. The day we went to Queenstown I must have walked at least 30 miles, besides the fatigue which arises from anxiety of mind, which to a certain degree must attach to every military operation, yet when I returned after being from 8 o'clock in the evening of the 12th to ten o'clock in the morning of the 13th on my feet, I was no more tired than if I had walked 3 miles and got on my horse & rode 6 miles, so you see I am not very bad, but the instant I come onboard I do suffer terribly and am so horribly low spirited. I rejoice for another reason at our having finished, I do not like what is perhaps a necessary part of our job, viz plundering & ruining the peasantry. We drive all their cattle and of course ruin them; and though I have clean hands as to individual plunder, I hate to see the poor Yankees robbed, and to be the *robber*. If we could take fairly I would not mind, but the rich ones escape; for the loss of a few cows and oxen is nothing to a rich one, but you ruin a peasant if you take his only cow. If the Government of America repay them and levy the whole loss like a tax I have no sorrow for them, but I am sorry for the wretches we punish in so individual a manner. However, no outrage has been committed on *persons*, though much on property unavoidably. I have taken off a horse, but I paid for him and made the Yankees put the value on him. By the way, I did try to steal a dog who would be stole and had no master; most beautiful, and who took a fancy to me and swam a mile and a half after us when we came away, but my conscience grew restive on the beach and I would not take him, for which I am very sorry, and wish my honesty at the devil; and if a boat goes on shore again, damn my wig but I'll steal the doggie; he liked to come and has a right to choose his master. I have not time to write more, so God bless you my dear Emily, give my love to dearest aunt and believe me ever your affectionate C Napier.

Camp above Halifax [Nova Scotia], 24 September 1813
My dearest [sister],
Let me give you an abstract of our proceedings, for I cannot promise you a detail, as it would not be amusing to you and very difficult to me. We left Chesapeake Bay, after a toilsome and exceedingly useless landing near St Michael's town after a voyage of a week in very fine weather and during which I was not sick 'that is *not* to *say sick*', but not quite *well*, we entered this harbour on the 20th of September after being on board since the *8th of June*, and on the 20th pitched our tents on a hill, in Nova Scotia, with the thermometer at 38°[F, 3°C]; after being in hot ships, with the thermometer at 96°[F, 36°C], a week before, and never under 80°[F, 27°C] for the six months in those latitudes. Now if our constitutions weather it they are *elegant adamants*. When we wake in the morning it is quite a concert to hear 1,600 men's teeth all chatter together, it screws my wounded cheek up wickedly; but as soldiers can't choose climate, and I don't think soldiers live long now-a-days, I have iron enough in me to knock off 20 years yet, if lead don't shorten the date. I wish Torrens & Louis Chabot[23] would let me into the 50th, I am heartily sick of this Transatlantic service and observe to *make it delightful* my last letter [received] bore date 6th of April! After this two packets were taken, a third sailed from hence to Bermuda, with all our letters 2 days before we arrived here, and the fourth came in yesterday (in twenty-nine days from England) and *not a line* from a mortal *for me*. No! not even from a dun![24] I would have given a guinea for a taylor's [sic] bill even. In short, I am afraid of a packet after so long a silence of 6 long *months*. The mischief is that I shall never get home, for nothing but getting into the *50th* can bring me home.

In April [1814] I expect to move with this brigade which I command (for Beckwith goes to Canada in two days) to Quebec. I shall not dislike this so much as being *afloat* and that I cannot stand, but fear I shall be so all winter. If I had any hopes of doing good I should not mind, but if Beckwith was too weak with the *whole* of our force to effect any action of consequence, what can I do with a smaller force? For he takes the 2nd battalion of Marines with him and a company of artillery, so that I shall not have above *1,000* men & 13 pieces of artillery. With this force wherever we land the Yankee *runs* away; and if he is decidedly able to face us, in *his* opinion he will not have less than *5,000* men, behind strong fortifications and heavy and numerous artillery. If I could get 5,000 in the open field I would not fear to attack them, but behind works, such an attempt would be throwing away lives without a hope of success. One may say, you may easily conceive that I speak as one who would willing[ly] try much for his own sake, and indeed for all our sakes, for our men are *tired* of *expecting* a fight and having had none of consequence. I believe it is good to indulge John Bull's taste for blood now and then. Had Moore sacrificed an army instead of saving one, he would have been perfect in the eyes of his country. Nothing but his unpardonable humanity, which fancied England cared for her *soldiers* as *he did*, would have made him act as he did. Had he saved his own life and contrived to get 20,000 men bayoneted, (and I firmly believe he was the only man in our army who could have saved us) he would have done England a job she would have made him anything he wished. But alas for her, he thought of everything but himself. Fortunately another hero has shone forth, but we wanted both. By the way what will be the result of Lord Wellington's great victory at Vitoria & the *greater* one we have an impertinent rumour of here? I expect to be up the Missouri and Mississippi Rivers in the course of 3 months, making a diversion in the *south*. I get a little sketch in your books now & then just to remember you. God bless you my precious Em, I do think I see your beloved face before me every night & morning when my mind rests from the worry of business & people I don't care for, and turns to all I love on earth, then the faces I love come to me and tell me a soldier is a miserable exile, labouring in his bloody vocation, living to destroy & destroying to live & yet you know I hate it so I won't say a word more.

Charles wrote his reflections on the Chesapeake campaign:

A commander should use his best troops at the outset; success then will give spirit, and though the loss of good men is to be regretted, yet the saving them for harder work creates that work, and in the sequel greater loss is incurred. If I go to the south, as Sir John Warren proposes, my intent is to give the 102nd the lead in every attack, they are better disciplined, more obedient and handy than the Marine battalions, and will if the first blow succeed, try anything. The Marines will thus be excited to emulation, and will soon be well in hand, for they are willing to learn. The stupid Craney Island blundering has indeed damped us all, but the 102nd have a good spirit and will, like all young soldiers, dash boldly; they know I had nothing to do with [the] Craney blunders, and their confidence in me is not lost. My design is to fall on some place where we can easily succeed, and then try some tougher job, for a successful skirmish gives the spirit which secures victory in a hotter day.

Our good admirals are such bad generals, there is little hope of doing more than being made prisoners on the best terms. We shall form three plans, or as many as there are admirals; and to these mine will be added. From all, perhaps all bad, a worse will be concocted and of course fail. We failed at Craney, because two admirals and a general commanded, and a republic of commanders means defeat. I have seen enough to refuse a joint command if ever offered to me; it is certain disgrace and failure from the nature of things; the two services are incompatible. A navy officer steps on shore, and his zeal, his courage, his ignorance of troops and the very nature of a campaign, makes him think you are timid. Discontent follows and if it does not alter your views, it certainly augments your difficulties to find an adviser, or opposer, in one whose rank entitles him to speak strongly, though his habits have not enabled him to be the judge he thinks himself. For the same reason, a landsman onboard a ship has no right to speak or advise. If I command this expeditionary force my request to Sir John Warren shall be, not to let any naval officer land except one or two of my own choosing, who will, and who do, for I have my eye on them, think themselves sailors, not soldiers. A general in a blue coat or an admiral in a red one is mischief!

Reflection has strengthened my first resolution. If we attack New Orleans, or New London, on our road, as the general talk indicates, the 102nd shall lead everywhere. My regret will be keen at losing those fine fellows in greater proportion than the rest, but the first blow is half the battle. I will not however let them be used to attack armed vessels; let the sailors and Marines work at their own trade. I have no prejudice against blue jackets, but hate to have men attempt what they cannot understand. We who spend our lives in trying to be soldiers make but bad ones; how can sailors suddenly start into generals?

Yet Cockburn thinks himself a Wellington! And Beckwith is sure the navy never produced such an admiral as himself! Between them we got beaten at Craney. But even now the notion of attacking New Orleans is only known to me from officers who hear it talked of in the streets. We always take care to knock at a man's door and say, *'Good sir, barricade and load your blunderbuss, we are coming to rob and murder you at night.*' Great therefore as this command is, for me my hope is not to go, being sure such bad arrangements as were made in the Chesapeake and at Ocracoke will not succeed. I do not know if my head is strong for good arrangements, but it can certainly note bad and their effects in perspective. Cockburn's confidence in his luck is the very thing most to be feared; it is worse than 1,000 Yankees. Luck is a good thing on a pinch, but sometimes it gives a pinch! I suspect it is inclined to follow good arrangements.

Chapter 10
Southern France 1814

George returned to the Peninsula carrying dispatches to the Duke:

On the 1 January 1814, I went to Falmouth; embarked, encountered a severe gale of wind and was nearly lost; but in five days from the time I left London carrying dispatches to Lord Wellington, I delivered them to his lordship at St Jean de Luz in the Pyrenees. The next day I left headquarters, and arrived at the cantonments of the Light Division, where I found my friend Colborne in command of a brigade and in consequence I had the command of the regiment, to my very great satisfaction. Here we remained a few weeks till the rains were over, which are so constant and heavy at that season in the Basque country that all the roads are rendered impracticable for any army to march on, and consequently we were forced to remain quiet. While here, Lord March came and asked my advice about joining the regiment, in which he was a captain, in order to learn his duty practically as a light infantry officer, he having been always on the Staff of Lord Wellington. I strongly advised him to do so, and he took my advice like a good soldier as he ever proved himself to be. Just before the weather cleared up and we were in daily expectation of advancing, a senior officer[1] to Colonel Colborne joined the division, so he lost the command of the brigade and I that of the regiment. In consequence of this, Sir Edward Pakenham, the Adjutant General of the army and my intimate friend, spoke to Lord Wellington to place me on the General Staff, and I was much surprised at seeing myself in orders as Assistant Adjutant General to the 6th Division. This being quite unsolicited by me was very kind and flattering in the commander in chief and Sir Edward Pakenham; but I did not like leaving my old regiment and the Light Division, where I was certain of seeing all the fighting that might take place, so I wrote to beg leave to decline the situation, and this being acquiesced in, though not without a good deal of correspondence and remonstrance upon the part of my sincere and kind friend Sir Edward, I remained as second in command of the regiment, most of my friends thinking me very foolish to give up so good a Staff appointment. My reason for it was that the great object of my wishes was to get the command of a light infantry regiment, and I knew that the best way to qualify myself for it was by doing regimental duty in the regiment and the division I was then in. I also knew that the Duke of York wished officers to remain with their regiments, and that by doing so his Royal Highness would be more inclined to give me the command I wished than if I went upon the Staff; and I was right, for I received a very flattering letter from the Duke's [Military] Secretary, Colonel [Henry] Torrens, written by his command, to inform me that he was highly pleased with my declining the Staff situation and remaining with my regiment; that he wished so good an example was more followed, and that his Royal Highness would take the first opportunity of showing his sense of my conduct. My kind and valued friend Sir Edward Pakenham was at first vexed with me, but as anger never entered the breast of that most delightful of all characters, he very quickly forgave me; and as I shall not have another opportunity of mentioning him, I must here describe him.

... As soon as the rainy season had a little abated we were put in movement, as Lord Wellington was determined to give Soult no rest. We made a delightful march through a most beautiful country about Pau and had famous quarters in the Basque towns and villages, where we got plenty to eat and drink; and as we paid well the people were very civil and even kind, for they looked upon us as the harbingers of *peace*, Napoleon's star being on the wane. Besides, the whole French nation was tired of war, endless war! particularly as '*La Belle France*' was full of foreign enemies of all nations and her citizens now felt at their own doors the horrid evils of war and suffered in proportion as they had devastated other countries, by whose armies France was now in her turn scourged on every side ...

William continued his flow of letters home to Caroline from the final campaign:

1 January 1814
My dearest Caroline,
We have had no fighting since I last wrote to you & I hope we shall have none as the speech of Bonaparte is so pacific; I suppose the Allies will not be fools enough to follow the ravings of our beasts of newspapers. I have had no letters later than the 7 December, a long time and a very anxious one for me, my love ... I have been just breaking a muleteer's neck for beating his mule unmercifully. I pulled him off into the mud and his head stuck so firmly in it that I forgot he was *killing*, but the doctor was by and he recovered, much against my inclination. You know I am a beast about animals. Yours my own darling Carro, W Napier.

9 January 1814
My dearest Caroline,
... Lord Castlereagh has arrived at Morlaix to negotiate, and I think peace must be the consequence. If it is not, I *will* quit the Army, sell or no sell. We have had a bad 4 days' of operations; Raining in bivouacs in January is bad fun. Soult made some move and we opposed it; it ended in smoke, and the delightful news that my Lord was at Morlaix, from Soult himself ... Yours W Napier.

Arrauntz, 15 January 1814
My dearest Caroline,
... George came here about 4 days ago looking very well. He brought me the latest letter from you. Send the enclosed letter to Margaret,[2] who has laid me under contribution for a correspondence on the state of George's health at all times; but as I look upon it as a tyranny, I shall shake off the yoke as soon as possible, as the man is able and willing to write himself ... Tom Napier goes home shortly, and you must have a knife like George's ready for him when he calls upon you and if you should be at Stone Hall, send it to my mother who will give it to him. Patrickson I am told is going to sail for this country; when he *comes* I shall go home *cierto*,[3] as any refusal to give me leave shall be followed up by my resignation. When I go, I give my chestnut mare, who is without exception the best in Europe, to March and my grey one to George. This is very extravagant as they are worth 200 guineas; but March gave me one once, and George you know has a right to the other, and the honourable money has made you so rich that we shan't starve; besides my beasties will be better taken care of as gifts than they would be as sales, because they can't be bad people that I make presents to. Margaret has persuaded George that he has no money and must starve in a little time, and it is very funny to see the distress he is in, between his fears and his natural disposition, which leads him to be more than liberal. One of his ways to prevent expense was funny enough; for fear things should be dearer at quarters than at St Jean de Luz, he bought at the last as much as would feed his whole regiment for a month ... Poor Lady Elizabeth Monck's brother, Saunders Gore,[4] was murdered by some Spanish soldiers in the most inhuman manner at Vitoria the other day, not secretly but by order of the governor, who sent an Alcalde or constable with four soldiers to his house to force a girl who lived with him away. Gore very naturally drove them out of the town but as he was shutting the outer door after having done so, they fired at him and killed him, *nothing of course* will be done to punish them and the only chance

that I see of revenge is that the Spanish people are going to declare war on England and if they only do it before we embark, what a dressing we will give them. Yours my darling ever William.

6 February 1814
My dearest Caroline,
… The people of Bayonne sent word to their friends here last night that peace was signed upon the 1st of February: this I take to be premature, but I have no doubt it will take place soon … ever my darling your own William.

Arrauntz, 12 February 1814
My dearest Caroline,
… Your fears of no peace seem to have too much foundation, but I am rather amused at the march you have cut out for us across France, all at the order of Bunbury, forgetting that it is 400 miles, and that *one* Soult has 60,000 men, whose leave we must ask first, and that we have not above 50,000 as a recommendation to him; nevertheless I will not conceal from you that I think it very likely we may make a march towards Bordeaux soon, but I hope the peace may still take place [in] time enough to stop us … my darling soul William.

George wrote in detail:

Battle of Orthez, 27 February 1814

At Orthez, a town in France about twenty miles from Pau, we came up with Marshal Soult's army, which was posted on a long range of very high ground, with a large plain in its rear over which passed the roads to Bayonne, Bordeaux and Toulouse; and in front of the enemy's position and immediately in its centre was a deep marsh through which ran a small rivulet, but of no note; indeed, in summer it is dry. On the right was a village in which Soult had placed a very heavy column of infantry and artillery. This he considered the key of his position, as he did not fear for his front or centre in consequence of the marshy ground. His left was just above the town of Orthez which he held, and here he had placed General Foy with a strong force also. Our army, which had passed the river during the morning at various fords (and which I am surprised that Soult permitted us to do so easily), had assembled in different columns, waiting the order of attack. General Picton's column was on the right, facing the enemy's left; the Light Division, consisting principally of the 52nd Regiment (as the 43rd had gone to the rear for clothing), was to attack the centre of the French in line; and General Cole commanded the left column which was to attack the village already mentioned on the enemy's right. While we were waiting for the signal to attack, I happened to be near Lord Wellington who was observing the enemy with his telescope, and perceiving an alteration in Marshal Soult's movements, he immediately altered the plan of his own attack and ordered the 52nd Regiment to form line and march straight through the marsh and attack the centre of the enemy's position without delay. In a few minutes we were in full march, up to our knees every step in the bog, the enemy pouring a heavy and well-directed fire upon us from the height above, which we could not return. I never saw our fellows behave more steadily or more gallantly; but owing to the ground, our line was not very *correct*. My horse floundered in the bog, and in spite of all my spurring and Lord March's beating and kicking him, we could not make the poor brute stir, so I was obliged to leave him to my servant and take his. At last, we made the enemy retire and gained the brow of the hill, and then dressed our line and commenced a heavy rolling fire in our turn, advancing at the same time. During our advance through the bog the left and right of our army attacked, but made no impression; indeed our left column of attack under Sir Lowry Cole was driven back several times and suffered severely, the enemy being in great force in the village and much too strongly placed for our people to force them from their position. However, when Marshal Soult found that our regiment had succeeded in gaining the centre of his position and was steadily advancing, he gave orders for retreating, which was done in the best order possible; and as night very soon came on, we gave up the pursuit and bivouacked. And thus ended the battle of Orthez, without much loss on either side; I suppose not twelve hundred on our part and perhaps a few hundred more on that of the French; except that we took great numbers of conscripts prisoners.

Just before we had completely driven the French from their position I had ridden to the right of our regiment, when Lord March, who was a captain in it and had joined from Lord Wellington's Staff, came up to me and said, '*George, you see I am not hit yet though you swore I should be as soon as I left the Staff and joined my regiment,*' alluding to a joke of mine a few days before. I answered, '*Do not holloa till you're out of the wood; the action is not over yet, my Lord March.*' I had not gone a hundred paces when a sergeant came running after me, saying, '*Oh, sir, Lord March is killed!*' I went to him and found my gallant, high-spirited, young friend lying with his head in my brother William's lap, to all appearance a lifeless corpse. I was deeply shocked; I dismounted from my horse; I kissed his forehead and took his cold hand in mine; but my duty called me elsewhere, and I left him with my brother (whose regiment was not in action and he was therefore at leisure), in the full persuasion that I had parted with him forever. However, thank God I was wrong, for he recovered; though the ball is to this day in his chest; and was sufficiently well to join us at Toulouse, to the great joy of the 52nd Regiment, the Light Division, and I may say the whole army, for he was known by all, and to know Lord March was sufficient to love him. It was impossible for any young man to be more popular, or to deserve it better, both as a gentleman and a soldier.

... Lord March was conveyed to the town of Orthez to a quarter there, as it was made the hospital for the wounded. The next night after he was wounded he was in so dangerous a state that Dr Hare[5] of the 43rd, who attended him, had given positive orders that no noise should be made and that as he should himself remain up all night with Lord March, if anyone wanted to come into the room they should not speak, but be as quiet as possible. About the middle of the night, as Dr Hare was sitting dozing in a chair opposite Lord March's bed, who had fallen asleep, the door of the room gently opened and a figure in a white cloak and military hat walked up to the bed, drew the curtains quietly aside, looked steadily for a few seconds on the pale countenance before him, then leaned over, stooped his head and pressed his lips on the forehead of Lord March, heaved a deep sigh and turned to leave the room, when the doctor, who had anxiously watched every movement, beheld the countenance of *Wellington!* His cheeks wet with tears. He had ridden many a mile that night alone, to see his favourite young soldier, the son of his dearest friend. He then returned to his headquarters, having first made every inquiry respecting the sick and wounded and given such orders as were necessary. Does this betray a want of feeling in the Duke? It needs no comment; the fact speaks for itself.

William's short letters gave only the merest details:

Orthez, 28 February 1814
My dearest Caroline,
I have only time to tell you that I am not wounded. The regiment was in the rear for clothing, I was in the action. George is also safe; his horse wounded and himself a little wounded. Poor March was wounded very badly;[6] I fear much that he will die. The only thing in his favour that I could see yesterday was that his face had no marks of immediate death about it; people mortally wounded have a very livid look about the lips, which he has not. It will be sad that the best of so large a family should

die so young; and doubly hard that the only person of rank I ever saw, with everybody his warm friend and nobody envious of him, should fall before his age gave him time to do that good that his noble disposition would lead him to do. Day after day the best of us go down and still no remorse, no check of conscience to those ruffians that constantly cry out *'War!'* Your affectionate husband W Napier

Chateau Papreon [?], 7 March 1814
My dearest Caroline,
March is declared out of all danger although the wound is very severe; I am delighted with it; I cannot well tell you how much I felt when I saw him extended on the field with all the marks of death about him. I have another piece of news for you, which I dare say you will not be sorry to hear. Patrickson has at last to my utter satisfaction now made his appearance in this country; when he joins, which will be in about a month, I shall ask leave to go home; I think about that time March will also go home, in which case I intend to take care of him. George is very well, we have been halted here a few days about Mont [-de-] Marsan; what is to be done I cannot tell. I should think, if Lord Wellington does not decide to go either to Toulouse or Bordeaux, that Soult will put the question out of doubt and send us back to St Jean de Luz again; he expects reinforcements from Catalonia … You may tell your brother Henry[7] that *the people here do not* like Bonaparte and if you may believe them, which I do *not quite*, they hate him. Peace they certainly wish for ardently on any terms, yet the country is rich and flourishing, full of everything you could wish for, as cheap as you have *heard* of things being in England 100 years ago and innumerable quantities of young able men. It is astonishing to see the clockwork obedience and regularity with which everything is carried on by the people at the orders of the mayor of any department. Bonaparte's genius is truly wonderful; the whole country is like a regiment and yet everything is done by the civil authorities, who are placed by the laws above the military and independent of them. Publick works upon a very superb scale are going on in Mont [-de-] Marsan, which is however only reckoned a small town; the conscription seems to be the great objection to his … Ever yours my darling Caroline, W Napier.

As I have paper, I don't see why I should not write you a little more. I am quite recovered from the illness I had some time back and of which George wrote you word. I was very ill and indeed for about 9 days, I got your letter of the 26 January yesterday, rather long coming. The Duke of Angouleme, *I am told* issued two days ago a proclamation declaring Louis

XVIII king, and Lord Wellington was very angry and supprest [sic] it. Did you ever hear of such consummate impertinence? under the cover of an English army, with an English minister treating with Bonaparte at a congress, to dare publish a document of that kind with[out] telling Lord Wellington of it! What would this stupid race of beasts the Bourbons not do if they had power. Once more my Caro, yours William.

Tarsack [Tarsac], 12 March 1814
My dearest Caroline,
To my utter astonishment Patrickson joined the regiment 3 days ago. I have lost no time in asking leave; I have not yet got an answer. In the said ball at the castle, while dancing with much vigour and great *eclat*, I put my foot in a hole in the floor and strained my ancle so badly as to prevent me from putting my foot to the ground, two days after I got a severe rheumatick [sic] *crick* in my neck, add to this riding all day and sleeping out in the night during very severe cold weather caused by constant snow and *hail*, and you will have a very good idea of the comforts I enjoy at present. This day however I am much better and not at all sorry, however all my attention [is] when I am going home to see you my darling thing … Believe me yours ever W Napier.

William returned home in March 1814. George was now the one who saw out the final days of the war. He resumes after the Battle of Orthez:

Next morning we pursued the French army, and General Hill's corps, which had passed higher up than the town of Orthez, came up with a part of the enemy at Aire [-sur-l'Adour], between Pau and Mont-de-Marsan, and immediately attacking drove them from their position. In a day or two we again came in contact with our enemy at Tarbes on the Toulouse road. Here the Light Division had a slight skirmish and drove a French brigade from their position on a woody hill; but it was done without loss on our part and scarcely any on that of the French; just a spirt of a moment to enliven us a little after some hours of a hot dusty march. The cavalry and sharpshooters of some of the other divisions had a *petite affaire* nearer the town of Tarbes on our right, in which an old friend of ours was killed, Colonel Sturgeon.[8] I may safely say one of the cleverest and most clear headed, experienced officers in the British army, and a man in whom Lord Wellington had the highest confidence and whose opinion (if he ever took any man's in preference to his own, which I doubt) he is said to have often asked and sometimes followed. But be that as it may, Sturgeon was held in high estimation by every officer in that army, and all deeply lamented his loss, the more particularly because a short time before he had been harshly treated by Lord Wellington and was very severely reprimanded by His Lordship in presence of a number of officers who were at dinner at headquarters. The thing was thus; Lord Wellington had made Sturgeon superintendent of the Post-Office and Despatch Department of the army, and also commandant of the Corps of Guides and Couriers, which it was of the utmost importance to keep in a constant state of readiness. The pay was very high and the Duke, from his confidence in and general liking for Colonel Sturgeon, put all these departments under him; at the same time he permitted him to be on the Quarter Master General's Staff at headquarters, and he was also major in the Staff Corps; so that his pecuniary emoluments were greater than those of any other man of his rank in the army, which no man envied, as he was so highly esteemed and looked up to both as a gentleman and an officer.[9] Well, after the Battle of Orthez, and a force having been sent under very peculiar circumstances towards Bordeaux, the Duke having written his despatches for England, with an account of the battle and also having others for Sir John Hope, who was blockading the fortress of Bayonne and with whom it was of the utmost importance to communicate, called for the couriers and guides who were to carry them, or rather to accompany the officers from relay to relay, when to his astonishment poor Sturgeon (who had totally forgotten all about them, being full of the grand movements of the army) had not a single courier or guide ready, nor indeed knew anything about them; neither had he made the slightest arrangement for the communications of the army, and his Corps of Guides had gone where they pleased. He could tell nothing about them, and in consequence the despatches were delayed several days! This made Lord Wellington furious, and he was so violent in his manner and harsh in his expressions that poor Sturgeon sunk completely under it, and a few days afterwards took the opportunity of the affair at Tarbes to gallop in among the enemy's skirmishers and got shot through the head!

After the business of Tarbes we pursued the French, who went off in the direction of Toulouse, which town they reached sometime early in May; and having long before prepared everything for its defence and formed an entrenched camp, Marshal Soult determined to give us battle under the walls of the ancient capital of the South of France. It is necessary here to state that during our march very few, if any outrages were committed by the British troops or Portuguese; but the Spaniards, under General Morillo, plundered and ravaged the country wherever they were quartered. Wellington did all he could to prevent it; but I must say I cannot see that the Spaniards were so much to blame as people think. How was it possible for these men to forget all the oppression, plunder and cruelties which the French army had committed upon them and their country? No! Of course they panted for revenge, and retaliated the moment it was in their power. I *regret* that they did so, but am not surprised; indeed, I should have been astonished had they done otherwise. Of course, the contrast between them and the Portuguese in this matter was very striking and glorious to that army, as I believe there was not an instance of a Portuguese soldier having committed a crime of any importance from their entry into France to the hour they left it on their return to Spain. However, we must take into consideration that they had a large number or British officers in all their regiments, and that they were nearly all under the command of Englishmen and were mixed with the British army in the various divisions and brigades. As we marched through France, I was surprised to see the depredations committed by the *French* army on their retreat and to hear the curses and execrations lavished upon them by their own people; and indeed they deserved it, for they showed very little compunction in robbing and pillaging every farm and village they passed, and the inhabitants told me they paid for nothing but took whatever was necessary.

On the arrival of the British army on the banks of the Garonne we went into famous quarters in the several small villages which are so prettily scattered about the neighbourhood of Toulouse. Part of the army had been detached under Lord Dalhousie[10] to Bordeaux, as the inhabitants of that city had declared themselves in favour of the Bourbons and had hoisted the *'drapeau blanc.'*[11] This and the portion of the army under Sir John Hope left to blockade the fortress and port of Bayonne, had reduced Lord Wellington's forces at Toulouse to a much smaller number than when he entered France in one large body; and this has given rise to an idea that he was nearly double the strength of Marshal Soult's army, which is very far from the truth, as I think he could not have had more than thirty-five thousand men, seven or eight thousand of whom were Spaniards, the rest British and Portuguese. The French acknowledge to twenty-two or twenty-three thousand in an entrenched position and well supported by forts &c. Every means of defence possible was at Soult's command, as the town itself made part of his position; so that the three or four thousand we had over his numbers were amply compensated for by the different position of the armies, and the circumstance of our being the attacking and his the defensive one. That he ably placed his army and gallantly and skilfully fought the battle, I deny not; but that he won it, as the French assert, is not true. Every fort was taken, his divisions driven into the town and the British army bivouacked upon the field of battle, and the next day entered the town which he had evacuated during the night.

Battle of Toulouse, 10 April 1814

The Duke of Wellington's first intention had been to cross the Garonne above the town of Toulouse, and he had accordingly been making every preparation for so doing. The pontoons for the bridge had arrived, and all being reported ready, we moved in separate columns towards the spot decided upon, when, lo! The engineer had miscalculated the breadth of the river and had not ordered up a sufficient number of pontoons to lay the bridge and we were obliged to abandon the project, as the enemy being now aware of our intention, it would not be possible to throw a bridge across at that spot. Lord Wellington was furious; I never saw him in such a rage, and no wonder; for this unpardonable mistake was the cause of many days' delay and forced us to cross lower down below the town, where the river was wider, deeper and much more rapid and the difficulties much greater than at the other place. When the new bridge was finished the Fourth Division, a part of the Sixth, and a brigade of Hussars; the whole under General Cole crossed over, and after driving in the enemy's outposts and having an affair of cavalry, bivouacked in front of the enemy's position, but at some distance. We were all to have passed over also, when a sudden storm came on and a deluge of rain, which so swelled the river that it carried away our pontoons and destroyed the bridge completely and left the troops which had passed over totally unsupported in case of an attack. And why Soult allowed them to remain unmolested for three days, which it took to make a new bridge, I cannot conceive. All his generals begged and prayed him to attack and as they said, annihilate this small force; but he would not run the risk, and (as I have understood from many French officers) said, *'You do not know what stuff two British divisions are made of; they would not be conquered as long as there was a man of them left to stand, and I cannot afford to lose men now.'*

When the bridge was ready, we all passed over as quickly as possible, and next day attacked the French in their position. The 4th, 6th and a Portuguese division under Marshal Beresford's orders, attacked the great fort on the right of the French, and here was the brunt of the battle, for the enemy was strongly posted and flanked by works, with trenches in their front and their best troops opposed to ours. But nothing could damp the courage of this column; the enemy's guns poured a torrent of fire upon it; still it moved onward, when column upon column appeared, crowning the hill and forming lines in front and on the flanks of our brave fellows who were near the top; and then such a roll of musketry accompanied by peals of cannon and the shouts of the enemy commenced, that our soldiers were fairly forced to give way and were driven down again. This attack was twice renewed, and twice were our gallant fellows forced to retire, when being got into order again and under a tremendous fire of all arms from the enemy, they once more marched onward determined *'to do or die'* (for they were nearly all Scotch) and having gained the summit of the position, they charged with the bayonet, and in spite of every effort of the enemy, drove all before them and entered every redoubt and fort with such a courage as I never saw before. The enemy lay in *heaps*, dead and dying! Few, very few, escaped the slaughter of that day; but *'Victory'* was heard shouted from post to post as that gallant band moved along the crown of the enemy's position taking every work at the point of the bayonet.

While the work of death was going on here, the centre of the French position was attacked by the Spanish column of eight thousand men, under General Freyre,[12] who had *demanded* in rather a haughty tone that Lord Wellington should give the Spaniards the post of honour in the battle. He acceded, but took special care to have the Light Division in reserve to support them in case of *accidents*. Old Freyre placed himself at the head of his column, surrounded by his staff, and marched boldly up the hollow way or road, which led right up to the enemy, under a heavy and destructive fire of cannon shot, which plunging into the head of his column made great havoc among his men; still they went steadily and boldly on, to my astonishment and delight to see them behave so gallantly, and I could not help expressing my delight to Colonel Colborne. But, alas! He knew them too well, and said to me *'Gently, my friend; don't praise them too soon; look at yonder brigade of French Light Infantry, ready to attack them as soon as the head of their column enters the open ground. One moment more and we shall see the Spaniards fly! Gallop off, you, and throw the 52nd Regiment (which was in line) into open column of companies, and let these fellows pass through, or they will carry the regiment off with them.'* He had scarcely finished the words when a well-directed fire from the French infantry opened upon the Spanish column, and instantly the words *'Vive l'Empereur! En avant! en avant!'* accompanied by a charge, put the Spaniards to flight, and down they came upon the 52nd Regiment, and I had but just time to throw it into open column of companies when they rushed through the intervals like a torrent and never stopped till they arrived at the river some miles in the rear. As soon as they had passed and I had formed the regiment into line again, we moved up and took the Spaniards' place, driving before us the enemy's brigade, who, being by this time completely beaten on the right and all his forts and trenches carried by Beresford's troops, had retreated into the town; so that we found the fort on that part of the position which we attacked quite abandoned, and we entered it without loss.

On our right the 3rd Division, under General Picton, was ordered to make a false attack on the canal bridge, which was strongly fortified and formed an impracticable barrier to that part of the town; but General Picton (who never hesitated at disobeying his orders) thought proper to change this false attack into a real one, and after repeated and useless attempts to carry it was forced to give it up, with an immense loss of officers; and to our extreme right and on the opposite side of the river General Hill was stationed with his corps in order to watch the bridge and gates of the town, and either prevent any attempt of the enemy to pass over a body of troops during the action to cut off our communications with the rear, or should he show any design of retreating that way, to impede him. However, all was quiet on that side, and now that every man of the enemy's army had been chased from the position the battle was won, and the roar of cannon, the fire of the musketry, and the shouts of the victors ceased. All was still; the pickets placed; the sentinels set; and the greatest part of the army sleeping in groups round the fires of the bivouac. I must here say that Marshal Beresford performed his part nobly that day; for had he not shown great determination and presence of mind in renewing his attacks so often and leading the troops so gallantly himself, the thing might not have been so successful. But to be sure, *'Old Douro'* (as the men always called him) was on the ground himself and gave all the orders, and on him alone rested any responsibility, so that Marshal Beresford was relieved from that burden, which is a heavy one to those who have not full confidence in themselves under all circumstances ...

George continued his account of the last days of the war, with news of a permanent rank:

... A few days after the battle of Toulouse I was appointed regimental Lieutenant Colonel of the 71st Light Infantry and immediately took the command of it, superseding who had been dismissed the service for cowardly conduct in the field, in leaving his regiment in action and going to the rear, where unluckily for him but luckily for the regiment and the service, Lord Wellington who was coming up, met him and reprimanding him on the spot told him to go back instantly and head his gallant regiment. Go back he did, but *head* the regiment, never in action! and Lord Wellington having reported his conduct to his Royal Highness the Duke of York, the

Prince Regent dismissed him from the army and I was gazetted in his place.¹³ He was a man of large fortune and a very old officer, just upon the point of being made by brevet a major general, but he was weak, overbearing and insolent beyond everything to all under him in rank, and by his conduct to the officers of his regiment had nearly extinguished the honourable spirit which had so long and so highly distinguished it under his predecessors, Sir Denis Pack and Colonel Cadogan.¹⁴ In short, to him and to him alone, belonged all the disorder which the 71st Regiment got into after poor Colonel Cadogan's glorious death at the battle of Vitoria; the proof of which was that in the course of a few months after I took the command, we received the thanks and approbation of the general commanding the division, Sir William Stewart, for its good conduct and high state of discipline. This I mention as a proof that the regiment's being in bad order was [Peacocke]'s sole fault, for had I been the cleverest commanding officer in the army it would have been impossible for me in so short a period, and under the circumstances of the time, to have made the progress I did if it had not been for the former system established by Pack and Cadogan … In this I succeeded, but not without some severity, for I found the discipline so relaxed that neither officers nor men were very well inclined to submit cheerfully to my orders, which were looked upon as too strict; and I am sorry to say I was forced to make some severe examples by flogging more men in the first two months I was with the 71st than I had witnessed or ordered during nearly as many years in the 52nd … Many people have a notion that Marshal Soult knew of the overthrow of Napoleon, and that the peace was signed before he fought the battle of Toulouse; but I think this must be a calumny invented by his enemies, and I feel the more convinced of this because it was against his interest and fame to have done so if he could have avoided it …

In a few weeks we received orders to prepare for returning to England, but before the army began to move we learned that a large force was to embark at Bordeaux for America, in order to finish the war with the United States, which had been rather unfavourable to our arms; the rest were to embark for England and Ireland, while the cavalry marched through France for Calais, in order to save the horses so long a voyage by sea. I was left with my regiment to remain in Toulouse for some days after the whole army had marched, in order to bring up the rear and clear the country of all stragglers and followers of the army, sick, stores, &c, &c; in short, to drive the *'tag, rag and bobtail'* before me. I had a very pleasant march (though dreadfully hot) through the south of France; everywhere receiving the greatest kindness and civility from the inhabitants. In almost every town we passed the night, they gave us a ball, where we met all the ladies, and my officers made themselves agreeable, dancing the whole night. I had but one *complaint* during our long march against our men, and that was on the second day's march, when a woman came to my quarters at the mayor's house, and crying and tearing her hair and wringing her hands, and accompanied by a mob of people, all talking and swearing that the soldiers were going to rob and murder the people and set fire to the town, she called on me for protection and justice. I, not knowing the nature of the French, supposed there was the devil to pay, so immediately demanding from madame what my soldiers had done, she answered, *'stole an old hen from her yard.'* *'Oh, oh,'* said I to myself, *'Is that all? thank God it's no worse,'* and I ordered my orderly bugleman to sound the assembly and told the lady she should go down the ranks of the regiment and point out the soldier who had committed the theft, as she said she would know him directly again. As soon as the regiment was formed, which was in about a quarter of an hour from her first coming to complain, I took her down the ranks, and upon coming opposite a company which I expected the fellow belonged to, she at once pointed him out. I asked him if he stole her hen; he resolutely denied knowing anything of the matter; upon which I ordered him to take off his knapsack and open it, when, sure enough, there was the old hen, dead as a ducat, with all her feathers on, so that the lady could swear to it. I instantly ordered a drum head court martial, tried my gentleman on the spot, and as he was proved guilty of plundering and sentenced to be flogged, I punished him accordingly before them all; and then the lady was furious with me, and all the people begged and prayed I would forgive him, and when they found I would not they abused me like a pickpocket ...

George then received alarming news about his wife:

On my arrival at Bordeaux, I received letters which alarmed me about my wife's health, so I instantly went to my friends Sir Edward Pakenham and Lord Fitzroy Somerset, who got me leave to go home without waiting for my regiment, which was ordered to Ireland. After a stormy and very unpleasant passage down the river, I got onboard a transport which was sailing for Plymouth; but I had a curious adventure while coming down the river. A brother officer who was with me, Colonel Charles Rowan[15] ... and I went on shore to look at a curious village cut in the rock. Each house was perfectly separate, but cut in the rock; bedrooms, kitchen &c, &c, with regular communications, exactly like the inside of a house; not the least difference, except that all the rooms were in a line and looking towards the river, otherwise there would have been a want of light; but there were chambers one above the other with steps cut in the rock to enable one to get up to each storey. As I had on my uniform, we were immediately known to be British officers, and as most of the male inhabitants were sailors just released by the peace from our prisons and hulks, where to the eternal disgrace and shame of the British government, they had been most infamously and inhumanly treated, they were determined to insult us and commenced throwing stones and abusing us most desperately. So furious were they that we deemed it the most prudent thing to retreat to our boat as fast as we could. However, as I was very angry, I drew forth one of my pistols and was just going to fire at them, but Rowan being a wiser and cooler headed fellow, very properly prevented my doing so, and luckily for us, as in a few moments the whole village turned out, and we had but just time to regain the boat and shove out and, a breeze springing up, we made all sail into the middle of the river, which was very broad, and escaped their fury, for they certainly would have murdered us without mercy. That night very late I was so ill from sea sickness that I swore I would not remain any longer in the cursed boat and Rowan very good humouredly got out with me, and we waded up to our middle through a long mile of mud, as the tide was out; and at last, having gained the bank, we made the best of our way to a light we perceived at some distance, where finding a house we knocked at the door, which was soon opened by a nice pretty French girl, and upon our saying we were English officers, a gentleman came forward and in broken English welcomed us to his house and said we should have every accommodation he could give us.

… in a few hours we arrived at the place for embarking, when we saw the ships *in full sail* for England. However, I soon overtook one of the large transports in a small boat which I hired for the purpose, and in a fortnight we arrived at Plymouth after a miserable passage. During the whole time I was as sick as a dog and lay upon the deck *night and day* without being able to move, and as it rained nearly the whole time and I had nothing to change; for I had left my servant in the boat with my baggage in the middle of the river; you may suppose I was as miserable as possible! As soon as I landed at Plymouth, I bought a couple of shirts and a pair of stockings and started that day on top of the coach for London, remained a few hours with my mother and went off at night by the mail to Edinburgh, where I arrived just five days after I landed at Plymouth, and I found my dear wife much better than I expected.

Soon after his arrival home, George received a great favour from the Duke:

> We remained in Scotland some weeks, when in consequence of the recommendation of the Duke of Wellington I was given a company in the 3rd [Foot] Guards as a reward for my services,[16] it being considered a great favour and honour to be a captain in the Guards, which ranks with a commanding officer of a regiment, but in a pecuniary point is much better, as when I got my company it was worth between six and seven hundred a year.[17]

Chapter 11
1815

The three brothers were not to be involved in the Battle of Waterloo, but two of the brothers were involved in the subsequent march to Paris. In December 1814, Charles was placed on half pay, and he immediately entered the military college at Farnham, where he was joined by his brother, William. Charles was in Belgium from March 1815, but his letters home only reveal his frustrations at not being able to gain a Staff role. However, he did play a part (as a volunteer) in the pursuit of the French army into France. A glimpse of him appears in the memoirs of Lieutenant John Hildebrand 35th Foot, who states that at Cambrai:

> I was the oldest subaltern and also in command of a company of what had but recently been organized under the name of sharpshooters under the superintendence and arrangement of Colonel Napier.[1]

Charles does not mention this incident, but given that Brevet Colonel Neil Campbell, 54th Foot, commanded the three light companies at the storming of Cambrai and that Charles records that he accompanied Neil Campbell and his troops to Aubervilliers only a few days later, it seems highly likely that Charles was at Cambrai, although in an unofficial capacity.

We can, however, be sure of William's involvement. The 1st Battalion, 43rd Regiment, had been present at the dreadful disaster of the Battle of New Orleans, but luckily escaped virtually unscathed as they were kept in reserve. Their transport ships arrived at Portsmouth on 1 June and the next few days, and they marched to quarters at Dover and Deal, where William re-joined them. On 16 June, the battalion, 1,100 men strong, boarded ships to proceed to Belgium. Landing at Ostend on 17 June, they arrived at Ghent on 19 June to hear news of the victory of Waterloo. They proceeded to Brussels, from where William wrote:

> Brussels, 25 June 1815
> My dear Caroline,
> You will have known before this, more of the battle than I can tell you. Poor Chambers[2] has been killed and Simpson[3] wounded. Tomorrow we

march for the army, but from the distance they are in advance I think it impossible to join them before another battle is fought. Lord Wellington's luck predominates over Bonaparte's; had the latter been two hours sooner in his advance, everything was lost; as it is I believe that a nearer thing never was ever; the loss in men I should think pretty even. Bonaparte lost about 40,000, of which 7,000 only are prisoners. We lost with the Prussians about 35,000; the latter lost 65 guns, but we have taken near 200 pieces of artillery. I have lost my two baggage horses and canteens and am in a very bad plight altogether; I fear the Prussians have robbed Southgate[4] of them if not killed him, this is their custom. The light cavalry behaved ill, the heavy cavalry very well. All the French cavalry fought in the most astonishing manner. Bonaparte charged at the head of his own Guards. He had about 90,000 in the field, we had including everybody 180,000, so that we were double his strength, everybody was beat but the British, but as usual we now say that he had an overwhelming force.

Charles, I believe, was not in the action. Henry Macleod[5] was run through, wounded in four places by the French lancers, but he is walking about and doing perfectly well. The regiment is in a shocking state and General Adam and the commandant here are doing what they can to make it worse. Your affectionate husband W Napier.

William marched his battalion into France, where they joined the army at St Denis on 4 July, being immediately placed in the 5th Division. William was an eyewitness to the formal entry of King Louis XVIII into Paris on 6 July. His favourable leanings towards Napoleon and against the Bourbons are patently clear in his later commentary:

The feelings of the British soldiers were unequivocally shown. Proud of their long victorious course against the French, they yet respected the latter as brave enemies and had a profound admiration, even love, for Napoleon. They thought of him, not as a foe but as a hero standing alone; a soldier to be hailed by all soldiers; as a man who had enabled them to gain the greatest possible glory by fighting him: a master of war and the fast friend of warriors. Their instinct as fighting men was for him and as freemen against the Bourbons. When Louis the Eighteenth entered Paris, [my] post being at the head of the picquets guarding the barrier of St Denis, was asked by the captain on duty there, if he was to salute? *'I have no orders on that head and give none'* was the reply. The king came up, crowds thronged forward and the words *'Vive and Roi'* were heard on all sides; but the last was generally preceded by the words '*L'Empereur et*', pronounced in a low tone.

The British soldiers, being left to themselves, brought down their muskets from the shoulder and placing their hands on the muzzles, fiercely regarded the approaching king. He seemed surprised, but soon his countenance assumed a look of such malignant ferocity, so fixed, so peculiar, as never to be forgotten. A number of mousquetaires [sic] in burnished cuirasses, their faces convulsed with anger, then rode up, shouting, gesticulating and brandishing their swords; but close behind the picquet was a wall and the swarthy veterans, hard as the steel of their bayonets and with wits as sharp, knew the advantage. Keeping their bronzed faces bent over their hands, their eyes glared sternly, yet no movement indicated that they were even sensible of the mousquetaires' presence, until the latter closed within a few paces and seemed dangerous; then suddenly, all their heads were lifted and streams of tobacco juice flew towards the shining cuirasses, whereupon the courtier soldiers followed the chariot of the king. A shout of delight arose from the crowd and many well dressed women embraced the British veterans.

However, his letter home dated just a few days later, betrays his annoyance at the welcome the king received:

Paris, 9 July
I have not had an opportunity of writing to you before since I left Brussels. I am much annoyed at finding how completely the French nation has lost all sense of shame, and my admiration of Bonaparte is increased tenfold when I find what very contemptible stuff he had to work with. Yesterday the King made his entree; I was on duty, and having placed myself between the palisades of the barrier had an opportunity of seeing everything. There was much shouting and noise, but it proceeded from a few women and gentlemen of his party, and from his bodyguard, which amounted to about 5,000; he had also his bodyguard of Swiss and some artillery. The day before at the same gate I saw the National Guard and the mob seize upon two men with white cockades, tear them from their carriage and stone them, swearing that they abhorred Louis and that he never should enter Paris. The next day the same people tore the tricolour from their own hats and stamped upon it!!! The general opinion seems to be that he cannot reign longer than while the allied troops are with him; but who can reckon upon such a people? The soldiers are all gone behind the Loire, still faithful to Napoleon. It is asserted here, but I do not believe it, that Napoleon is in

Paris and looked at the procession yesterday, laughing at the cry of *'Vive le Roi!'* It does not appear certain that the war is yet over ... If we should be settled and quiet I must contrive to get you over here even if I go to jail for it; but at present it is impossible. The fortresses are all besieging, and the stragglers and parties of all nations make it very dangerous; but you had better enter in a negociation [sic] about the little devils[6] with some friend to take them in charge. Could not my mother live at Farnham and take care of them? People tell me I am like Bonaparte; and the 43rd soldiers gave me three cheers when I joined the regiment at Ghent, which pleased me.

Charles returned home to continue his studies at the Military College, but nearly drowned when his transport ship was wrecked; life at sea was certainly not right for Charles! William was to remain in France, his battalion forming part of the Army of Occupation, until it was disbanded in 1818:

Chapter 12

Later Life

Thus, the three brothers ended their service with the armies of Sir John Moore and Wellington and they each sought their individual paths thereafter.

Charles Napier completed his studies at Farnham at the end of 1817 and in May 1819 he was appointed Inspecting Officer in the Ionian Isles and he contemplated leading the Greeks in their fight for independence from the Turks. Appointed Resident of Cephalonia, he remained there, until called home on the death of his mother in 1826. The following year he married Elizabeth Oakeley in April and the couple returned to Cephalonia but returned home because of her ill health in 1830. Charges were brought against him regarding his time in office at Cephalonia and he refused another appointment, rather than returning to the island. In 1833, he contracted cholera and lost his wife on 31 July, then devoting his life to educating his daughters, although he did remarry a widower, Francis Alcock (nee Philipps), in 1835. He was promoted to major general in 1837 and in 1839 he was appointed to command the Northern District. In April 1841 he was appointed to a command at Poona in India and over the next few years in a series of stunning campaigns he won Sind for the British. Promoted to lieutenant general in 1846, he resigned and sailed for home the following year, although he returned to India in 1849. He returned home again in 1851 and bought a property, Oaklands on the Hampshire Downs, he died on 29 August 1853.

As to George Napier, he continued serving with the 3rd Foot Guards until 1821, when he retired on half pay. He became a brevet colonel in August 1825, a major general in January 1837, lieutenant general in November 1846 and full general in June 1854. From October 1837 until December 1843 he was appointed Governor and commander in chief at the Cape of Good Hope. After his return in 1844, he generally resided in Nice and he died in Geneva on 16 September 1855.

Lastly, we have William Napier, who retired on half pay a year after the Army of Occupation had ended, in late 1819. His finances required him to continue to earn and he initially considered life as an artist, studying under George Jones. However, he also turned his hand to historical works and in 1823 he was persuaded by friends to embark on his six-volume *History of the*

Peninsular War. Volume one was published in 1828 and was critically acclaimed, although it proved to be a financial failure; the publisher declining to publish further volumes and William continuing by self-publishing. He then became embroiled with a number of officers who felt harshly treated by his *History* and a constant stream of claim and counter-claim did tarnish the work, which was undoubtedly biased towards those William admired. William was always a political animal and he was regularly offered seats in parliament, but refused all offers. In November 1841 he was promoted to major general and was appointed Lieutenant Governor of Guernsey, a post he held for six years. In 1848 he was made colonel of the 27th Inniskillings and in 1849 he bought and moved into Scinde House, Clapham Park. Promoted to lieutenant general in November 1851 and full general in October 1859. He died on 10 February 1860, Caroline surviving him by only six weeks.

Britain has rarely experienced the rewards of having three such brothers.

Notes

Foreword
1. Although almost all of William's and Charles's letters to their family are held in the files of the Bodleian Library, a few from which snippets were published in Victorian times appear to have gone astray, while others never previously published but found to contain interesting information were found in the files.
2. Emily eventually married Henry Bunbury, who was in the Army and rose to the rank of lieutenant general.
3. Richard eventually married Anna Stewart, daughter of Sir J Stewart.
4. Henry joined the Royal Navy and rose to the rank of captain.
5. Caroline unfortunately died in her twentieth year.
6. Cecilia unfortunately died in her seventeenth year.
7. Near Southampton.
8. General Francis Rawdon-Hastings, he succeeded to the title Lord Moira on the death of his father in 1793.

Chapter 1
1. HMS *Invincible* was a 74-gun ship built in 1765.
2. Captain the Honourable Thomas Pakenham, Royal Navy, was Captain of HMS *Invincible* in 1793–95.
3. Charles Cornwallis, 1st Marquess Cornwallis, Lord Lieutenant and Commander in Chief in Ireland.
4. Major General Sir James Duff commanded the Limerick District.
5. Lieutenant James Douglas, 42nd Foot.
6. Colonel Alexander Mackenzie, 78th Foot, was on the Home Staff in 1803–05. He took on the additional surname of Fraser in 1803.
7. 950 guineas.
8. Lord Frederick Bentinck had served as a captain in the 52nd Foot in 1803–04, before purchasing a majority in the 45th Foot in March 1804 and a month later purchasing a lieutenant colonelcy in the 7th Foot.
9. Then with the 59th Foot.
10. The Marquis of Hastings was a title created in 1816, in 1794 he was Earl of Moira.
11. The Londonderry Regiment was raised in 1794 and disbanded in 1795.
12. The men of the Londonderry Regiment were actually drafted into the 43rd and 31st Regiment.
13. General Charles Cornwallis, Marquess Cornwallis, was appointed Lord Lieutenant of Ireland in June 1798.
14. Lieutenant Colonel John Brown of the Quarter Master General's department.
15. *Whither Destiny Takes Me.*
16. Getting more abuse than good treatment.
17. General Henry Fox was the brother of Charles Fox the politician.

Notes 195

18. Major General Edward Paget.
19. Vice Admiral Cuthbert Collingwood.
20. Vice Admiral John Thomas Duckworth.
21. The *Lord Collingwood* was launched in 1806 serving as a transport ship.
22. Foot whipping.
23. Lieutenant Colonel Patrick Macleod commanded the 2nd Battalion, 78th Foot, and was killed at El Hamet on 21 April 1807.

Chapter 2
1. The Russians had been defeated at Friedland on 14 June 1807.
2. This would appear to refer to Lieutenant James Shaw, 43rd Foot, and Lieutenant Robert Shaw of the 3rd West Yorks Militia, who joined the 51st Foot as an ensign on 25 August 1807.
3. The powerful politician Henry Dundas.
4. Brevet Colonel Richard Stewart commanded the 43rd Foot at Copenhagen.
5. His brother, who was a midshipman.
6. Major General Charles Christian von Linsingen of the King's German Legion.
7. The British government suddenly suggested retaining possession of the Island of Zealand, but Admiral Gambier was clear that it would be impossible, both because the waters between the island and Jutland would freeze, allowing Danish and French forces to pass over to the island, and it would also negate the convention they had signed.
8. Earnest Augustus, the Duke of Cumberland, was the fifth son of King George III and would become the king of Hannover in 1837.
9. Major General Brent Spencer.
10. The boy's mother, Lady Sarah Lennox, daughter of the Duke of Richmond.
11. Sir Edward Knatchbull, 8th Baronet, was the High Sheriff of Kent and a Member of Parliament.
12. As a Captain William would receive £194 in Prize Money (worth about £10,000 today).
13. The Staff school of the day.
14. The great mystery.

Chapter 3
1. Typhus is generally spread by fleas and lice, therefore it was almost certainly contagious.
2. Some £80,000 in modern terms.
3. This seems unlikely, equating to eight pints of blood!
4. Brigadier General Robert Anstruther.
5. Brest was the major port in the north of France.
6. King Gustav Adolf IV reigned from 1792 until 1809, when he was deposed in a coup and the army prevented his son from inheriting the throne. His uncle was declared king, reigning as King Charles XIII.
7. HMS *Victory* of 104 guns.
8. Rear Admiral James Saumarez, 1st Baron de Saumarez.
9. Lieutenant General Sir John Hope.
10. Major John Colborne, 20th Foot, was Military Secretary to Sir John Moore.
11. Major the Honourable Hugh Arbuthnot, 52nd Foot.
12. 4th Swiss Regiment.
13. Colonel Francois Dominique Perrier.
14. General John Pitt, 2nd Earl of Chatham, was offered a command in Portugal, but declined, eventually commanding the force sent in 1809 to Walcheren.

15. If Colonel Richard Stewart sought to bring in a lieutenant colonel into the regiment and drive out a major, it did not occur.
16. This must refer to Major Edward Hull, who became a lieutenant colonel in the regiment in late 1808.
17. Napier's concerns about outsiders receiving the promotions to lieutenant colonel and lessening his chances for moving up in seniority were legitimate but never happened. At the time of the writing, he was the seventh senior captain in the regiment. Ten months later, due to promotions of officers senior to him, he was the fifth senior captain.
18. The Downs are an anchorage off Deal in Kent.
19. The news had just arrived that Sir Arthur Wellesley had just defeated the French in Portugal at Roliça and Vimiera and afterwards the French commander had asked for terms. The subsequent treaty, known as the Convention of Cintra, allowed the French Army to return to France with their baggage on British transports. The caused quite a scandal and both Dalrymple and Wellesley were recalled to England to testify at an inquiry.
20. Lieutenant General Sir David Baird was to command a force of 10,000 men, sent out to reinforce the army under Sir John Moore.
21. Charles had transferred into the 1st Battalion, 50th Regiment as a major, but commanded the battalion as Lieutenant Colonel George Walker was absent, having been severely wounded at the Battle of Vimiera.
22. Wellesley signed the preliminary agreement but refused to sign the final convention.
23. Lieutenant General Sir Harry Burrard did return to England in October 1808 to attend the enquiry into the Convention of Cintra.
24. William's choice of words is misleading. Age-wise, Moore was four years younger than Baird. However, as both were lieutenant generals with a date of 30 October 1805, Moore was senior because he was two places higher on the Army List.
25. Henry Richard Vassall Fox, the 3rd Lord Holland, was a Member of Parliament and a staunch abolitionist. He was a distant cousin. Napier's comment is curious, since Holland had accompanied General Baird to Spain and had to be in the vicinity of Corunna.
26. Captain Thomas Lloyd, 43rd Foot.
27. France and Russia were allies ever since the treaty signed on the River Niemen in July 1807, this must refer to overtures made to Britain for peace talks, but nothing came of them.
28. Marshal Jean-de-Dieu Soult.
29. General Pedro Caro y Sureda, Marquis of La Romano.
30. General of Division Charles Lefèbvre-Desnoëttes was not related to Napoleon.
31. Brevet Colonel the Honourable Charles Stewart, 18th Light Dragoons.
32. Chasseurs-à-Cheval of the Imperial Guard.
33. Lieutenant General Lord Henry Paget commanded the cavalry.
34. Captain Charles Pasley, Royal Engineers.
35. Major Charles Stanhope, 50th Foot.
36. Captain & Lieutenant Colonel Lord Frederick Bentinck, 1st Foot Guards.
37. Major General Sir Rowland Hill.
38. Lieutenant General Alexander Mackenzie Fraser, 9th Lord Fraser of Inverallochy.
39. The 3rd Division.
40. Captain Alexander Gordon, 3rd Foot Guards.
41. Colonel Sir Thomas Graham, 90th Foot. He was promoted to major general on his return home in 1809.

42. The Flank Brigades under Brigadier General Robert Craufurd and Brigadier General Charles von Alten retreated to Vigo.
43. This is incorrect. Lieutenant Colonel George Cookson, Royal Artillery, was given the job of blowing up the magazines. No Royal Engineer officer was killed by the explosion. Lieutenant Henry Davy, Royal Engineers, had been killed blowing a bridge at Betanzos and he has probably been confused with this later incident.
44. Captain William Clunes, 50th Foot.
45. Brevet Colonel George Walker, 50th Foot. He was severely wounded at Vimiera.
46. Brigadier General Henry Fane.
47. Lord Edward Fitzgerald was an Irish nationalist and was killed on the eve of an intended uprising in 1798.
48. Paymaster John Montgomery, 50th Foot.
49. Ensigns Robert Moore and William Stewart were both wounded, Moore died on 7 February 1809, Stewart died of his wounds on 24 February 1809.
50. Captain John Harrison, 50th Foot.
51. Lieutenants John Patterson and William Turner, 50th Foot.
52. Major Francis Brooke, 4th foot.
53. This occurred between 29 March and 12 May 1780.
54. I surrender.
55. General de Brigade Antoine Renaud.
56. Guerilla leader Don Julian Sanchez.
57. Marshal Michel Ney.
58. Then Second Captain Anne Clouet.
59. Hardinge Captain Henry, 57th Foot Deputy Assistant Quartermaster General.
60. Lieutenant Colonel Paul Anderson, 60th Foot, Deputy Assistant Adjutant General.
61. James Hamilton Stanhope, 1st Foot Guards, was the aide-de-camp to Lieutenant General Sir John Hope.
62. John George Woodford, 1st Foot Guards, Deputy Assistant Quartermaster General.
63. Ensign Paul Harry Durell Burrard, 1st Foot Guards, ADC to General Moore. He died of his wounds on 21 January 1809 at the age of 19. His father was Lieutenant General Harry Burrard.
64. William Clunes was slightly wounded in the battle.
65. Captain Henry Percy, 7th Foot, aide-de-camp to General Moore.
66. Captain Thomas Le Marchant Grosselin, Royal Navy, was the captain of HMS *Audacious*.
67. Lieutenant Colonel George Murray, 3rd Foot Guards, Quartermaster General.
68. Captain James Baird, 66th Foot, aide-de-camp to General Baird.
69. Ensign William Craig, 52nd Foot, died on 13 December 1809. His sister would later marry George Napier.
70. Lieutenant Colonel Robert Barclay, 52nd Foot.

Chapter 4
1. This claim is difficult to reconcile with facts. The route was about 65km (40 miles) and it took the division about twenty-five hours.

Chapter 5
1. Admiral Sir George Berkeley.
2. Dona Maria Amalia de Carvalho e Daun was the daughter of the Marquise of Pombal and Dona Maria Constancia de Saldanha Oliveira e Daun her daughter. The Marquise of Pombal had died in 1782.

3. General Juan de Contreras was promoted to field marshal in April 1810 and was appointed military governor of Corunna and the commander in chief of Galicia.
4. General William Carr Beresford was appointed Marshal of the Portuguese Army to improve the Portuguese troops.
5. Major General Stafford Lightbourne commanded an independent brigade in July 1809.
6. Brigadier Generals James Catlin Craufurd and Robert Craufurd arrived in Lisbon too late to participate in the Talavera Campaign.
7. The three brigades had just arrived in Portugal in June and, except for Robert Craufurd's Light Brigade, were not in a condition to undergo a campaign.
8. Overlooked by higher ground.
9. Oman states that the fortress numbered over one hundred guns, forty of which were of 18lb or greater.
10. Captain Henry Francis Mellish, 87th Foot, Deputy Assistant Adjutant General assigned to the Light Division.
11. Major General Martin Carrera commanded the Spanish forces in the area.
12. Colonel Henry MacKinnon, Coldstream Guards, commanded a brigade in the 3rd Division.
13. Colonel Edward Pakenham, 7th Foot, was the Deputy Adjutant General of Wellington's Army.
14. A country party.
15. Captain Georg Krauchenberg, 1st King's German's Legion Hussars.
16. Captain John Belli, 16th Light Dragoons.
17. Captain Hew Ross, Royal Horse Artillery.
18. Lieutenant Colonel George Elder had been a major in the 95th Rifles, but was seconded to the Portuguese Army in 1809. He commanded the 3rd Caçadores.
19. General Andrés Perez de Herrasti was the governor of Ciudad Rodrigo.
20. Brigadier General William Cox was a British officer serving in the Portuguese Army and the commandant of Almeida.
21. To run into something more powerful than what was expected.
22. Lieutenant Colonel Neil Talbot, 14th Light Dragoons, was killed on 11 July 1810.
23. General of Division Louis Loison commanded the 3rd Division in Marshal Ney's 6th Corps.
24. This refers to the 2nd Battalion, 50th Regiment, which were on Home Service.
25. Ciudad Rodrigo surrendered on 10 July 1810.
26. Captain Isaac Hewitt, 6th Foot, who was made a prisoner of war when Almeida surrendered, remained such until 1814.
27. Captain Robert Campbell, 52nd Foot.
28. This 'tower' was actually the base tower of a ruined windmill.
29. Lieutenant Colonel Robert Barclay, 52nd Foot.
30. Major Charles Macleod, 43rd Foot.
31. Lieutenant Colonel Thomas Sydney Beckwith, 95th Rifles.
32. Captain Charles Rowan, 52nd Foot.
33. Captain Robert Dalzell, 43rd Foot.
34. Captain Christopher Patrickson, 43rd Foot.
35. Craufurd had been forced to surrender there in 1807.
36. William disagreed with Charles, stating that 'This was a mistake, the bone was injured and the recovery slow; two months.'
37. Charles grossly overestimated the number of casualties. Recent research shows that the division had 333 killed, wounded or missing.

38. Lieutenant Colonel Edward Hull.
39. Connected series of events.
40. Spanish General Miguel de Alava y Esquivel was appointed as Military Attaché to Wellington, who appointed him one of his aide de camps.
41. Wellington's force was in the region of 52,000 men.
42. Massena's force numbered 65,000, of which 8,500 were cavalry, which could not participate in the battle.
43. General Edouard Simon.
44. No officers, but three men of the 5/60th were killed.
45. Lieutenant John Winterbottom, 52nd Foot.
46. Captain Charles Napier was present merely as an amateur on leave from his and got hit in his leg. He wrote to the Admiralty '*Sir, my leave of absence is just out. I don't think it worth remaining here, for I expect you will give me a ship, as I am almost tired of campaigning, which is a damned rum concern. CN.*'
47. Head.
48. Assistant Surgeon Nicholas Fitzpatrick Royal Artillery.
49. I cannot identify any such person in either the Army or Navy.
50. Charles Napier, Royal Navy, was his first cousin. He was on half pay and decided to visit his three cousins in Portugal. He too was wounded at Busaco.
51. Major General Galbraith Lowry Cole.
52. Toujours gai – forever cheerful.
53. Captain the Honourable William Pakenham RN, he was appointed to HMS *Aquilon* in January 1811, but transferred to HMS *Saldanha* in May 1811 and drowned on 4 December 1811 along with all 252 crew.
54. Situated just west of Derry, Londonderry.
55. A number of court martials of Brunswick Light Infantry troops occurred in early 1811. On 19 January Privates Liebental, Lange, Morentye and Getterman were found guilty and sentenced to be shot. Privates Henrich, Schneider, Rafineti, Knies, Friess and Barens were found guilty on only one charge and sentenced to 200 lashes each, but were pardoned.
56. General Dupont's force had been forced to surrender at Bailen in 1808. Dupont and his Staff were repatriated to Rochefort, while his men were to repatriated by Cadiz. However, the Spanish Junta refused to sanction the treaty and the Frenchmen were kept on prison hulks, but after an attempted escape, the remainder were placed on Cabrera Island. Less than half were still alive when the war ended in 1814.
57. They were actually dispersed throughout the army as skirmish companies in the various divisions.
58. A non-commissioned officer.
59. Lieutenant Colonel Charles Macleod, 43rd Foot.
60. There was Jonathan Ash in the 1st Battalion, 95th Rifles.

Chapter 6

1. Lieutenant Richard Burke, 45th Foot.
2. Captain William Mein, 52nd Foot.
3. Lieutenant John Winterbottom, 52nd Foot, was an ex-sergeant major.
4. Major General Sir William Erskine.
5. Lieutenant Colonel John Ross commanded the 52nd Foot.
6. Major John Stewart, 95th Foot, died of his wounds on 16 March 1811.

7. Lieutenant Theophilus Gifford, 52nd Foot, was killed at Casal Nova on 15 March 1811.
8. I suspect that he refers to Sir William Erskine, who commanded the Light Division temporarily. He committed suicide at Lisbon on 14 May 1813.
9. Lieutenant Charles Lennox, Lord March, 13th Light Dragoons, was an aide-de-camp to Lord Wellington.
10. Lieutenant William Light, 4th Dragoons.
11. Light quit the Army as a major in 1821, he later married and worked as Surveyor General in South Australia.
12. The records differ slightly with this account. John Dunn was invalided on 15 June 1811 and transferred to the 2nd Battalion on 24 February 1812. James Dunn was recorded as missing on 2 September 1811 and discharged on 24 December presumed dead.
13. The only officer of the 43rd to be killed at Sabugal was Lieutenant John McDearmid.
14. This was incorrect, the bullet damaged the spine, but luckily did not sever it.
15. François Étienne de Kellermann, 2nd Duc de Valmy, was 38 years old at Vimiera.
16. A local corps called out to defend the local area. It was not as well equipped or trained as the militia.
17. Captain Thomas Erskine Napier, Chasseurs Britanique, was a Deputy Assistant Adjutant General. He was Charles' first cousin.
18. At Casal Novo.
19. Colonel George Drummond commanded a brigade in the Light Division.
20. Napier's 1st Battalion, 50th Foot, was in Major General Kenneth Howard's Brigade of the 1st Division.
21. The General Order of 16 March 1811 requested the commanding officers of the three regiments to name one sergeant each for promotion to ensign.
22. His horse. It was a white half Arabian from Morocco, with the reputation of showing good judgment.
23. Blanco was Napier's horse.
24. The Bishop of Guarda was Jose Pinto de Mendonca Arrais.
25. Marshal André Masséna was born in Nice in 1758, which was part of the Kingdom of Sardinia at the time.
26. General of Brigade Pierre Soult commanded a light cavalry division in the 2nd Corps.
27. General of Division Jean Reynier, commander of the 2nd Corps in Massena's Army.
28. There were no Italian regiments in Massena's Army.
29. *Le Moniteur* was the official newspaper of the French government.
30. General Antoine Brenier de Montmorand was wounded and captured at the battle of Vimeiro on 20 August 1808. While he was prisoner, he stayed at their mother's house until formally exchanged in April 1809.
31. Fought near Cadiz on 5 March 1811.
32. General Sir David Dundas was Commander in Chief of the Forces from 1809 to 1811, following the scandal that forced the Duke of York to resign.
33. Captain Lord Fitzroy Somerset, 43rd Foot, Wellington's Military Secretary.
34. The Honourable Edward Acheson, 67th Foot, got his brevet lieutenant colonelcy dated 30 March 1811. Charles did not get his until 27 June 1811 by exchanging.
35. Formed at a projecting angle with the line.
36. Brenier exploded the fortress and escaped through the allied lines on the night of 10–11 May 1811.
37. Erskine commanded the 2nd Cavalry Division.
38. Major General Alexander Campbell commanded the 4th Division.

39. He is referring to the Battle of Albuera, which was fought on 16 April.
40. The ride was about 200 miles or 320km.
41. Robert Bellarmine was a Roman Catholic Cardinal who had condemned Galileo for claiming that the sun rather than the earth was the centre of the universe.
42. He was promoted to brevet major on 30 May 1811 and to major without purchase in the 52nd Foot on 27 June 1811.
43. Lieutenant Colonel John Ross, 52nd Foot, did transfer into the 66th Foot on 18 July 1811.
44. Lieutenant Colonel Robert Barclay, 52nd Foot, died of his wounds on 3 May 1811.
45. Captain the Honourable Henry Powys, 83rd Foot, died of his wounds on 6 April 1812. He was a brother of Thomas Powys, 3rd Baron Lilford.
46. John Colborne exchanged into the 52nd Foot on 18 July 1811.

Chapter 7

1. Two companies each of the 43rd, 52nd, 95th, 1st & 3rd Caçadores.
2. It is clear from other Light Division eyewitnesses that they passed this river having previously removed their boots and socks, to avoid trench foot.
3. Lieutenant General Sir Ralph Abercromby had led a force which landed in Egypt in 1801, he was mortally wounded at the Battle of Alexandria.
4. Captain James Ferguson, 43rd Foot.
5. Captain William Jones, 52nd Foot.
6. Captain Samuel Mitchell, 95th Rifles.
7. Lieutenant John Gurwood, 52nd Foot.
8. Assistant Surgeon Thomas Walker, 52nd Foot.
9. Brevet Colonel George Elder of the 3rd Caçadores. He was an ex 95th man.
10. Or Faussebray, was a lower defensive wall in front of the main wall.
11. Then Lieutenant William Staveley, Royal Staff Corps.
12. Colonel, His Serene Highness Prince William of Orange was an extra aide-de-camp to Lord Wellington.
13. Major General John Ormsby Vandeleur.
14. Staff Surgeon George Guthrie.
15. Staff Surgeon John Robb, who was ex-95th Foot.
16. Surgeon John Maling, 52nd Foot.
17. Lieutenant Colonel Charles Stewart, 50th Foot.
18. Lady Louisa Conolly (nee Lennox), an aunt of the brothers who married Thomas Conolly in 1758.
19. Major General Henry Mackinnon was killed at Ciudad Rodrigo.
20. George's sister Emily Louisa.
21. Brevet Major the Honourable Alexander Gordon, 3rd Foot Guards, aide-de-camp to the Duke of Wellington.
22. A litter stretched between poles.
23. He was promoted to brevet lieutenant colonel on 6 February 1812.
24. Captain William Kent Royal Navy.
25. HMS *Latona*, a 36-gun frigate.
26. Major Daniel James Hearn, 43rd Foot, was going home sick, while Major Joseph Wells, 43rd Foot, had been severely wounded at Badajoz.
27. Possibly Captain Alexander Macdonald, who arrived with A Troop, Royal Horse Artillery, in the Peninsula at this time.
28. Now a suburb of Badajoz.
29. John Duffy had been made a brevet major on 6 February 1812.

30. Sir Henry Bunbury was Under Secretary of State for War and the Colonies from 1809 to 1816.
31. There is a memorial tablet to him in the Chapel of John the Baptist in Westminster Abbey.
32. Private Edward Feagan, William's soldier servant.
33. Lieutenants James Considine, who was 19 years old, and Edward Freer, who was about 20 years old.
34. Captain James Hull, 43rd Foot, was allowed to resign his commission.
35. General Hill's troops surprised the French garrison and destroyed the boat bridge there.
36. Lieutenant Colonel Elder was seriously wounded at Badajoz several times and developed lockjaw. He was not expected to survive his wounds. His serious wound forced him to return to England and he did not come back to the Peninsula until July 1813, when he was promoted to colonel and given command of the Portuguese 6th Infantry Regiment.
37. The French had converted three old convents into forts with supporting arcs of fire.
38. A force of Sicilian and British troops was planned to land on the eastern coast of Spain and to coordinate with local Spanish forces, keeping the French forces there fully occupied.
39. Major General Barnard Bowes was killed on 24 June 1812.
40. During the sieges of Ciudad Rodrigo and Badajoz, the Light Division lost its commander, both brigade commanders, and three of its five battalion commanders. Napier was the second senior officer in his brigade in June 1812.
41. Lieutenant John Westmacott, Royal Staff Corps.
42. Lieutenant General Thomas Graham was 63 years old and suffered with ophthalmia.
43. This is curious, as there is no evidence that William gained a brevet Lieutenant colonelcy prior to November 1813. He had only become a substantive Major on 14 May 1812. It is likely that he joked, elevating himself to lieutenant colonel as he commanded the battalion in the absence of Lt Colonel Gifford.
44. Brevet Major Ulysses Burgh, 92nd Foot.
45. Colonel William Gifford, 43rd Foot.
46. The 102nd had been ordered to Bermuda.
47. Lieutenant General Sir Stapleton Cotton.
48. The Battle of Salamanca.
49. Lieutenant Charles Synge, Portuguese Army, aide-de-camp to Brigadier Denis Pack, was not killed.
50. General Cole was wounded in the body not the arm.
51. Leith was severely wounded but he did not lose his arm.
52. Colonel William Spry commanding a Portuguese Brigade, I can find no evidence he was wounded.
53. He was accidentally shot by a Portuguese sentry after the battle.
54. Major General John Gaspard Le Marchant was killed.
55. Marshal Marmont was seriously wounded in the right arm but did not lose it.
56. Major General John Gaspard Le Marchant, commanding a brigade of heavy cavalry.
57. Among the British generals wounded were Marshal William Beresford, Lieutenant Generals James Leith, Galbraith Cole and Stapleton Cotton and Major General Victor von Alten. Portuguese Brigadier General Conde de Rezende was also wounded.
58. The eagle of the 62nd Ligne was captured by Lieutenant Pearce, 44th Foot; the eagle of the 22nd Ligne was taken by Captain Jeronimo Pereira da Vasconellos, 12th Caçadores, although Ensign Pratt, 30th Foot, is sometimes credited.
59. Major Thomas Lloyd, 94th Foot, was not wounded.
60. Major General Edward Pakenham commanded the 3rd Division.

61. Emperor Vitellius (AD 15–69).
62. Napier is referring to an Army Gold Medal that was awarded to commanders after a significant victory. He was awarded one for commanding the 43rd Foot at Salamanca.
63. General Claude François Ferey.
64. A false identification.
65. Geographical Atlas of Spain and Portugal by D. Tomas Lopez published in 1804.
66. Brevet Major Ulysses Burgh, 92nd Foot, aide-de-camp to Wellington.
67. Ensign George Campbell, 43rd Foot.
68. A horse.
69. Unusual, shocking.
70. Lieutenant General Frederick Maitland led an expedition of 5,000 men to the east coast of Spain.
71. Christopher Patrickson was the senior major in the 43rd Foot.
72. Cox & Greenwood Army Agents of Craig's Court, London.
73. A palace in central Madrid that was turned into a fort during the French occupation.
74. Spanish for head.
75. Colonel James Willoughby Gordon, Quartermaster General to the Forces.
76. Lieutenant General Sir Edward Paget, commanding the cavalry Reserve, was captured on the retreat and remained a prisoner of war until April 1814.
77. Lieutenant Colonel Andrew Francis Barnard, 95th Rifles.
78. Napier is writing about the Combat of San Munoz.
79. Lieutenant George Ridout, 43rd Foot, died of his wounds on 23 November 1812.
80. George married Margaret Craig on 22 October 1812. They were to have five children together.
81. Captain Henry Dawson, 52nd Foot, was killed at San Muñoz.
82. Captain Thomas Fuller, 52nd Foot.
83. Charles Macleod's memorial was sculpted by John Bacon the Younger.
84. About £15,000 in today's terms.
85. Grimaldi was slang for a clown.
86. Lieutenant colonel Charles Rowan, 52nd Foot.
87. The French.
88. Joseph Bonaparte was the elder brother of Napoleon who installed him on the throne of Spain.
89. *Junius* was the pseudonym of the author of a series of letters published between 1769 and 1772, discrediting the ministries. His identity has never been established.
90. All attempts to identify this individual have failed.
91. Slang for the United States.
92. The USS President was a 53-gun frigate.
93. Commodore John Rodgers, US Navy.
94. Praties – informal term for potatoes.

Chapter 8
1. Lieutenant William Havelock, 43rd Foot.
2. This is a gross exaggeration, the channel is about 1 mile long.
3. Sorauren.
4. *Memoires sur la derniere guerre entre la France et l'Espagne dans les Pyrenees occidentales par le Citoyen B**** was published anonymously in 1801, but it is widely accredited to a Mr Beaulac.
5. San Marcial on 31 August 1813.

6. Major General James Kempt was Napier's brigade commander, but was in temporary command of the Light Division.
7. Major General John Oswald temporarily commanded the 5th Division.
8. Brevet Lieutenant Colonel John Philip Hunt was seriously wounded leading the volunteers, but survived until 1857.
9. The Adjutant General of the Army
10. Lieutenant John O'Connell, 43rd Foot.
11. Brevet Major George Marlay, 14th Foot.
12. He means Thomas Heaphy, who went out to the Peninsula to make a large number of small watercolour portraits of the senior officers of the army, in preparation for a large atmospheric group portrait entitled *'The Duke of Wellington in consultation with his officers previous to a general engagement'*. The present whereabout of the original painting is not known.
13. Lieutenant Edward Fox Fitzgerald, 10th Light Dragoons, was the son of the infamous Lord Edward Fitzgerald who had led an attempted rebellion in Ireland.
14. French Marshal Jean Bernadotte was elected the heir to King Charles XIII of Sweden in 1810. He chose the name of Charles XIV John and became the regent and commander of the Swedish armed forces. He led the Swedish contingent against Napoleon in central Europe in 1813 and was the commander of the Allied Army of the North.
15. Major General Samuel Gibbs led a British expeditionary force to northern Germany in 1813.
16. Colonel Henry Torrens, was the Military Secretary to the Commander-in-Chief of the British Army.
17. General of Division Dominique Vandamme commanded a corps and was captured at the battle of Kulm on 30 August 1813.
18. Major General James Kemmis commanded a brigade in the 4th Division. He was born in 1751 and would have been 61 when Napier wrote the letter.
19. Lave – wash.
20. Colonel Frederick Adam serving on the east coast of Spain.
21. This would appear to be Private Benjamin Lingham, 43rd Foot.
22. Lieutenant the Honourable William Cecil Percy, 59th Foot, was the son of the Earl of Limerick. He was in the 95th Rifles from August 1810 until October 1811, when Napier was the brigade major. When he says deserter, he almost certainly means that he was absent without leave.
23. The Crossing of the Bidassoa, which was fought on 7 October 1813.
24. Brevet Colonel Colin Halkett, commanding a brigade in the 1st Division.
25. Colonel Anne-Louis Clouet was wounded and made a prisoner at the Battle of Dennewitz.
26. Napier appears to be exaggerating. Six officers junior to him were given brevet promotions to lieutenant colonel before him; Lord Fitzroy Somerset (43rd Foot), William Mein (52nd Foot), George Napier (52nd Foot), Alexander Cameron (95th Rifles), John Henry Algeo, 34th Foot, who was seconded to the 1st Caçadores, and George Elder, ex-95th Rifles, who was seconded to the 3rd Caçadores.
27. A gold medal for commanding a battalion in action.
28. Captain Robert Murchison, 43rd Foot. He died of his wounds on 11 November 1813.
29. 14 March 1811.
30. Actually Lieutenant the Honourable Charles Gore, 43rd Foot.
31. I have been unable to identify this man.
32. Colonel John Colborne had become Lord Seaton.
33. Lieutenant Alexander Steele, 43rd Foot.

34. A report by the Duke of Wellington dated 13 November states 4 officers and 7 men killed, 5 officers and 58 men wounded. Captain Thomas Capel and Lieutenant Edward Freer were killed outright, Captain Robert Murchison and Lieutenant John Angrove died of their wounds.
35. Quoted in *A Brotherhood of Heroes*.
36. Thomas Lloyd was serving in the 94th Foot when killed.
37. Barnard was to live until 1855.
38. Some sources give the date as 22 November.
39. These included Captain Robert Simpson's, Captain Thomas Champ's and Captain Samuel Hobkirk's companies.
40. Lieutenant Mackay Hugh Baillie was shot in the forehead.
41. Captain Samuel Hobkirk, 43rd Foot.
42. Lieutenant Alexander Steele, 43rd Foot, was wounded in the leg.
43. Lieutenant George Hennell, 43rd Foot, who participated in the fight, states in a letter two days later, that he heard General Kempt gave the order to move forward.
44. His eldest sister.
45. Captain Thomas Erskine Napier, Chasseurs Britannique, was William's first cousin.
46. He was awarded a gold medal for commanding the 43rd Foot at Salamanca, Nivelle and Nive. Only one medal was given, with a clasp added to the ribbon for subsequent awards. If an officer received four gold medals, he would receive an Army Gold Cross, with the names of the battles on the arms of the cross and further battles would then be added as clasps to the ribbon. Napier never received the Army Gold Cross.

Chapter 9

1. Private Joseph Burke was found guilty of gross insolence and disgraceful conduct on 4 December 1812 and was confined for one month.
2. Ensign Arthur Greuber, 102nd Foot?
3. Lieutenant RT Hume, 102nd Foot?
4. Ensign Thomas Ker, 102nd Foot?
5. Lieutenant J Lyster, 102nd Foot?
6. Lieutenant Colonel Richard Williams, Royal Marines.
7. His brigade included two independent companies of foreigners, which were mainly composed of French deserters, who enlisted rather than be prisoners of war.
8. A sans-culotte was a French soldier recruited from the lower classes of society during the early days of the French Revolution. Sans-culotte meaning they had no breeches.
9. Craney Island off Virginia had a fort built on it by the Americans in early 1813 to protect Norfolk and Gosport Naval Base.
10. Captain Samuel John Pechell Royal Navy, commanding HMS *San Domingo* of 74 guns.
11. This refers to the capture and burning of Hampton. Claims of plunder and rape were greatly exaggerated by American newspapers.
12. Ocracoke Island, North Carolina.
13. Two privateers were captured: the 18-gun brig-sloop *Anaconda* and the 13-gun schooner *Atlas*.
14. Rear Admiral Sir George Cockburn commanded the expedition.
15. The *Anaconda* was a privateer, mounted eighteen 9-pounders.
16. He actually means *Yaupon*, traditionally used by native Americans to brew a type of tea.
17. Admiral Sir John Borlase Warren was commander in chief on the America station.
18. Kent Island, Maryland, is the largest island in Chesapeake Bay.
19. St Michael, Maryland, is on the eastern peninsula of Chesapeake Bay.

20. Queenstown, Maryland, is just to the east of Kent Island. A force of 300 men attacked the town, but because of a premature fire, the local militia were able to retreat to safety.
21. Lieutenant General Sir George Prevost, Commander in Chief in North America.
22. Before the 'Great Flood'.
23. Lieutenant Colonel William Chabot, 50th Foot.
24. An overdue bill.

Chapter 10
1. Brevet Colonel Andrew Barnard, 95th Foot.
2. George's wife.
3. True.
4. Captain the Honourable Saunders Gore, 94th Foot.
5. Assistant Surgeon Archibald Hair, 43rd Foot.
6. He was shot in the chest and survived his wound. The ball was never removed.
7. Caroline's brother Henry Fox, was a British diplomat.
8. Brevet Lieutenant Colonel Henry Sturgeon Royal Staff Corps, Assistant Quarter Master General, was killed at Vic-en-Bigorre on 19 March 1814.
9. A major in the Royal Staff Corps was paid 19 shillings a day or £346 15 shillings per year. As an Assistant Quartermaster General, he received an additional 14 shillings a day or £255 10 shillings a year. His total pay would be £1 13 shillings per day or £602 5 shillings per year. This was more money than an infantry or cavalry regimental colonel made.
10. Lieutenant General Lord Dalhousie commanded the 7th Division.
11. The white flag of the Bourbons.
12. General Manuel Freire de Andrade.
13. George was promoted to lieutenant colonel in the 71st Foot on 24 March 1814; superseding Lieutenant Colonel Peacocke, who was given the choice of resigning or face a court martial. He chose to resign.
14. Lieutenant Colonel the Honourable Henry Cadogan, 71st Foot.
15. Brevet Lieutenant Colonel Charles Rowan, 52nd Foot.
16. In 1814 the Army rewarded eighteen officers from outside the Foot Guards by giving them promotions in a Guard Regiment. The majority of these officers had distinguished themselves in the Peninsula, most on the Army Staff. All of the promotions from outside the regiment were to the rank of captain. George Napier was one of five officers who were brought into the 3rd Foot Guards. Among those who were brought into the Guards were his friends Henry Hardinge and Fitzroy Somerset.
17. This is a slight exaggeration. In 1814, a captain in the Foot Guards was paid £301 per year plus £228 subsistence allowance.

Chapter 11
1. *Fighting Napoleon*, Gareth Glover, 2016.
2. Captain Newton Chambers, 1st Foot Guards, was an aide-de-camp to General Picton and was killed shortly after him.
3. Lieutenant James Simpson, 1st Foot Guards, was seriously wounded at Quatre Bras on 16 June.
4. His servant.
5. Captain Henry Macleod, 35th Foot, was serving in the 1st Corps as a Deputy Assistant Quarter Master General.
6. His two daughters, Francis Louisa and Emily Ann, both less than two years old.

Bibliography

Bruce, HA, *Life of General Sir William Napier (2 Volumes)*, London, 1864
Butler, Sir W, *Sir Charles Napier*, London, 1890
Glover, G., *Fighting Napoleon: The Recollections of Lt John Hildebrand, 35th Foot in the Mediterranean and Waterloo Campaigns*, Barnsley, 2016
Gwynn, Stephen, *A Brotherhood of Heroes: Being Memorials of Charles*, London, 1910

George & William Napier
Napier, Sir CJ, *Lights & Shades of Military Life*, London, 1850
Napier, William, *Passages in the Early Military Life of General Sir George T*, London, 1884
Napier, William, *The Life and Opinions of Sir Charles Napier (4 volumes)* London, 1857
Napier, William, *Sweat, Blood & Dust: The Military Career of Charles Napier During the Peninsular War & War of 1812*, Leonaur, 2017

Index

102nd Foot viii, 109, 112, 156, 157, 162–165, 168–9
11th Light Dragoons 129
12th Light Dragoons 129, 166
13th Light Dragoons 105, 166
14th Light Dragoons 20, 65, 129
16th Light Dragoons 61, 63
1st Division 72, 143
1st Hussars KGL 62
24th Light Dragoons ix, 1
27th Foot 130, 193
2nd Division 72, 100
33rd Foot vii
35th Foot 13, 188
3rd Cacadores 115, 126
3rd Division 72, 115, 116, 132, 183
3rd Foot Guards ix, 192
40th Foot 130
42nd Foot 37–8, 40, 42, 44, 47
43rd Foot x, xi, 3, 4, 13, 16–7, 26, 27, 54, 60, 66–7, 68, 70, 71, 73, 90, 99, 100, 101, 114, 115, 133, 139, 141, 143, 146, 148, 150, 153, 175, 176, 188, 191
46th Foot ix, 2
4th Division 79, 143, 181
4th Dragoons 93
4th Foot vii, 36, 37, 38, 39, 44
50th Foot viii, 6, 18, 32, 36, 40–4, 46–9, 51, 58, 64, 106, 156, 160, 166, 167
52nd Foot ix, 1, 2–5, 7, 51, 66–9, 70, 73, 74, 89, 90, 94–5, 99, 100, 111, 114, 115, 118, 121, 142, 146, 150, 154, 174, 175, 176, 182, 184
5th Division 142, 143, 189
60th Foot 75
62nd Foot ix
66th Foot 111
6th Division 127, 171, 181
71st Foot ix, 183, 1284
89th Foot vii
90th Foot 3
92nd Foot 15
95th Regiment vii, 15, 27, 65, 66, 67, 85, 99, 100, 114, 126, 141, 146

Acheson Lt Colonel the Honourable Edward 67th Foot 106
Adam Colonel Frederick 145
Agincourt HMS 121
Agueda River 57

Alava y Esquivel, General Miguel de 71, 77–8
Alba de Tormes 130
Albergaria a Velha 108
Albergueria de Arganan 105, 106
Alcantara 125
Alcock Francis (nee Philipps) 192
Alfaiates 101, 122
Alicante 133
Almaraz 55, 56, 126
Almeida 60, 63–70, 101–2, 105–8
Alten General Charles 135, 143
Alten General Victor 130
Amiens Peace of ix, 2
Anderson Lt Colonel Paul 60th Foot 48, 49, 50
Angouleme Duke d' 177
Anstruther General Robert 22
Arbuthnot Major 52nd Foot the Honourable Hugh 25, 74
Arcangues 152
Army of Occupation 191
Army of Reserve x
Arrauntz 173–4
Arzobispo 55
Ash Private Jonathan 95th Foot 85
Ashford viii, 20, 21
Astorga 31
Audacious HMS 50
Austria 141, 144, 146

Badajoz viii, x, 56, 97, 109, 111, 112, 114, 121
Baillie Lieutenant Mackay 43rd Foot 152
Baird Captain James 66th Foot 50
Baird General Sir David 27, 30, 33, 34, 48, 50
Baltimore 160
Barba del Puerco 57, 131
Barclay Lt Colonel Robert 52nd Foot 51, 66, 67, 73, 74, 111
Barquilla 64
Barrosa 105–6
Bathurst Lord 144
Bayonne 174, 179, 180
Beckwith Colonel Sidney 57, 66, 73, 100, 103, 157, 163, 164, 165, 166, 167, 169
Beckwith General Sir Thomas viii
Bellarmine Cardinal Robert 109
Belli Captain 16th Light Dragoons 63
Benavente 31
Bentinck Colonel Lord William 1st Foot Guards viii, 33, 37, 41, 44, 47

Bentinck Lt Colonel Lord Frederick 7th Foot 4
Beresford Marshal William Carr 59, 105, 108, 110, 111, 130, 181, 183
Berkeley Lady Emily 98
Bermuda viii, 129, 132, 137, 138, 155, 156, 160, 167
Bernadotte Crown Prince of Sweden Jean 144, 147, 148
Bonaparte Joseph 137, 141
Bordeaux 174, 177, 179, 180, 184, 185
Boulogne 3
Bowes Major General Bernard 127
Brenier de Montmorand General Antoine 105, 106, 107, 108
Brunswick Oels Corps 83
Bunbury Sir Charles vii
Bunbury Sir Henry 123, 124, 125, 140, 142, 143, 145, 148, 174
Burgh Major Ulysses, 92nd Foot 129, 132
Burgos 133, 134, 135
Burke Private Joseph 98th Foot 156
Burrard Ensign Paul 49, 51
Burrard General Sir Harry 24, 27, 51
Busaco Battle of viii, ix, x, xi, 72, 77, 85, 97, 101, 102, 131, 146

Cacadores 66, 67, 115, 126
Cadiz 83, 133, 137, 139
Cadogan Lt Colonel the Honourable Henry 71st Foot 184
Cambrai ix, 188
Campbell Captain Robert 52nd Foot 66
Campbell Colonel Neil 54th Foot 188
Campbell Ensign George 43rd Foot 132
Campbell General Alexander 108
Campbell Private 50th Foot 156
Campo Maior 56
Canterbury 3
Cape Corps viii
Carrera General Martin 61, 63
Casal Nova ix, x, 90, 94, 149
Cathcart General William 13, 16, 17
Celorico da Beira 59, 69, 99
Cephalonia 192
Ceuta 9
Chabot Lt Colonel William 50th Foot 167
Chambers Captain Newton 1st Foot Guards 188
Chamont Monsieur de adc 46
Chasseurs Britaniques 100
Chatham vii, 3
Chatham General John Pitt, Earl of 25
Chesapeake 164, 165, 166, 167, 168, 170
Ciudad Rodrigo ix, 44, 57, 60, 61, 62, 63, 65, 101, 105, 112, 114, 117, 118, 119, 120, 125, 135
Clinton General Sir Henry vii
Clouet Colonel Anne Baron adc 47, 53, 148
Clunes Captain William 50th Foot 36, 49
Coa, Action of viii, x, 64, 65–6, 68, 69, 78, 120, 131

Cockburn, Admiral Sir George viii, 159, 163, 165, 169, 170
Coimbra 59, 69, 76, 78, 79, 97, 99, 100, 102, 103, 110, 121
Colborne Colonel John 52nd Foot 24, 50, 111, 112, 113, 114, 116, 117, 121, 122, 146, 171, 182
Cole General Sir Galbraith Lowry 72, 79, 80, 89, 130, 175, 181
Collingwood Admiral Lord Cuthbert 7, 8
Concepcion Fort 64, 107
Condeixa-a-Nova 92, 97, 98, 99
Congreve Rockets 161
Conolly Lady Louisa 118
Contreras General Juan de 58
Copenhagen x, 13, 14, 15, 16, 18, 19,
Cornwallis Marquess General Charles 1, 5, 6
Corunna viii, ix, x, 27, 28, 29, 30, 31, 32, 34, 35, 36, 46, 51, 52, 53, 103, 106, 118, 124, 134
Cotton General Sir Stapleton 130
Cox & Greenwood Army Agents 133
Cox General William, Governor of Almeida 63, 64
Craig Ensign William 52nd Foot 51, 104
Craney Island 158, 162, 164–5, 169
Craufurd Brigadier General James Catlin 59
Craufurd Brigadier General Robert viii, 27, 30, 34, 51, 55, 58, 59, 60, 63, 64, 65, 66, 67, 68, 69, 70, 73, 75, 76, 90, 110, 111, 113, 114, 116, 118, 119, 120
Cumberland, Ernest Duke of 15

Dalhousie Lt General Lord 180
Dalzell Captain Robert 43rd Foot 198
Dawson Captain Henry 52nd Foot 135
Deal viii, 3, 7, 11, 13, 27, 54, 188
Deleitosa 55
Dobbs Captain Joseph 52nd Foot 90, 94–5, 119
Douglas Lieutenant James 43rd Foot 2
Downs The 12, 27
Drummond Colonel George 97
Duckworth Admiral Sir John Thomas 7, 8
Duff Major General Sir James vii, 2
Duffy Major John 43rd Foot 123, 126, 127, 139, 149, 150
Dundas General David 106
Dundas Lord Henry 13
Dunn Private John 43rd Foot 93
Dupont de l'Etang General Pierre 84

Echalar (Etxalar) 140
Elder Colonel George 3rd Cacadores 63, 115
Elvas 25, 56
Elvina San Vicenzo de 36, 39, 44, 46, 48
Encina La 122–6
Erskine Sir William 90, 97, 105, 108
Essling Prince of See Marshal Massena
Etna Mount 9

Falmouth 27, 171
Fane General Henry 37

Ferguson Captain James 43rd Foot 114, 115
Ferrey General Claude 131
Fitzgerald Lieutenant Edward 10th Light Dragoons 144
Fitzgerald Lord Edward 37
Fitzpatrick Ass Surgeon Nicholas RA 77
Flogging 14, 18, 21–2, 25, 29, 123, 145, 153, 155–6, 184, 185
Fox Caroline Amelia x, 121
Fox General Henry Edward vii, x, 7, 20, 78, 121
Foy General Maximilien 174
Francois, servant of Sir John Moore 50
Fraser Francis Paymaster 43rd Foot 133
Fraser General Alexander Mackenzie 33, 34
Freer Ensign Edward 43rd Foot 151
Freire General 182
Fuentes d'Onoro viii, ix, x, xi, 106, 107
Fuller Captain Thomas 52nd Foot 135

Gallegos de Arganan 57, 60, 62, 63, 117–8, 135, 136–7, 139
Gazan Madame 140
Geneva 192
George III King 5
Gesso 10
Ghent ix, 188, 191
Gibbs Maj General Samuel 4, 144
Gibraltar 8, 11, 24
Gifford Colonel William 43rd Foot 129, 136
Gifford Lieutenant Theophilus 52nd Foot 91, 98, 100
Good Hope Cape of 192
Gordon Captain Alexander 3rd Foot Guards 33, 50, 119
Gordon Colonel James, Quarter Master General 135, 127
Gordon Lord William vii
Gore Captain the Honourable Charles 43rd Foot 149
Gore Captain the Honourable Saunders 94th Foot 173
Gosling Captain RN 50
Gottenburg 11, 23
Graham General Sir Thomas 34, 50, 106, 128, 143
Guards 7, 11, 28, 31, 389, 47, 48, 77, 99, 136, 137, 187
Guernsey viii, 4, 6, 11, 109, 112, 119, 137, 160, 193
Guides Corps of 179
Gurwood Lieutenant John 52nd Foot 114, 115, 116, 118–9
Guthrie Staff Surgeon George 116

Hair Surgeon Archibald 43rd Foot 176
Halifax, Nova Scotia viii, 132, 160, 164, 167
Halkett Colonel Colin 147
Hardinge Captain Henry 57th Foot 48
Harrison Captain John 50th Foot 39, 40, 41, 43
Hastings Marquis of See Moira
Havelock Lieutenant William 43rd Foot 139, 140

Hearn Colonel Daniel 43rd Foot x, 131, 133, 134, 135, 1346, 146, 148
Helsingor 14
Hennessy Private John 50th Foot 43, 44, 45
Herrasti General Andres 63, 64
Hewitt Captain Isaac 6th Foot 64
High Wycombe 19
Hildebrand Lieutenant John 35th Foot 188
Hill General Sir Rowland 33, 60, 62, 72, 111, 126, 147, 178, 183
Hobkirk Captain Samuel 43rd Foot 152
Holland 5
Holland Henry Fox, Lord 28, 47, 141
Hope General Sir John 24, 33, 48–9, 50, 106, 179, 180
Hull Captain James 43rd Foot 125
Hull Lt Colonel Edward 43rd Foot 68
Hunt Lt Colonel John 52nd Foot 142
Hythe vii, viii, 3, 6, 13, 21

Invincible HMS 1
Ionian Islands 192
Ipswich 16
Ireland vii, ix, x, 2, 4, 5, 14, 128, 142, 184, 185
Irun 140
Italy 23, 141

Jones Captain William 52nd Foot 114
Junot General Jean 97

Keene Sergeant 50th Foot 38
Kellerman General Francois 96
Kemmis Major General James 145
Kempt Major General James 141, 146, 147, 148, 149
Kent Captain William RN 121
Kent Island 164, 166
Kioge Battle of 15, 17
Krauchenberg Captain Georg 1st Hussars KGL 63

La Rhune mountain x, 147, 148, 153
Latona HMS 122
Lefebvre-Desnouettes General Charles 31
Leith Lt General James 130
Lennox Charles, 2nd Duke of Richmond vii, viii, x
Lennox Lady Sarah vii
Light 93
Light Brigade/Division viii, ix, x, 55, 56, 58, 62, 72, 83, 88, 91, 92, 97, 99, 100, 105, 110, 112, 113, 114, 116, 118, 119, 120, 122, 125, 126, 129, 130, 131, 132, 136, 141, 142, 143, 148, 171, 174, 176, 178, 182
Lightbourne's Brigade 59
Limerick vii, 2, 4
Lingham Private Benjamnin 43rd Foot 141–2, 145
Linsingen Major General Charles KGL 15, 17, 18

Index 211

Lisbon viii, x, 25, 28, 54, 59, 71, 79, 80, 81, 86, 92, 99, 110, 121–2, 124, 131, 134, 139, 156
Little Hampton USA 160, 162, 165, 166
Liverpool Lord 142, 144
Lloyd Captain Thomas 43rd Foot 29, 67, 68, 69, 71, 74, 85, 95, 130, 131, 151
Loison General Louis 63, 64, 69, 88
Londonderry Regiment 5
Louis XVIII King 189, 190
Lugo 28, 29, 31

Mackenzie General Kenneth 2, 3, 111
Mackinnon General Henry 119
Macleod Lt Colonel Charles 43rd Foot x, 66, 67, 85, 121–2, 123–4, 127
Mafra 96
Magee Sergeant 50th Foot 38
Maitland Lt General Frederick 133
Maling Surgeon John 52nd Foot 118
Malta 141
March Lord 13th Light Dragoons 171, 175–6
Marchant Le General John 130
Marine Artillery 165–6
Marines 157, 160, 162, 164, 166, 168, 169
Marlay Major George 14th Foot 143
Massena Marshal 72–3, 76, 82, 86, 87, 97, 99, 100, 101, 105, 106, 108, 134
McDonald Captain Alexander RHA 122
Medellin 109
Mein Captain William 52nd Foot 89, 112, 148
Mellish Captain Henry 87th Foot 60
Messina 9, 10
Milazzo 10
Military College ix, x, 188, 191
Mitchell Captain Samuel 95th Foot 114
Moira Lord, General Francis Rawdon-Hastings viii, 5, 22
Molinos de los Flores 61
Mondego River 97
Mont de Marsan 177, 178
Montgomery Paymaster John 50th Foot 37–8
Moore Ensign Robert 50th Foot 38
Moore Sir John vi, viii, ix, x, 2, 3, 4, 5, 6, 7, 10, 11, 20, 23–5, 27–8, 29, 30, 31–2, 33–7, 40, 41, 44, 45, 48, 49–50, 52, 59, 73, 85, 105–6, 111, 127, 128, 152, 168, 192
Moreau General Jean 147
Morillo General Pablo 179
Mulgrave Lord 52
Murchison Captain Robert 43rd Foot 148–9, 150, 151
Murray Lt Colonel George 50

Napier Captain Charles RN 75, 78
Napier Emily vii, 152, 154, 160, 163, 166, 167
Napier George Colonel the Honourable vii
Napier Henry vii, 14, 15, 19, 177
Napier Lady Sarah 16, 76, 96, 117, 118
Napier Louisa vii, 118

Napier Richard vii
Napier Tom 97, 153, 154, 173
Napoleon Bonaparte vi, ix, xi, 3, 22, 23, 29, 30, 31, 54, 172, 177, 178, 184, 189, 190, 1291
National Guard 190
Nave de Haver 107
Nelson Admiral Horatio 7
Netley Camp vii
New London 169
New Orleans 169, 188
Ney Marshal viii, 44, 46, 47, 51, 53, 57, 58, 60, 61, 62, 69, 70, 76, 89, 120, 145
Nive Battle of x, xi, 153
Nivelle x, xi, 147, 148
Norfolk, Virginnia 164

Oakeley Elizabeth 192
Oakes General 11
Oaklands 192
O'Connell Lieutenant John 43rd Foot 143
Ocracoke 159, 163, 170
Oporto 105
Orange William Prince of 116
Ordenanza 97
Orthez ix, x, xi, 174–6, 178, 179
Ostend ix, 188
Oswald General John 142, 143

Paget Major General Henry 7, 9, 30, 31, 33, 34, 51
Paget Major General Sir Edward 135
Pakenham Captain Thomas Royal Navy 13, 81, 82
Pakenham General Edward 61, 131, 142, 146, 148, 172, 185
Palermo 11
Pamplona 141
Paris ix, xi, 127, 188, 189–91
Pasley Captain Charles RE 31
Passages (Pasaia) x, 140
Patrickson Captain Christopher 43rd Foot 67, 133, 134, 136, 137, 139, 173, 177, 178
Patterson Lieutenant John 50th Foot 39
Pau 172, 174, 178
Peacocke Lt Colonel 184
Pechell Captain Samuel RN 158, 163
Percy Captain Henry 7th Foot 50
Percy Lieutenant Cecil 59th Foot 146
Phillipon General Armand 123
Picton General Sir Thomas 72, 100, 115, 174, 183
Pinhancos 59
Pinhel 57
Plasencia 54, 128
Plymouth 52, 121, 137, 138, 139, 185, 186
Pollock Elizabeth vii
Pombal x, 58, 77
Ponte de Mucela 97–8, 101
Poona, India 192
Portsmouth 6, 11, 52, 54, 139, 188
Potomac River 160

Powys Captain the Honourable Henry 83rd Foot 111
President USS 137
Prevost Lt General Sir George 164

Queenstown, Maryland 166

Ramsgate 12, 14
Redinha x, 88, 89, 90, 97
Regent Prince 106, 109, 184
Renaud General Antoine 44, 45
Retiro 134
Reynier General Jean 100, 101
Ridout Lieutenant George 43rd Foot 135, 136
Robb Staff Surgeon John 118
Rolica 59
Romana Marquis de 30
Roskilde 14, 15
Ross Captain Hew RA 63, 73, 90
Ross Lt Colonel John 52nd/66th Foot 111
Rowan Charles 52nd Foot 3, 66–7, 69, 136, 185, 186
Royal Horse Guards ix, 20
Royal Irish Artillery ix
Royal Military Canal viii
Rueda 128–9
Russia 29, 140, 147

Sabugal 95, 100, 122
Sacavem 58
Sahagun 30
Salamanca xi, 30, 59, 105, 127, 130, 135
San Domingo HMS 160, 166
San Sebastian 140, 141, 142, 146
Sanchez Don Julian 44, 61, 62
Santarem 82, 86, 96
Scinde House 193
Seia 100
Shorncliffe vii, ix, 3
Sicily ix, 7, 9–10, 141
Simon General Edouard 74
Simpson Lieutenant James 1st Foot Guards 188
Somerset Lord Fitzroy Lt Colonel 43rd Foot 116, 137, 148, 185
Soult General Pierre 100
Soult Marshal Jean-de-Dieu viii, 30, 31–2, 44, 45, 46, 51, 52–3, 55, 76, 131, 134, 140, 143, 146, 172, 173, 174, 175, 177, 179, 180, 181, 184
Spencer Major General Brent 11, 15, 99
Spry Colonel William Portuguese Army 130
St Denis 189
St Estevan 140
St Jean de Luz 9, 140, 147, 171, 173, 177
St Jean Pied de Port 140
St Michael's Town, Maryland 167
Staff Corps vii, 1, 6, 115, 128, 179
Stanhope Captain James 1st Foot Guards adc 48, 50
Stanhope Major 50th Foot 32, 36, 38, 39, 48, 58
Staveley Captain William Staff Corps 115
Steele Lieutenant Alexander 43rd Foot 150
Stewart Colonel the Honourable Sir Charles 31, 118
Stewart General Richard 15, 16
Stewart Major John 95th Foot 91, 93
Stewart Sir William 11, 38, 100, 184
Sturgeon Colonel Henry 178–9
Suchet Marshal Louis 141, 143, 146
Synge Lieutenant Charles Portuguese Army 130

Tagus River 55, 59, 82, 145
Talavera de la Reina 54–5, 56, 59, 60
Talavera la Real 109
Talbot Lt Colonel Niel 14th Light Dragoons 63, 64, 65
Tarbes 9, 178, 179
Tetuan Bay of 8, 9
Tordesillas 129
Torrens Colonel Henry Military Secretary 109, 145, 152, 154, 167, 172
Toulouse ix, 174, 176, 177, 178, 179, 180, 181, 183, 184
Turner Lieutenant 50th Foot 39–40

Utterslev, Sweden 14

Vale da Mula 64
Valenciennes xi
Valladolid 132
Vandamme General Dominique 145
Vandeleur Major General John Ormsby 116, 119
Vedbaek 14
Vera/Bera 10, 140, 141, 143, 144, 145, 147, 148
Vienna 144
Vigo 34, 51, 52
Vilafranca de Xira 97
Vilar Formoso 107
Villafranca del Bierzo 29, 31
Vimiera viii, 24, 37, 96
Vitoria 139, 141, 168, 173, 184

Walker Assistant Surgeon Thomas 52nd Foot 114, 118
Walker Lt Colonel George 50th Foot 37
Warren Admiral Sir John Borlase RN 163, 165, 168, 169
West India Regiment x
Westmacott Lieutenant John Staff Corps 128
Westphalia 141
Williams Lt Colonel Richard Royal Marines 157
Winterbottom Lieutenant John 52nd Foot 75, 89
Woodford Captain John 1st Foot Guards 49

York Duke of 108, 154, 172, 183
York Militia 13